DECOMPILE YOUR MIND

AN ENGINEER'S GUIDE TO THOUGHTS AND EMOTIONS

AUDREY GILFILLAN, LPC
ALISON WEST, LPC, LAC

Cover design & illustrations by Alison West
Editing by Colin West, Colleen Ehrnstrom, Stacy Gerberich, Lisa West, & Laura Pasquale
Interior layout by Taryn Nergaard

ISBN 979-8-9917821-3-5 (Paperback)
ISBN 979-8-9917821-1-1 (eBook)

DISCLAIMER

The authors have made every attempt to provide information that is accurate and complete; however, this book is not intended as a substitute for professional medical or psychological advice. This book is not meant to be used, nor should it be used, to diagnose or treat any medical or psychological condition.

TABLE OF CONTENTS

TABLE OF IMAGES

INTRODUCTION

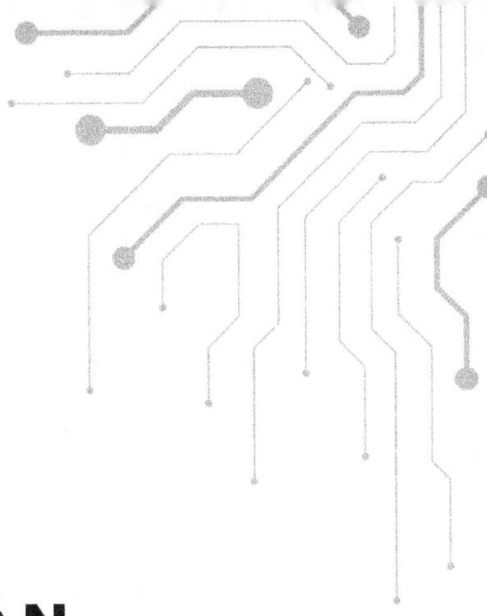

HUMANS ARE NOT WIRED TO UNDERSTAND THE ONES and zeros in a computer code. To compensate for this, programming languages (Java, Python, C++, etc.) have been invented to function as translators between the computer, which does speak in ones and zeros, and the human programmer. These programming systems take human-comprehensible language and *compile* it into code that the computer understands. The compiled code is compact and efficient, optimized for the computer to run as fast and as smoothly as possible.

This is the way most people interact with a computer: we see it doing things but have no access to what is going on behind the scenes. Most of the time we do not **want** to have to think about this deeper level, so long as the machine is doing what we need. And even if we did try to peek, all we would see is an inscrutable collection of bytes.

But sometimes, experts who know what they are doing desire to do the reverse, to take the ones and zeros and *decompile* them into a programming language, allowing humans to make sense of those digits. There are at least two reasons for this. First, experts might intend to change the program, to add some new feature, remove some bug, or patch some vulnerability. Generally speaking, this is much easier to do in the decompiled code; it is unpacked into its different components, with the connections and relationships between the different objects and functions laid bare. Second, sometimes a programmer wants this level of clarity simply so that they can read and better understand the program, even without making any updates. Sometimes, when they can read the uncompiled code behind a program, they discover why the limitation they found so vexing was essential for the program's overall functioning. Sometimes they find features and capabilities that they did not know existed. Sometimes, they recognize an area where the program could be improved *if* they had the time and resources. Even if they don't, it can be a comfort just to know why the computer works as it does.

Similarly, in the neurological realm, observing the brain in action is like watching the ones and zeros filtering through the memory of a computer: on its own, the activity gives no insight into the human experience. The interactions between the neurons, synapses, and neurotransmitters appear random and senseless without a translation device. Moreover, the psychological experience of thoughts and emotions, grounded in those neurological systems, can also be incomprehensible without an intermediary process to make sense of their meaning.

To offer such an intermediary process, this book decompiles the psychological activity of thoughts and emotions that are not always comprehensibly available to human conscious awareness. That is, we aim to lay out the inner workings of the mind in a manner that lets you see the unexpected connections, the inevitable vulnerabilities and workarounds, and the bugs that may in fact be features. Like using decompiled code, we hope to provide the ability to make small updates where you would like to see change. And just as importantly, seeing how it all works behind the scenes might provide more peace and understanding, just by virtue of greater self-knowledge.

Decompiling your thoughts and emotions equips you with usable data that depict your underlying needs. After all, the purpose of psychological thought and emotion is to meet the needs of human beings. Emotions drive humans to meet their biological needs, such as connection, belonging, and safety. Thoughts allow humans to reason and perceive the world around them, supporting their survival. The brain's systems evolved for the survival of early humans in their prehistoric environment. The intuitive, unequivocal functioning of thoughts and emotions worked well in that past landscape. However, while these systems still persist, the environmental and social constructs that exist today are quite different.

As the world has changed, the mechanisms of the human mind have not. These systems have been slow to adapt to demands of the modern world. The disconnect between the evolutionary origin of thoughts and emotions and what the world requires of humans today creates challenges in accurately understanding the data—and the needs they reflect—from these systems. And what would an engineer do with a piece of equipment that was no longer functioning as expected, perhaps because the decades-old software that controls it is now running in a much more modern computing environment? The first step to resolve this kind of potential mismatch is to decompile the code and seek to understand it.

As authors of this book, we care not just about human survival, but also the capacity to live a life full of meaning and purpose. Beyond building insight into your survival needs, the decompiling process offers discernment of your values as well, thereby aiding in the examination of what is most important to you and what impact you want to have on the world. Thoughts and emotions, when decompiled, reveal what you need and care about. In this way, the process becomes more complex and challenging than just debugging software. Software has needs and requirements, but not wants, desires, hopes, or dreams. Expect the mind to be a complex place, even when decompiled.

As we provide guidance on how to access inner thoughts and emotions, you can move forward with actions that more effectively meet underlying needs and values. Knowing how the mind works, you can identify opportunities to feel more connected, engaged, and fulfilled in life, opportunities that might have otherwise been missed.

Without this kind of data and information, the brain falls back on learned behaviors as a "best guess" for what actions will lead to the desired results. For engineers in particular, these learned behaviors often include problem-solving, reasoning, attention to detail, and perseverance. After all, these strategies work wonderfully in their engineering projects! However, context matters, and the same go-to behaviors are not always the most effective response to emotional or cognitive distress. In fact, these same actions that serve engineers so well in their day-to-day work can sometimes exacerbate their distress related to thoughts and emotions. In other cases, the engineering skills are still extremely helpful. The trick is knowing when and how to apply these skills, and when to incorporate new ones.

This book is designed to give information needed to relate to internal experiences, and the underlying significance reflected by those experiences, more effectively. It is structured in three sections: decompiling emotions, decompiling thoughts, and applying what is learned to respond more effectively in various circumstances, especially those that commonly impact the engineering experience.

As therapists who work within an engineering college, we have gained insight around common trends in engineering as well as effective interventions for this population. This book, then, is a unique curation of psychological research, neuroscience, counseling frameworks, insights shared by engineers, and our personal observations, all framed to resonate with engineers. We use flowcharts, personal anecdotes, analogies, vignettes, and exercises to help you imagine and apply the content reviewed. With or without personal experience in therapy, this book offers glimpses into our therapy offices, showcasing ways to change one's relationship with inner thoughts and emotions.

While written with an engineering population in mind, you do not need to be an engineer to find value in this book. We have noticed trends that correspond with engineers and have intentionally chosen content to align with those trends. Humans, however, no matter their chosen professions, are more similar than different. Some of the research we draw from is specific to the engineering population, while much of it was conducted with broader populations.

It is also okay if you *are* an engineer and find that the specific framing of this book does not resonate. While we have observed trends, we have also observed individual differences. So, we invite you to read this text with an open mind, taking what is helpful and leaving the rest.

HOW TO APPROACH THIS BOOK

Changing your learned responses to thoughts and emotions in a way that better serves you is complicated and takes time. We want to encourage you to approach this book with a few things in mind. These following tips will help optimize your integration of these concepts.

Keep in mind that we all have thoughts and emotions.

If you are human, you have a brain. If you have a human brain, then of course, you have thoughts and emotions. Experiencing thoughts and emotions is related to wellbeing and mental health. Mental health can range from very healthy to very unhealthy. Fluctuations in mental health are natural, depending on life circumstances, just as is true for physical health. Mental health can also vary across different areas, such as mood, focus, and motivation. Perhaps, as you read, it's more apt to view mental health as multidimensional—existing as a collection of separate yet interrelated parts. These parts can and do change over time, depending on factors such as life circumstances and/or the tools and resources to handle them.

Mental health and mental illness are not synonymous. This book will address mental health broadly rather than review specific mental illnesses. Generally, mental illness is a set of diagnosable conditions, recognized by the *Diagnostic and Statistical Manual of Mental Disorders (DSM).* For the purposes of this book, we frame mental health this way: "Mental health includes our emotional, psychological, and social well-being. It affects how we think, feel, and act, and helps determine how we handle stress, relate to others, and make choices"("What is mental health?", n.d.). Thus, all humans have some level of mental health, yet only a portion of humans also have diagnosable mental illness. That being said, *a diagnosed mental illness does not define one's mental health.* For example, a person given a diagnosis of an anxiety disorder might also have the tools and skills necessary to manage this disorder and effectively maintain their overall mental health.

Whether or not you have personal experience with mental illness(es), we are hopeful that this book will provide helpful insight. Again, we do not review treatment of any specific diagnoses or conditions, so if you identify with a diagnosis or suspect that you may be affected by such a condition, it is important to also seek support from a qualified, licensed healthcare provider. Even if you do not personally identify with a diagnosis, therapy and other mental health resources can be extremely effective in helping manage life's difficulties.

An important note: this book is not a replacement for therapy or any other formal treatment. Please view it as a tool to help build insight about yourself and your mental health. We encourage you to see it as a supplement to other resources.

Hold a "both/and" position.

In efforts to cope with contradictory information, humans often take a strong stance on one side or the other. For instance, blaming oneself **or** blaming something external are common thinking patterns to cope with unfortunate circumstances. This limiting black-or-white thinking framework could exist among engineers: it is either the system's fault for not providing adequate resources and support, **or** it is the individual's fault for not doing enough to prioritize their wellbeing. In an either-or mindset, it cannot be both.

It is much harder to hold the honest truth that *both* the system and the individual may have a role to play. The system may be neglecting important responsibilities, for example, for their employees or students, **and** individuals might not use their own agency to protect their mental health. We encourage you to make space for both of these realities. Here, we also honor the true feelings of sadness, grief, and anger that arise when the systems do not meet individual needs. We aim to offer insight, language, and support to navigate thoughts and emotions in the ways that are within the individual's control.

Go slowly.

This book is structured with a combination of explanatory text, examples, and exercises. The text highlights the broad theory, the vignettes are generalized ways theory could be put into action, and the exercises help put the theory into action in the context of real life. Although it might be tempting to speed through the activities and examples with the goal of getting through the content, consider going slowly. Learning a new concept or process requires practice repeatedly before it becomes automatic. Start slowly, with reflection and practice, so that they become habitual. Perhaps you remember a time when your physics professor told you that just sitting back in lecture was not going to be enough, and that you actually had to try the problems for yourself, get stuck, start over, and work the details out by hand in order to really get the material. Well, the same is true here.

To get the most out of this book, we suggest reading a chapter or less at a time, completing the activities, and challenging yourself to access emotions as they arise. This moderate, interactive process will help shift the neural pathways, deepening learning. If time restrictions are a factor, another option is to read the book quickly to understand the content and revisit it again later. Keep in mind that reading quickly will not provide the full benefits, but it will offer a foundation to build upon at a future time.

Connect with others.

Humans are social beings. Psychological systems have evolved to rely on connection with others. Although working through this book independently will offer a foundation for change, making changes means practicing these skills **in the context** of relationships. For many, vulnerability in relationships is scary and can often be a barrier to change. We have intentionally written this book from our personal and professional perspectives, as a way to facilitate a relational connection between you, the reader, and us, the authors, often writing in the way we speak in therapy with our clients.

Again, increasing connection and vulnerability is a gradual

process, and it is okay if you do not feel confident in all these areas. For the time being, stay within your current comfort zone of connection while engaging with this text. Also, if you are not comfortable engaging with others around this information, read the book and complete the exercises independently for now. Later, if you have a few people you can be vulnerable with, consider bringing these concepts into conversation and into practice with those people.

Evaluate your readiness for change.

In our experience, decompiling can be dramatically different from how engineers previously learned to relate to their thoughts and emotions. And it can be exceedingly painful to challenge the assumptions that they have held onto for years. Assumptions can bring a sense of security and confidence in the world as well as provide a sense of control that offers protection from the unknown. Challenging these assumptions and learning a new way to relate to emotions and thoughts, then, is no easy task. Depending on context and life circumstances, you may be more or less ready to face the risks required in challenging these assumptions and moving toward change. If you personally feel ready to take these risks, even knowing you may experience some turbulence as your brain works to integrate these new concepts, that is okay. If you are not feeling ready to face the predictable destabilization in the process of change, that is also okay.

Be kind to yourself.

The process of change brings awareness of the behaviors that have not always worked. This awareness might bring some discomfort, regret, guilt, or even shame. These emotions are uncomfortable and might be associated with self-doubt and self-blame. So, be kind to yourself as you build awareness of the patterns that are not serving you well. You likely adopted those patterns for important, valid reasons. Perhaps those patterns served you well in the past. For instance, today, a pattern of yelling at others might currently harm you and your relationships; however, in your past, yelling may have been the only way that you were able to be heard or to protect yourself. Or maybe anger protected you from feeling other underlying emotions, such as sadness or fear, that were not accepted in your family or social groups.

Keep in mind that regretting past actions is often an indicator of growth and psychological health, as it allows an examination of past behaviors and a motivation for positive change. Our intention is to help increase awareness of current patterns that are not serving you while offering guidelines for change. If you notice uncomfortable emotions or self-critical thoughts while reading, this is normal and a sign of capacity for growth! If you feel overwhelmed, you can pause or seek additional support. For now, though, let's start decompiling!

DECOMPILING EMOTIONS

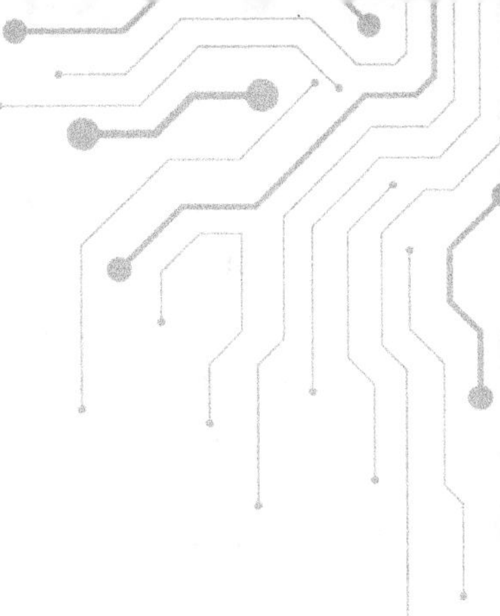

CHAPTER 1

EMOTIONS 1.0

WHAT COMES TO MIND WHEN THINKING ABOUT HOW emotions influence your life? Where do emotions sit at the table when it comes to making decisions—are they at the head or off to the side? Do they even have a seat?

As an engineer, leading with emotions can be ineffective or even downright dangerous, especially when running experiments or creating products with people's safety on the line. The engineers we have worked with are some of the brightest and best problem-solvers we have had the pleasure of meeting. Rationality has gotten them very far in life. While rational problem-solving works well in the lab, leading with logic in *all* of life's decisions and experiences does not seem to have the desired effect. For example, if a romantic couple is having a disagreement, attempts to determine who is "right" typically lead to circular arguments that leave both parties frustrated. Conversely, engaging with these emotions while actively listening to each other's perspectives is likely to bring the couple closer to some type of understanding.

Humans have evolved to experience emotions. Why might this be? Emotions are motivating, and they direct one's attention toward what is important. Understanding one's emotions is arguably one of the most important things a person can do, because

19

humans' relationships with their emotions influence their perceptions, attitudes, and habits. While emotional exploration is valuable, it can come with trepidation. Many engineers we have worked with fear that giving attention to emotions will lead to a loss of control. They are wary of involving emotions in the decision-making process, concerned these feelings will "interfere" with their goals. They worry that if they take time to experience the emotions, they will get distracted and derailed.

Paradoxically, when humans do not allow themselves to feel, they end up with even less control. When effort is exerted to consciously and unconsciously get rid of painful emotions, more immediate consequences drive the decisions. Decisions are then made based on how to eliminate emotions rather than what is most important in the long run. The conundrum here is that often the decisions that are best aligned with one's needs and values are accompanied by very uncomfortable emotions.

What could life be like if you were willing to experience difficult emotions? What if feelings of embarrassment, rejection, or sadness did not prevent you from taking risks or pursuing your passions? What could you accomplish if your challenging emotions did not have to be experienced as threats, but were instead perceived as data to collect and analyze? When you consider the long-term costs, you may find that your comfort zone is actually very *un*comfortable, and even costly.

Despite the quick and instinctive nature of emotions, processing and regulating these emotions is far from intuitive. Instead, these skills are developed with practice and an open mind. "Emotion regulation" (also referred to as emotional regulation) is the ability to manage and respond to emotions in a way that meets your needs and moves toward your values. Rather than reacting impulsively to emotions or avoiding them, learning how to decompile them to reveal their underlying meaning allows you to respond to them more effectively.

In the coming chapters, we will review what research says about emotions, provide evidence-based approaches to effectively understand and respond to emotions, present opportunities to learn from examples, and offer practice steps in decompiling emotions. At the end of this section, we've created a streamlined approach to the decompilation process. With practice, this new way of relating to emotions can become integrated into a decision-making process, to help you better meet your needs and move toward what is most important.

The content of this section is dense, so again, take time to reflect and practice. Taking breaks can also help with understanding and adopting these new practices. So, move through this section slowly. Fully engage in the exercises in order to increase self-reflection and integration of these skills.

A COMMON THEME

Before diving into the process steps, consider a theme we have observed in our sessions with engineers: an eagerness to immediately engage the prefrontal cortex, the area of the brain associated with problem-solving and planning, when any emotion arises. This engagement often shows up in attempts to answer two questions: 1) "Why am I feeling this way?" and 2) "How can I fix it/make it stop?"

Do you also ask these questions? If so, then while reading this book you might attempt to "debug" emotions in this way. Although this urge is not unusual, let's leave these questions out of the process for now. These "Why?" and "How?" questions are not inherently unhelpful or bad. It's simply that they are so familiar they might block alternative ways of relating to feelings, perhaps leaving a bias that limits growth. Instead, we want to build techniques that can lead to unexpected avenues of innovation in personal development.

In his book *Think Like an Engineer,* author Mushtak Al-Atabi, PhD, also suggests leaving the "whys and hows" for later. Al-Atabi describes various thinking and ideation techniques including "trimming" (Al-Atabi, 2014). Trimming is the process that attempts to improve a system by considering how it can operate *without* one of the components. A list of trimming steps (adapted from Al-Atabi's book) follows:

1. Break the product or system into its individual main sectors.

2. Identify the functions of each of the sectors.

3. Select a sector with a significant function, and mentally "trim" it.

4. Consider how to make the system work without the removed sector.

This method targets personal cognitive biases, requiring one to imagine radically different versions of products or systems that have become familiar.

Al-Atabi uses the example of eyeglasses. Though it is difficult to imagine anything but a classic pair of glasses, using trimming to break the concept into the two sectors (frames and lenses), and then to remove one of them (e.g., the frame), the product appears in an entirely new way. Exploring the function of the lens without the frame resulted in the concept of contact lenses. In this way, trimming can lead to exciting discoveries!

Using trimming, we are going to break down an entire system of emotional regulation and identify the functions of each component. We are going to decompile emotions without reflexively relying on the "Why?" and "How?" questions. Later, by reintegrating the "Why?" and "How?" questions, we'll develop a more thorough understanding of the answers.

WHAT ARE EMOTIONS, REALLY?

An article in *The Atlantic* (Beck, 2015) titled "Hard Feelings: Science's Struggle to Define Emotions" outlines the ways philosophers and scientists have studied and debated the concept of emotions for centuries. One famous study, conducted by Paul Ekman, tackled the universality of emotions. Ekman's work focused on measuring facial movement across Eastern, Western, and preliterate cultures. Participants matched photographs displaying certain facial expressions to particular emotions and were able to correctly categorize the expressed emotions at rates well above chance (Ekman, 1971). Ekman concluded that certain "basic emotions" are universally identified and expressed.

While this result certainly sounds impressive, the study's critics have had a lot to say about the study itself. One main critique, for example, is that the study included only six emotion words to choose from–leaving ample room for correct guesses. And while Ekman and Friesen (1971) found that humans belonging to a preliterate culture came close to matching the photographs at a comparable rate, researchers who repeated the study with separate preliterate groups were unable to replicate Ekman's results (Gendron et al., 2020).

In "Are Emotions Natural Kinds?" author Lisa Feldman Barrett, PhD, tackles the assumption that certain emotions (including anger, sadness, fear, disgust, and happiness) are globally consistent (Barrett, 2006). Barrett also challenges the idea that observable expressions (i.e., facial movements, blood pressure, vocal signals) reliably measure emotion. Instead, she proposes that emotions manifest in diverse ways, based on one's unique environment. She concludes that it all comes down to context: culture, language, and individual differences can profoundly impact how one experiences emotions.

To date, there is no consensus on a definition of emotions. Scientific measurements can only give so much insight. Ultimately, we believe that the only way to fully understand how another human is feeling is to listen to them. This can be unsatisfactory for some—especially scientifically-minded individuals who make sense of the world through precise data and elegant theories. Yet even scientists understand that their theories must account for the messiness of reality rather than the other way around.

In the early 1930s, for example, physicists felt they were close to a complete description of atomic nuclei in terms of fundamental particles called "quarks." Two quarks, the "up" and "down" quarks, sufficed to describe the nuclear structure of all known varieties of atoms and molecules. And yet, in 1936, scientists discovered a third quark, the "charm quark": a particle so unexpected and seemingly unnecessary that it prompted the physicist I.I. Rabi to quip, "Who ordered that?!" It turned out that nature was more complex—almost *needlessly* more complex—than scientists had expected. Yet, the presence of rare and exotic particles like the charm quark, and later the "strange," "top," and "bottom" quarks, ultimately produced a new and richer-if-messier understanding of the universe. That said, we take the universe as we find it, even when it is complicated or unfamiliar. Anything less means ignoring the truth of what is out there.

The boundless nature of the emotional experience can also be welcomed and appreciated. Sometimes humans react in ways that are shocking or surprising and, perhaps, even seem inappropriate or unnecessary. But the emotional states of others, and even of oneself, *can* be taken as they are found. In reality, an individual's expressed experience of emotion cannot reasonably be challenged or disputed. Their experience is indisputably their own, as they describe it.

Emotions are complex; humans can feel many different things

at once, and the feelings can all be connected. Thus, what other people see on the outside is only a small piece of what is happening on the inside. Laughing at a funeral or crying while angry is not necessarily inconsistent with the internal experience; instead, these very human responses simply require stretching our conceptions of what emotions are and can be. When emotions defy expected categorization, instead of questioning the validity of these internal *experiences,* questioning the *categories* might be more effective.

DEFINITION OF EMOTIONS

The American Psychological Association's definition of emotion captures the complexity of the topic while highlighting three different elements that an emotion might entail. The APA defines an emotion as a "complex reaction pattern, involving experiential, behavioral and physiological elements" (American Psychological Association, n.d.c). In the field of psychology, it is agreed that "emotions" are short-lasting and represent one's immediate internal responses. "Moods" on the other hand, are less intense, general states of feeling that do not necessarily result from a particular cue and sustain over a longer period of time (American Psychological Association, n.d.e). In this book, we use the words "emotions" and "feelings" interchangeably.

Emotions arise in response to external and internal situations or "stimuli." For example, an emotion can be elicited after receiving a grade on an exam (external) or in response to a thought about the grade (internal), possibly including excitement, regret, or embarrassment. Experiential reactions are felt internally in response to the stimulus. They are entirely subjective. This subjective experience is the first of three elements of emotions.

Emotions that arise in response to stimuli also depend on one's culture and background. For example, during a speech to a large audience, one might feel fear, anxiety, excitement, and even happiness. The reaction depends on life experiences, including past experiences with public speaking. Similarly, a person from a culture that relies on direct communication might feel relief and appreciation in response to a straightforward comment, whereas someone with a different cultural background might respond to that same comment with anxiety or shock.

The second element of an emotion, the behavioral response, refers to physically expressing the emotion to others (e.g., a smile, frown, or laugh). It often also involves more subconscious changes to non-verbal expressions like body language, posture, and tone of voice. These physical expressions can provide others with clues about how one is feeling. A surprise gift, for instance, might cue the behavioral response of smiling. However, differences in culture, context, and life experience might lead others to interpret these behaviors in ways that do not match the subjective, internal experience of the emotion. Some might interpret the smile as representing happiness and gratitude, while others might interpret the response as subdued, perhaps with the absence of a big hug as a sign that the present is not appreciated.

The third and final element, the physiological response, refers to the body's innate response. The autonomic nervous system activates an involuntary response to prepare the body for what might come next. For example, fear and anxiety might result in an increased heart rate, enhanced blood flow, and released adrenaline. Relief and satisfaction might show up physiologically as a lower blood pressure, and a slower rate of heart beats and breathing. The function is not communication, but survival. This leads us to the evolutionary benefits of these responses.

EVOLUTIONARY PSYCHOLOGY'S PERSPECTIVE

Evolutionary psychology conceptualizes emotions as adaptive responses to basic human needs: responses supporting the survival and procreation of humankind. That said, all emotions—even the unpleasant ones—can be beneficial. When met with a predator, early ancestors felt the emotion of fear. And it's a good thing, too! Without fear, they might have gone about their day unbothered by a beast three times their size, likely resulting in tragedy. Even if they intellectually understood there was a threat but did not *feel* the emotion, they might have spent too long analyzing the situation and theorizing about the best way to respond.

Leaning into intellect in such a situation is arguably as dangerous as not recognizing a threat at all. While fear can feel unpleasant, it signals that some type of action is required. Human minds use emotions to inform what steps should be taken next. Most importantly, they can (adaptively) make this happen quickly.

The areas of the brain responsible for autonomic emotional processes are called the amygdalae (plural of "amygdala"). The amygdalae are a pair of almond-sized structures embedded deep in the brain, roughly at the level of your eyes. They are located in the limbic system, which is broadly responsible for lower-order emotional processing. While the amygdalae facilitate a variety of affective responses to emotions, they are known mainly for their link with the emotion "fear." Therefore, amygdalae are known as the brain's "danger monitor." True to this nickname, amygdalae have the important job of responding to threatening stimuli.

When experiencing fear, the amygdalae are urgently communicating the danger to another part of the brain called the hypothalamus. The hypothalamus then activates the sympathetic nervous system, flooding the body with protective hormones.

Among these hormones is adrenaline, which provides the increased energy to do something about this urgent message. At the same time, a cascade of other physiological responses also occur including an increase in heart rate, a decrease in digestive processes, and a quickening of breath—all bodily changes that give an increased chance of survival in the face of a physical threat.

This rapid, involuntary response is often referred to as "fight or flight" because when it kicks in, the body prepares itself to either approach or run away from the threat. More recently, two more stress responses have been recognized. The first, "freeze," involves a slowing of the body, which can involve stopping movement or speech, and even dissociating as a means of survival. Additionally, there's "fawn," which involves seeking others for help, reassurance or comfort. All of these very different responses transpire *before* the logical part of the brain, the prefrontal cortex, has a chance to evaluate the situation. In other words, the emotional system has specifically evolved to outrun the logical part of the brain, in order to increase the chances of survival.

This is not to say that logic has not had its own place in human survival. While emotions provide immediate responses, logic enables planning for longer-term survival. Humans, perhaps the most self-conscious animals, developed a rational system of functioning including the ability to draw on one's past *and* imagine the future. This perspective afforded human ancestors the ability to anticipate danger and to problem-solve before facing that danger. Hunters, for instance, learned to set traps for predators instead of simply reacting to threats by fighting or fleeing. Rational thought also allowed gatherers to breed plants and provide year-round food sources. Clearly, both systems—rational and emotional— have helped humans to survive and even to thrive. On balance, effective survival requires a reliance on both emotional reactions and logical reflections.

SUMMARY

Emotions are behavioral and physiological responses to internal and external cues. While some emotions bring pleasure and others bring pain, all emotions serve a function. They exist to drive behavior to support survival. The skills tied to decompiling these emotions, which will be reviewed in the rest of Section I, will help you to respond to emotions more effectively. Understanding the core functions of emotions will also allow you to make decisions and to take action that is accurately aligned with the underlying needs.

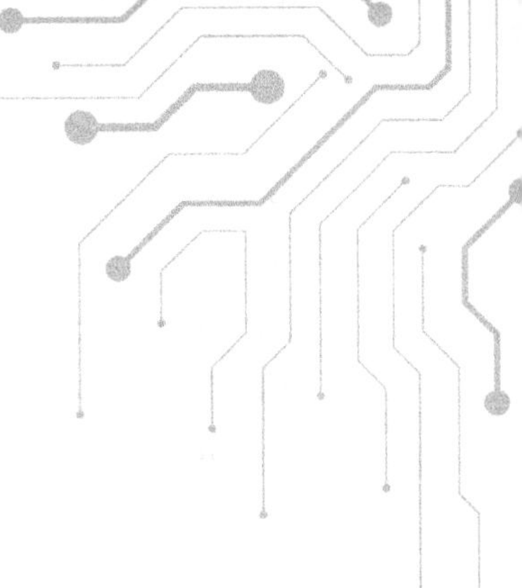

CHAPTER 2

EMOTIONAL AVOIDANCE

WHILE RELYING ON EMOTIONS IS ESSENTIAL, IT IS also difficult, because the human threat-response system is wired to avoid pain. Often, when our clients come in to start therapy, they express wanting to stop feeling particular emotions, such as anger or anxiety, altogether. They perceive emotions as problems that need to be overcome. This perspective is understandable as it is common to receive a message in childhood, whether explicitly or implicitly, that feelings such as sadness, anxiety, anger and fear, for example, are not okay.

Moreover, emotions can be uncomfortable and painful; they are often a reaction to something going wrong. Emotions might even feel intolerable, so of course, people are driven to get rid of them. Let's take a look at rejection. As social creatures, humans are particularly sensitive to this experience. It can bring up a wide range of feelings such as sadness, anger, shame, and fear. Using fMRI and meta-analytic research, Kross et al. found that "social rejection and physical pain are similar not only in that they are both distressing—they share a common representation in somatosensory brain systems as well" (Kross et al., 2011, p. 6273). This means that the pain of a stomach ache due to the flu and a stomach ache due to anxiety after a first date activate the same neurological channels. The neurological overlap between emotional pain and physical pain highlights the significance of our emotions, invalidating the expression, "Sticks and stones may break my bones, but words can never hurt me." The truth is that words can and do hurt.

Our clients are often surprised when we tell them that the function of therapy is not to get rid of painful emotions, but to relate to painful emotions in a new way. Embracing emotions rather than viewing them as burdens that should be avoided or challenged requires a significant paradigm shift. In the remainder of this section, we will reframe emotions. We will examine the common ways emotions are avoided, the consequences of doing so, and an alternative (more effective) way of responding. We have structured this content in a way that concretizes the often overwhelming and ambiguous world of emotion.

EMOTIONAL SUPPRESSION

The human brain can be quite creative in finding ways to avoid feelings. Often, this takes the form of what is called "emotional suppression," an attempt to push the unwanted emotions completely out of conscious awareness. Examples of suppression include scrolling on your phone, binging television, or using substances instead of feeling the emotions. Suppression can also include getting immersed in work or projects, again with the drive to avoid emotions.

The act of suppression can occur both consciously and unconsciously. Someone might actively choose to watch television instead of broaching a challenging conversation that will bring up anger and sadness. Alternatively, someone might automatically, outside of their conscious awareness, scroll on their phone without even recognizing that they are avoiding feelings of boredom or anxiety.

In some cases, these acts of suppression are essential for safety. In physically unsafe situations, short-term emotional suppression can allow someone to focus on an urgent task at hand, like running away from a threat. Paying too much conscious attention to the fear might prevent them from reacting to the immediate needs of the situation. Another example of suppression being helpful is in response to a difficult health diagnosis. For some, it might be beneficial to temporarily suppress the emotions that arise after immediately receiving a diagnosis in order to focus attention on necessary logistical tasks, such as scheduling a surgery or calling the insurance company. Emotional suppression is also protective in psychologically unsafe environments. Suppressing emotion in the presence of a judgmental boss might prevent further criticism or other negative consequences. In these cases, this temporary suppression maintains safety and allows the person to focus on necessary, even urgent action.

While temporary emotional suppression can be useful sometimes, it does not get rid of the emotion. Emotional suppression will change or limit the behavioral *expression* of the emotion, but it does not decrease the *experience* of the emotion (Gross, 2002). For instance, suppressing sadness might lead to less crying and better posture; however, the sadness will persist and continue to be impactful. This is also true for physical pain. Although someone cannot *force* themselves not to feel the sensation of a papercut, they might be able to successfully hide their reaction to the pain from others. But the ability to physically control their facial muscles and expressions does not neutralize the stinging sensation in the moment or prevent that same sensation later (when they accidentally cover the cut with hand sanitizer!).

Along with not being able to erase emotions, emotional suppression has been shown to lead to a whole slew of other challenges. Not only is emotional suppression associated with anxiety and depression (Dryman & Heimberg, 2018), but it is also associated with higher levels of pain among individuals with chronic illness (Thomas, 2006; van Middendorp, 2008) and even potential threats to cardiovascular health (Quartana & Burns, 2010). Researchers have also found an association between continual emotional suppression and poorer social adjustment, lower levels of positive affect, and decreased well-being (Gross & John, 2003). Interestingly, emotional suppression is also associated with *higher* negative affect. Said differently, those who attempt to push away painful emotions through suppression can experience greater painful emotions. The truth is that eliminating unwanted emotions is an impossible task, and ironically, attempts to do so intensify the very emotions being suppressed.

Metaphor for Emotional Suppression

The "beach ball" metaphor demonstrates the nature of efforts to suppress unpleasant emotions (Jepsen, 2012). Imagine that you are at a pool with a beach ball, whose buoyancy naturally causes it to float on the surface of the water. Now, picture yourself trying to suppress the beach ball's natural tendencies by forcing it underwater. As you can imagine, it takes considerable force to keep it there, and also requires your constant attention. The beach ball held underwater is in a state of unstable equilibrium; that is, you can maintain it so long as nothing disturbs it. But if the ball begins to roll even slightly out from under your hand, you can quickly lose control and find it shooting above the water and into the air, revealing itself even more dramatically and explosively than before.

Now imagine that others have joined you at the pool to enjoy a nice summer day. They have brought snacks and beverages and games. While the others surround you, you are still focused on keeping the ball underwater and are determined to prevent the ball from popping up to the surface. With this determination, your thoughts stay focused on the ball. It is difficult for you to engage in conversation with others because your thoughts are so consumed by the task at hand. You are not able to join in the games or have a snack because your hands are occupied with the ball. No matter how long you are able to keep it underwater, as soon as your attention falters, the ball will jump back up.

This metaphor reflects long-standing research on emotional suppression. Wegner et al. (1993) conducted a study that assessed participants' abilities to control their moods under different circumstances. Just as humans can be reasonably effective in suppressing a beach ball when that is the sole focus, Wegner found that participants were able to control their mood for short periods of time while undistracted. However, while engaging in a cognitive task like memorizing a nine-digit number, the participants' efficacy in controlling their mood decreased. In fact, efforts to control their mood while memorizing the number led to changes in mood opposite from what was intended.

Trying to hide or suppress painful emotions, like this interaction with a beach ball, might be effective for short periods of time without distraction, but it takes away from engaging in life. Also, the emotions do not actually disappear; they just live underneath the surface. Note that in this example, we do not blame the beach ball as the reason we are not able to fully engage at the pool party. Nor is it painful emotions themselves that hold us back from engaging in life. Rather, it is the attempts to *suppress* the beach ball, or the emotions, that limits our ability to be fully present.

INTELLECTUALIZATION

Another common method that humans use to avoid emotions is called intellectualization, or an attempt "to keep the entire spectrum of disturbing emotions at bay" by focusing on cognitive reasoning (Burgo, 2012, p. 148). Given the reasoning and problem-solving skills required of many engineering professionals, we have noticed intellectualization is a popular avoidance method among these analytical thinkers. Intellectualizing directs one's attention to the intellect and away from the bodily sensations of emotions. This process might look like asking "why" and "how" questions after a painful experience, rather than allowing the sensations of the emotion to be felt. Engaging in problem-solving and existential questioning are other ways intellectualization can show up. Those who regularly engage in intellectualization often are not aware that physiological sensations are arising even as they are preoccupied by their logical thoughts.

We certainly recognize how intellect and logic are valued in many professional communities. In interviewing engineers, we received many comments that these skills are necessary for their work, and that they are often rewarded for leading with their intellect. While these are powerful, important skills, it is important to note that leading exclusively with intellect while also dismissing the somatic experience of emotions has consequences.

For instance, intellectualization can lead to difficulty relaxing the mind, contributing to sleep concerns (Burgo, 2012). Of course, those who spend time in the middle of the night working out how they are feeling by getting lost in their thoughts do not do this because it is enjoyable. Instead, intellectualization can be used as an unconscious tool to cope with the discomfort of uncertainty. When the uncomfortable emotions that accompany uncertainty (such as anxiety and dread) feel intolerable, leaning on hypotheses about why something is happening can bring temporary relief.

While the insight that comes with intellectualization can bring comfort, the effort required to engage with critical thinking in response to every challenging moment is costly. In addition to sacrificing sleep, maintaining an intellectual disposition during challenging times can actually limit one's ability to move through them. For one, emotions play an essential role in creating opportunities for human connection. Attunement with your emotions allows you to feel and receive empathy, bringing you closer together with others. This closeness supports one's ability to cope and recover from stressful times. When you rely on your intellect and ignore your emotions, you risk making decisions and forming perspectives without the meaningful data that your emotions can supply (more on this later).

Signs of intellectualization include:

- Being aware of thoughts while struggling to notice the physiological experience of emotions

- Tending to assess or debate after/during a stressful experience

- Attaching a sense of self-worth to being smart or insightful

- Getting stuck in rumination

- Struggling to empathize with others' points of view and to accept a different way of perceiving a situation

- Circling around the same content in disagreements without accessing a deeper meaning or understanding of the emotional root of the disagreement

EXERCISE: EMOTIONAL AVOIDANCE

Take a few minutes to reflect on the ways you might avoid emotions. Please keep in mind that emotional avoidance is the mind's way of protecting itself. If you notice any shame or guilt arising during this reflection, know that you are not alone, and that avoiding pain is an inherent part of the human experience!

VIGNETTE

To demonstrate how emotions can be exacerbated when they are avoided, we are going to share a vignette of a dynamic that we frequently observe in our work. This vignette, along with all other vignettes in the book, features a fictional person who represents a compilation of experiences that we often observe in our clinical work. As you read, consider what parts of these vignettes you can relate to and what feels different from your experience:

Elena has an upcoming work project that is really important. She knows that her boss is expecting a lot from her, and Elena cares about doing her best. Elena feels nervous about the project and experiences a queasiness in her stomach and tightness in her body. She also feels "antsy" and struggles to sit still.

Because this is an uncomfortable situation, Elena is driven to get rid of these feelings. She tries to distract herself with her phone and video games. While those distractions work for a while, the nerves come back immediately once she puts the device away. She also tries to brainstorm ways to get out of the nerve-wracking situation, including asking for a project extension. She uses logic to try to reason her way out of the nerves, justifying why she should not feel nervous.

Elena perceives her nervousness as a burden and worries that she will not be able to perform sufficiently if she does not get the nerves under control. Because she is now also nervous about her nervousness, her emotions escalate to dread and anxiety. As soon as the queasiness hits, another wave of anxiety and dread arise in response, on top of the nervousness. She feels frustrated that she is not able to rid herself of those feelings.

After working hard to try to get rid of those feelings and discovering that if anything, they have intensified, Elena starts to experience feelings of shame as well. She does not want to think of herself as an anxious person and feels weak for not being able to control her emotions. Before long, Elena finds herself in a shame spiral and feels paralyzed by self-criticism and a sense of dread. What started as a natural response to a high-pressure situation has resulted in an overwhelming sense of despair and self-hatred.

CONSIDERATIONS

As in Elena's case, the futility of exiling unwanted emotions does not stop people from trying. After all, in modern society, there is easy access to all kinds of avoidance tools: alcohol, drugs, food, screens, overworking, and more. The constant temptations to numb emotions through stimulating experiences greatly tests one's willpower. And these tools *can* bring relief, even if only for a moment.

Barring safety concerns, occasional avoidance can be fairly harmless in the short-term. After a long and stressful day, who doesn't want to zone out and watch a comfort show or surrender to the social media algorithms? More active distractions, such as trying to solve someone else's problems, can also offer temporary relief from personal stressors. But emotional avoidance becomes more concerning in the long-term if the uncomfortable emotions are not processed or revisited later. Avoidance is also problematic if it limits or prohibits completing necessary tasks.

The pressures and obligations of modern life also compete with the needs of emotional wellness. Emotional avoidance can become a necessity in a system that does not always make space for emotions. Many people work long hours at stressful jobs with limited opportunities for social connection. As a result, these individuals might navigate life without social support structures in place. And perhaps their bosses or organization leaders do not fully acknowledge their employees' humanity and need for connection, rest, and play.

Emotional processing can create a sense of vulnerability and risk when in a context that judges or punishes these human reactions. Even in private moments or with people who are accepting and empathetic, people in these contexts might experience depleted levels of energy and might not have the mental and emotional resources to make space for emotions. Understandably, the default of zoning out, numbing, distracting, or intellectualizing might become more compelling.

While we want to empower you to make space for and embrace emotions, we also acknowledge that time and other resources are not equally accessible to everyone. For instance, some work multiple jobs to meet their and their family's basic needs. Trauma history, life circumstances, and other individual differences can all impact how much space is needed for emotional processing. That said, we hold space for a "both/and" approach, encouraging individuals to prioritize their emotions

and to consider the environmental barriers that impact their ability to safely embrace their emotions.

Emotional avoidance is not an ideal long-term solution for wellness, and, it is often a strategy that is necessary for pragmatic safety and functioning. We recognize that it can be challenging to hold these two, seemingly contradictory, truths. To help address this tension, when presenting suggestions for effectively decompiling emotions, we will also offer guidelines for navigating the nuances of individual circumstances, especially when access to the necessary time and resources for emotional processing are not available.

SUMMARY

Humans are "wired" to avoid pain. Emotional and physical pain is the body's cue that a situation or stimulus is dangerous, and that action should be taken to avoid the danger. This instinctual response works well in some contexts, like the instinct to avoid a hot stove by pulling your hand away. However, when it comes to emotional pain, this instinct is often not helpful. Avoiding the emotional pain that arises in response to internal and external cues often leads to exacerbated distress and symptoms. While there are circumstances where short-term avoidance is necessary or unavoidable, avoiding emotional pain is not a sustainable approach to wellness.

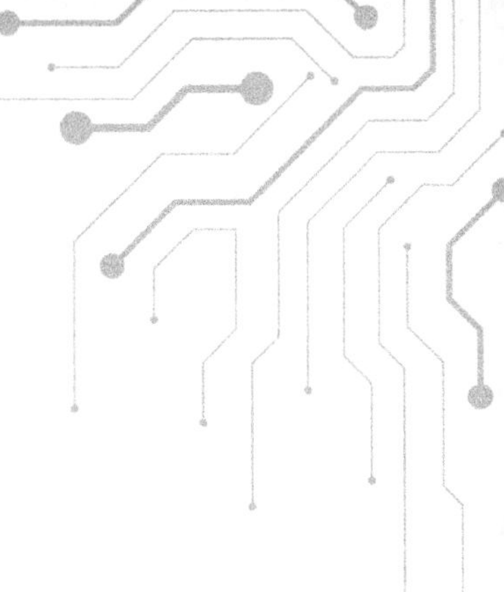

CHAPTER 3

THE FUNCTION OF EMOTIONS

WE'VE SEEN THE VALUABLE ROLE EMOTIONS PLAYED in keeping the hunter-gatherer ancestors safe. Understanding the role that emotions play in our modern world is also helpful in overcoming emotional avoidance. After all, if the purpose of pain can be acknowledged, it is easier to accept and engage with it. In therapy, we often encourage clients to consider what the arising emotion is trying to do for them. We find that this can help clients feel less resentment or shame for their emotions while also building some insight into the needs being highlighted through the presence of the emotion. For instance, one might realize their emotion of anxiety indicates that they care about their professional goals, and it is the mind's way of trying to motivate them to prepare thoroughly.

Developing an understanding of emotions and their evolutionary functions, then, can bring a sense of normalization and connection to humanity (Lench & Carpenter, 2018). Emotions are inherently human and serve a variety of functions in support of survival. Moreover, emotional awareness can provide a "richness to experience" (Lench & Carpenter, p. 5), connecting the broader context of an emotional reaction in a given moment. This awareness also increases the capacity of appreciation for others' experiences.

UNDERSTANDING THE FUNCTION OF EMOTIONS

Emotions are there to help. It can be useful to ask, "What is this emotion trying to do for me?" The key word here is "trying." Emotions are helpful data, but the instinctual response to the emotion is not always effective. Lench and Carpenter (2018) note the discrepancy between the evolutionary purpose of the emotion and its functional impact in the modern world.

Let's take another look at anxiety. Evolutionarily speaking, anxiety is a means of preventing harm from potential future threats (Parsafar & Davis, 2018). The emotion of anxiety is perfectly natural and often does help people to prepare and to avoid future harm. Experiencing anxiety before a white-water rafting trip, for example, will likely help us remember to make sure the equipment is safe and to take necessary training courses beforehand.

But many experience a level of anxiety that escalates to a point where it is no longer adaptive. In the modern world, people are aware not only of the potential threats in their immediate sphere, but also globally. In addition to upcoming stressors in their personal lives, such as a work deadline and a family conflict, modern technology allows humans to be ever more aware of threats such as political upheaval and climate change. In these complex and broad spheres, individuals have limited direct or immediate control. The instinctual responses to anxiety, such as preparing and worrying, then become overwhelming and unmanageable. Thus, anxiety becomes ineffective, as the "what ifs" and sense of uncertainty become immobilizing.

The evolutionary functions of emotions continue to be helpful in the modern world, yet it is up to the individual whether adaptive or maladaptive behaviors result. Knowing the complex nature of emotions also leads to some big questions. If emotions are inherent to the human experience and yet can sometimes lead to destructive actions, how does a person accept the emotions without acting out in ineffective ways? How do they reap the benefits of understanding the function of emotions without acting on the innate reactions that may not serve them? Throughout the remainder of this section, we will engage with these inquiries and explore how to decompile emotions in order to respond effectively.

Given the messiness of the questions above, as well as the complicated nature of the human mind and society, let's set some expectations. We will not be able to provide answers perfectly fitted for every scenario. We can, however, help to put these questions into context and frame them in a way that might offer new insight. We'll offer an alternative way to understand and relate to emotions in a way that fosters wisdom and thoughtful responses. To start, we have created a table that describes the function of various emotions and also provides examples of how they can show up in the modern world.

Function of Emotions

Emotion	Function(s)	Example of when emotion is experienced
Fear	Fear provides you with protection and avoidance of harm from immediate and actual threat	When a car is swerving toward you
Anxiety	Anxiety provides you with protection and avoidance of harm from distant and potential threats	Possibility that a future presentation will not go well
Sadness	Sadness fosters cognitive change which allows cognitive restructuring to take place and new goals to be developed after you experience a loss or setback; it elicits aid from others during a time of vulnerability; it conserves energy through low arousal during a time of compromised immune system	After being rejected for a conference proposal
Grief	Grief motivates others to offer aid after a loss and fosters the experience of compassion from others; it helps you reflect on values and meaningful connections	After being laid off from a job
Boredom	Boredom motivates behavior change to increase your cognitive engagement; it motivates more optimal use of conscious awareness, given that resources are finite	Engaging in a mundane task that is not perceived as important

Emotion	Function(s)	Example of when emotion is experienced
Anger	Anger motivates you to set boundaries in order to protect yourself; it motivates others to change their actions by giving negative consequences for undesired behavior	A co-worker is not meeting expectations
Admiration	Admiration motivates you to improve your skills in order to emulate others that you respect; it contributes to a sense of affiliation with a respected person	Interacting with a co-worker perceived to be good at their job
Happiness	Happiness fosters social bonding; it increases your ability for flexibility in your thinking and focus	Achieving a promotion that you have worked toward for the last six months
Pride	Pride fosters actions that are consistent with your self-driven goals	Solving a problem that supported the team

Note. This table is based on research from several authors (Andrews & Thomson, 2009; Bench & Lench, 2013); Danckert et al., 2018; Huron, 2018; Karnaze & Levine, 2018; Klinger, 1975; Parsafar & Davis, 2018; Rachman, 1998; Reed & DeScioli, 2017; Roseman, 2018; Storbeck & Whyte, 2018; Williams, 2028; Wrosch et al., 2003).

Understanding the function of emotions is an essential first step to building insight into your underlying needs. The next table gives examples of potential needs different emotions might reflect. Please keep in mind that this list is not exhaustive, but a tool to start thinking about needs in relation to emotions. Our emotions and their respective needs cannot always be taken at face-value. Later in this section, we'll be exploring ways in which emotions can be layered on top of one another, and how to discern which needs are at the root of the experience.

Identifying Needs

Emotion	Possible need(s)
Sadness	Acceptance of circumstances in order to make new goals; connection or support from others
Anger	Enforced boundaries; awareness that boundaries are being crossed
Fear	Safety or the acceptance of limited safety in current circumstances
Grief	Processing the loss of a relationship or expectations; support from others
Boredom	A new activity, or acceptance that activity is not engaging at this time yet with recognition that there is value in continuing with the activity
Happiness	Continued engagement in current behaviors and connections to others
Anxiety	Preparedness for upcoming circumstances; acceptance of uncertainty

VIGNETTE

Take a moment to recall Elena's situation. Consider how Elena could use the previous table when she notices anxiety about her work project. While reviewing the table, Elena might see that anxiety is the body's way of preparing for possible danger. In contrast to the immediacy of fear, Elena would see that the anxiety probably denotes that there is no current danger, but that preparation for future circumstances might be necessary. While reviewing the needs indicated by the emotion, Elena could then direct her attention to preparing for the project as well as to acknowledging and accepting the uncertainty of the situation. Rather than fighting the anxiety or blaming herself for not controlling it, Elena can be more accepting of her anxiety, viewing it as a human emotion trying to be helpful and motivating.

SUMMARY

Recognizing that emotions have functions is a key step in being able to decompile them. Even when emotions feel like a burden, or the instinctual responses to emotions create additional hurdles, the evolutionary root of these emotions centers on survival. While these instinctual responses are not always adaptive in the modern world, their presence points to a core need.

CHAPTER 4

MINDFULNESS

AS PREVIOUSLY DISCUSSED, OUR CLIENTS' INITIAL response to an emotion is often to use their prefrontal cortex—the reasoning center of the brain—trying to understand *why* they are experiencing that emotion and *how* to solve the problem of that emotion. In some ways, this response makes a lot of sense! The reasoning skills offered by the prefrontal cortex have served these intelligent adults extremely well, and they have been significantly rewarded for their ability to quickly and effectively assess and solve problems.

Yet asking "Why?" and "How?" typically pulls them out of the moment by centering their attention on the past and future, respectively. In this mode, engineers can spend hours analyzing why they are experiencing an emotion by repeatedly reviewing past events. They can also spend just as long thinking about how they might resolve the uncomfortable emotion or strategizing ways to avoid emotional discomfort in the future. But what about the present? How much time is allotted to just...feel?

Mindfulness offers this option. A concept with its roots in Hindu and Buddhist traditions which has been extensively researched and documented in Western psychotherapy, mindfulness has gained traction as an effective tool in many realms, including business, medicine, and psychotherapy. This research emphasizes the wide range of benefits. To name a few, mindfulness practices are linked to a decrease in depression (Kuyken et al., 2015), a reduction in anxiety and stress (Steffen et al., 2017), improvements in short-term memory (Greenberg et al., 2019), enhancements in emotion regulation skills (Frank et al., 2014), improvements in cognition including flexible thinking (Zou et al., 2020), and improvements in physical health conditions such as fibromyalgia (Cash et al, 2015).

Pretty impressive, right? So, what *is* it? The American Psychological Association provides the following definition (American Psychological Association, n.d.j):

Mindfulness is awareness of one's internal states and surroundings. Mindfulness can help people avoid destructive or automatic habits and responses by learning to observe their thoughts, emotions, and other present-moment experiences without judging or reacting to them.

Although it is natural to dislike certain emotions, thoughts, or physical sensations, mindfulness does not view these experiences through a lens of morality. Thoughts, emotions, and physical sensations are neither "right" nor "wrong," or "good" nor "bad." They are just hard-wired responses to the environment. Mindfulness fosters an understanding of these sensations as data points that give information about current experiences. When conducting research, judging individual data points in a research study as "good" or "bad" is an easy recipe for generating biased results. Similarly, judging your internal experiences can lead to misinterpreting the information provided.

RIDING OUT AN EMOTION

Emotions can be challenging. Sometimes it is not physically or psychologically safe to access emotions in certain contexts, especially when trauma is involved. Trauma can be defined as a "disturbing experience that results in significant fear, helplessness, dissociation, confusion, or other disruptive feelings intense enough to have a long-lasting negative effect on a person's attitudes, behavior, and other aspects of functioning" (American Psychological Association, n.d.h). Because of those long-lasting negative effects, those with a history of trauma may find that confronting painful emotions is extremely overwhelming and dysregulating. The Decompiling Emotions section of this book addresses processing emotions *unrelated* to trauma. Later in this chapter, we will discuss how to determine whether or not the decompiling process is an effective approach to processing an emotion.

It is not uncommon to worry that uncomfortable emotions will not stop once they begin; this concern can make allowing oneself to experience emotions feel risky. However, research shows that the average emotion lasts less than two minutes (Taylor, 2006). Neuroscientist Jill Bolte Taylor posits that an emotion arises as a 90-second chemical experience, in reaction to an environmental cue. That said, it can be helpful to think of emotions as waves that come and go, knowing that an emotion has a beginning, a middle (which peaks in intensity), and an end.

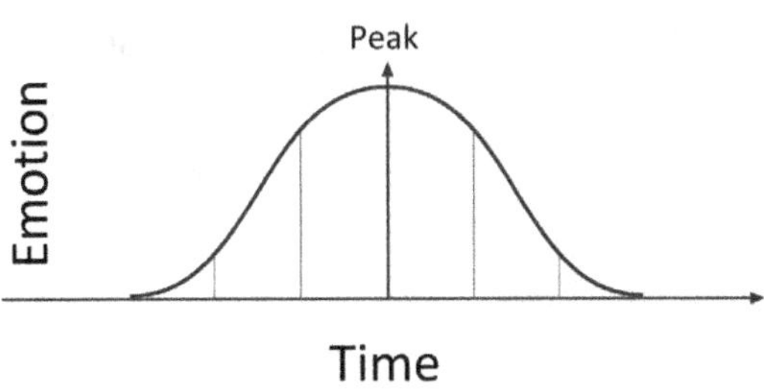

You might be thinking, "My emotions last longer than that!". Taylor addresses this very experience, explaining that any remaining emotional response after the 90 seconds is perpetuated by what she calls "emotional loops" (Taylor, 2006). These loops consist of reactive and often avoidant thoughts, which evoke the body's physiological response over and over again. While the initial experience of sadness might last around 90 seconds, resistance to the sadness via these reactive or avoidant thoughts might prolong the experience and feed into these loops.

In other words, resistance prevents a person from fully moving through the sadness in that moment; the emotional flow is interrupted with various protective systems. For example, the thought "I shouldn't have to be in this unfair situation" might subconsciously show up as a way to avoid feeling sadness, thereby blocking the full wave of the emotion. Each time a glimmer of sadness arises, immediately focusing on thoughts about the unfairness of the situation prevents the full processing of sadness and prolongs the experience.

The emotional system will continue to revisit the avoided sadness until given space to ride the wave. This is not to say that riding the wave means never having to experience that emotion again. It does, however, move you one step closer to effectively moving through the emotion tied to that particular life event.

Riding the wave is productive, helping you process and move forward from an emotion. Many biological, social, cultural, and psychological factors can influence thoughts and how they sustain these loops. We will explore some of these when discussing the decompiling process. For now, let's explore how we can feel emotions without distraction by staying in the present moment.

LIVING IN THE PRESENT

What does inhabiting the present look like? For starters, it involves paying attention to the physiological experience of emotions. As thoughts can block the processing of emotions, noticing the physical sensations can be an anchor that aids the processing of emotions without getting lost in the distracting thoughts. If suppressing or intellectualizing has been your typical way of responding to emotions, allowing yourself to focus on the physiological experience of emotions can feel foreign.

To remain present, it is important to sit in the discomfort of the emotion and observe it. While "sitting" and "observing" may seem to be simple tasks, for most, this practice of attention can be extremely uncomfortable. It can contribute to feelings of helplessness and fear when acknowledging that "doing" or "solving" is not effective at this point. It can be humbling to allow the body to take the lead in the emotional regulation process. Many minds have automatic thinking patterns (e.g., rumination, intellectualization, and self-criticism) that are difficult to distinguish from deliberate observation. It takes active, intentional effort to pick out these thought patterns and to reposition oneself back into neutral observation. (In this section, we'll offer exercises involving sitting and observing internal experiences in order to identify the emotions.)

Collectively, these tasks are aspects of mindfulness. Jon Kabat-Zinn, developer and founder of an evidence-based practice called "mindfulness-based stress reduction" (MBSR), defines three components of mindfulness: it's on purpose, in the present moment, and non-judgmental (Kabat-Zinn, 1994). The first component, "on purpose," implies approaching awareness with intentionality. For example, we can purposefully notice the breath and direct attention to the sensations of inhaling and exhaling.

In his book *The Principles of Psychology, Vol. 1,* psychologist William James wrote: "My experience is what I agree to attend to" (James, 1890, p. 402). In other words, *choice* is inherent to experience. Imagine purposeful attention as the beam of a flashlight in a dark room; it takes forethought to turn the flashlight on, point it, and observe what is visible in the contained pool of light. The light cannot cover the entire room at once. Instead, attention will only focus on one thing at a time, eventually mapping the entire room.

The second component is being "in the present moment," directing attention to thoughts and sensations in the *here and now.* While controlling all thoughts, feelings or physiological experiences is not possible, it is possible to intentionally direct attention. We are not referring to the act of *keeping* attention (many people struggle with focusing on one subject or task for a length of time). Being in the present means the act of consciously choosing to redirect attention after the mind wanders. In fact, the act of noticing this wandering is an effective way to connect to the here-and-now.

The third component of mindfulness is "non-judgmentally." Whatever arises in the present moment is met with kindness, curiosity, and non-judgment. Often, this component of mindfulness is the most challenging, because internal experiences can be quite difficult. Associations of harsh self-criticism with particular thoughts, feelings, or sensations can also be a barrier to noticing with non-judgment.

Let's imagine feeling envy towards a coworker because they were chosen to receive a promotion. If you view envy as unacceptable, you might get stuck in self-critical thoughts, judgment, and shame, all distractions from feeling the envy itself. Thinking "They don't deserve the promotion" might feel more distressing if this coworker is also a close friend, leading to feelings of guilt for having this thought. These critical thoughts and guilt can compound, leading to self-criticism and shame about the critical thoughts and guilt. In this swirl of critical thoughts, the original emotion of envy gets lost. Mindfulness can be helpful in slowing down and noticing the initial emotion.

Engineers like those we work with already possess an essential skill that can help when practicing mindfulness: the ability to *objectively observe.* Like discerning different reactions in the lab, quantifying the uncertainties of results, or detecting trends in data, mindfulness encourages the observation of thoughts, feelings, and physical sensations just as they are, without immediately trying to change them. While change may be necessary—such as strategically taking out or re-measuring outliers in the data—it is important to first observe and take note of what exists before intervening. Similarly, when being mindful, the job is to simply pay attention.

MISCONCEPTIONS

The growing popularity of mindfulness is a double-edged sword. On one hand, it is amazing that such an effective, useful skill is widely known. On the other hand, the more popular it becomes, the more likely that "mindfulness" as such will be incorrectly communicated to the public. One recent study found that a significant number of lay people incorrectly view mindfulness as a "passive endorsement of experience, undermining engaged problem-solving" (Choi et al., 2021, p.1). In this misapprehension, practicing mindfulness is thought to mean surrendering to and disengaging from life's challenges. Of course, we assume most people do *not* want to resign to their challenging circumstances—quite the opposite!

Mindfulness involves acknowledging one's experiences

directly. Acknowledgement is not an act of complacency. It also does not mean ignoring one's values or letting go of one's goals. And it certainly does not mean putting up with circumstances causing great pain. The type of acknowledgement mindfulness requires is not passive at all. When mindfully "sitting with" uncomfortable thoughts, emotions, and physical sensations, one is acknowledging them first, not trying to change or deny them.

Brains generate automatic thoughts, emotions, and physical sensations; these internal experiences are not chosen. By the time an uncomfortable emotion occurs, you are already feeling it; what you are trying to fix or avoid has already happened, whether you choose to pay attention to it or not. (One might take steps to address future occurrences of this negative emotion, but that happens later.)

The first step is to accept that you have already felt the emotion. We have often heard our clients say, "What is the point of letting myself feel sad if it won't change my situation?" What we are saying here is that mindfulness *does* lead to change. In fact, it arguably leads to more effective change than reflexively reacting without bringing awareness to internal experiences. Building insight into these experiences helps people understand what type of change they need. Having done this, they can take action with clarity. As in engineering, if a prototype is behaving incorrectly, then, absent safety concerns, you might let the "malfunction" play out, paying careful attention to form an accurate impression of the scope and source of the problem.

Another common misconception about mindfulness centers on what it means to "notice" or "pay attention" to emotions. In a certain sense we "notice" our emotions every time we experience them. We typically will not feel sad while also being completely unaware of that feeling.

But the experience of an emotion as we are swept up in it

is not what mindfulness implies. A mindfulness perspective means noticing the emotion from a distance, experiencing the emotion while maintaining awareness that *we* are separate from the emotion itself. This is also why mindful observance is said to be "dispassionate" or "non-judgmental." If we notice we're feeling angry about something and respond to this emotion with judgment, then we can be overtaken by the resulting emotional loops, swept away with the current.

To help distinguish "noticing an experience" versus "being immersed within it," consider a morning commute to school or work (or, in this work-from-home era, perhaps consider a trip to the supermarket). Traveling the familiar route, you are undoubtedly "experiencing" the trip. Your brain makes all the correct turns, takes note of all the stoplights, and carefully monitors for obstacles, detours, and traffic jams.

But suppose one day you challenge yourself to really *study* the route, perhaps intending to describe it to a friend who has to make the same trip. You will find a wealth of information that your brain quite reasonably tunes out or aggregates during a more ordinary experience of the trip. Did you actually know the number of the exit? Or do you simply remember it as "the first exit after the Arby's sign?" Did you realize that the road narrows from four lanes to three at a certain point, and could that be why you always feel more stressed on the second half of the drive? If you walk or bike there, which segments of the sidewalk were most recently repaved? What birds or animals can be heard along the way? Is there a certain car that is always parked by the side of the road?

You can take note of these and other details because you are now *observing* the experience of the commute from the outside, rather than going through the motions on autopilot. In the same way, there are likely emotional journeys in your lives that are so familiar, so overwhelming, or both, that they sweep you along, providing the illusion that you realize what is happening but without giving you the chance to see the bigger picture. Real mindfulness challenges you to break that pattern, to be "on the ride" but also outside it, cataloging what happens while setting aside judgment about the experience.

EXTERNAL AND INTERNAL

Mindfulness can be practiced by engaging with any or all of our senses: sight, sound, touch, taste, and smell. These senses help bring awareness to the external world. For instance, when smelling a flower, we engage with something that is outside of ourselves.

In *Mindfulness for Beginners,* Jon Kabat-Zinn (2016) writes about how mindfulness also includes the mind, or the mind's awareness, as the sixth sense. Awareness is a tool to orient to place (space), or what happened before this moment (time). As with the five traditional senses, awareness can be taken for granted because this process happens fairly automatically. Slowing down and intentionally observing the present moment fully engages the senses, which helps us connect to the external world (what you see, hear, touch, smell, and/or taste).

Senses then connect to the internal (thoughts, emotions, and physical sensations) differently. In this way, Kabat-Zinn says, "... everything can become our teacher of the moment, reminding us of the possibility of being fully present: the gentle caress of air on our skin, the play of light, the look on someone's face, a passing contraction in the body, a fleeting thought in the mind. Anything. Everything. If it is met in awareness." (2016, p. 55).

While practicing mindfulness, awareness can be directed toward the external world, the internal world, or both. Some mindfulness exercises focus on one or the other, but there is no wrong way to practice mindfulness as long as the three pillars of mindfulness are in place: on purpose, in the present moment, and non-judgment.

A WORD OF CAUTION

As with any inner work, painful thoughts and feelings can and likely will arise when practicing mindfulness. Again, mindfulness can often help in processing painful thoughts and emotions. Yet sometimes, these thoughts and feelings can feel so overwhelming that the work needs to be gradual and/or supported by a mental health professional, especially if an individual has a history of trauma.

In his book *Trauma-Sensitive Mindfulness,* David A. Treleaven, PhD, (2018) provides insight into how trauma can impact one's experience of mindfulness. He also discusses warning signs that indicate when mindfulness practices might be activating these experiences rather than being helpful. While his book is written to help practitioners support their clients, we believe that just about anyone concerned with or interested in the topic can benefit from its content.

Thus far, we have discussed how avoidance of inner pain can add additional stress and even amplify unwanted emotions or thoughts. And while studies show that such experiences occur in some cases, this paradoxical phenomenon does *not* apply to trauma as it is a "different kind of pain" (Trelevaen, 2018, p. 67). Treleaven goes on to describe how the avoidance of traumatic pain can be "an intelligent, survival-based response" (p. 67). It is true that avoidance can prolong suffering. It is also true that it can be protective.

Trauma is more than a challenging emotional experience.

When someone experiences a traumatic stress response, the brain and body respond as though the trauma is happening all over again. Safety becomes the priority, and the brain and body work hard to survive the re-experienced moment. During a traumatic stress response, one can experience an excess of arousal (hyperarousal), which can cause disorganized cognitive processing, hypervigilance, overstimulation, and difficulty paying attention (Trelevaen, 2018). This is the mechanism that supports our capacity for fight or flight. Another experience can be too little arousal (hypoarousal), which can disable cognitive processing altogether, making the individual feel apathetic, removed, or immobilized. This is the mechanism that aids the stress response to freeze. It is also possible to oscillate between the two; together, hyperarousal and hypoarousal make self-regulation extremely challenging.

One particularly severe hypoarousal response is called "dissociation," which is "a defense mechanism in which conflicting impulses are kept apart or threatening ideas and feelings are separated from the rest of the psyche" (American Psychological Association, n.d.b). Someone who experiences dissociation feels disconnected from their feelings, thoughts, behaviors, and/or surroundings. They can lose their memory, sense of time, and orientation to their surroundings. Some describe an out-of-body experience, as though they are watching themselves experience life. Others describe a disconnect from their environment, feeling like the world around them is "fake."

Most people experience dissociation at some point as it is the brain and body's normal response to extreme stress and trauma. In addition, there are varying degrees of dissociation, and it is not necessarily an indication of a serious disorder. Nonetheless, it can be very distressing.

Between hyperarousal and hypoarousal lies the "Window of Tolerance," a concept created by Dan Siegel (Siegel, 1999). When inside this window, people can experience challenging emotions such as anger, frustration, sadness, and fear while remaining able to effectively process and integrate their emotional experiences, as well as cope with their stress. They are also able to take in new information, practice curiosity, and remain oriented to themselves and their environment—no matter what kinds of emotions they are experiencing. According to Siegel, people differ in the emotional intensities and tolerable levels of stress. Also, their windows can change over time. For those who have experienced extreme stress or trauma, the tolerable range often narrows as a safeguard against threats.

The Window of Tolerance

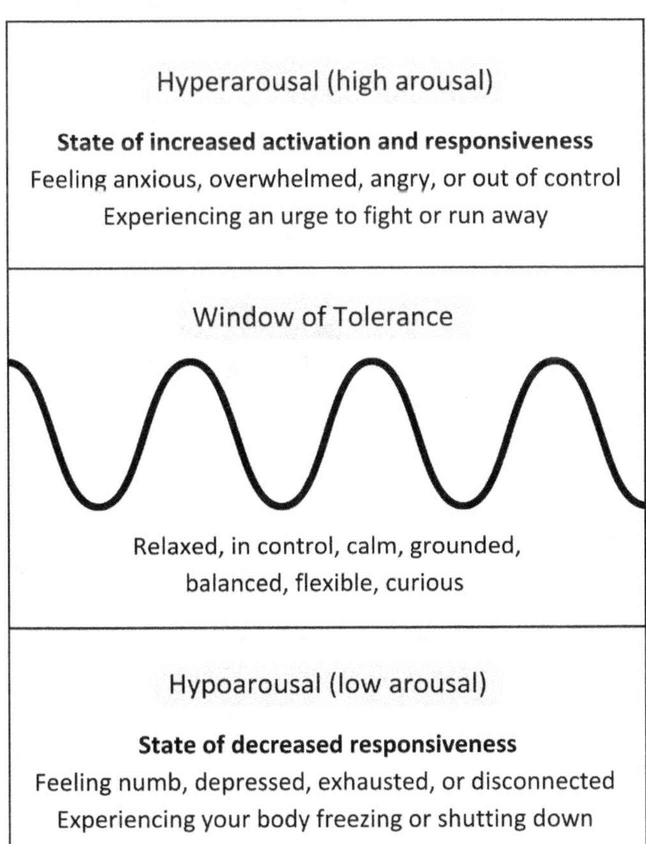

As you approach the exercises in this book, please keep the Window of Tolerance in mind. Inside your window, emotions are able to ebb and flow without leading to dysregulation. While some of the exercises might elicit discomfort, they are not meant to cause distress. Also, please know that turning attention towards inner experiences has the potential to push you outside of your window, depending on your specific levels of tolerance. And as you've just read, practicing skills outside of your window can be unproductive; when the brain and body respond to a perceived threat, fighting, fleeing, or freezing become the brain and body's priority, not emotion regulation or learning something new.

Remember: you are in the driver's seat, and you have the agency to decide when an exercise or topic feels safe, and when it does not. To build insight into your own Window of Tolerance, please refer to the following table.

Window of Tolerance

State	Indications
Hyperarousal	Significant increase in heart rate Significant increase in heart rate Racing thoughts Panic Difficulty concentrating Feeling overwhelmed Hypervigilance, feeling unsafe Tightening or tensing of muscles, which can lead backaches, headaches, neck and jaw pain Eruptive, reactive emotions Overwhelming irritability or anger Feeling out of control Flashbacks or intrusive memories or images

State	Indications
Window of Tolerance	Feeling calm, present, alert, engaged, curious, grounded Oriented to what is happening, the time, personal identity, and physical surroundings. Feeling the full range of emotions while also staying oriented to the environment. Feeling able to take in new information.
Hypoarousal	Emotional numbness Feeling empty Operating on "autopilot" Chronic fatigue Chronic lack of motivation Difficulty concentrating Memory issues, trouble recalling information Dissociation Feeling outside of the body or as though the immediate surroundings are not "real"

Engaging with the content of this book will be most impactful while within the Window of Tolerance. As mentioned earlier, everyone possesses different levels of tolerance. Learning your personal signs that you are outside of that window is important. And recognizing hyperarousal or hypoarousal as it is happening can be a very challenging skill. If you have any difficulty distinguishing between levels of arousal, or have a history of extreme stress or trauma, please approach the mindfulness exercises with caution and possibly the support of a therapist. If you stray outside of the Window of Tolerance, then 1) stop engaging with the activating exercise or stimuli, and 2) prioritize becoming regulated.

Grounding for Regulation

To help with regulation, let's explore how to use "grounding." Grounding is a skill which can be used to regulate intense anxiety or overwhelming feelings, with the goal of returning to the Window of Tolerance. While some grounding and mindfulness skills overlap, the two serve very different purposes.

The goal of mindfulness is to tune in to the present moment without judgment. These skills involve observing inward experiences (i.e., thoughts, emotions, and body sensations) as well as outward experiences (e.g., observing surroundings, noticing the texture of different objects, etc.). When pushed outside of the Window of Tolerance, observing inward experiences (paying attention to an overwhelming experience) can exacerbate the stress response. Grounding, on the other hand, is designed to help move attention *away* from distressing thoughts, emotions, and body sensations by focusing either on outward experiences or mentally-engaging distractions. The goal of grounding is to feel safe again.

The three types of grounding skills are: physical, mental, and soothing. Different skills can be effective at different times. And certain skills might not help certain people. It may take time to find what works. In the following table are examples of grounding techniques in each of the three skill categories.

Grounding Techniques

Category	Actions
Physical	**Move** your body. This can include: standing, stretching, push-ups, jumping jacks, shaking your arms, or moving your shoulders in a circular motion. **Place your hands under running water.** Notice how the water feels. Change the temperature from warm to cold, and back to warm again. **Breathe** deeply. Place your hand on your belly and slowly inhale. Feel your hand rise as your belly inflates like a balloon. Hold your breath briefly before exhaling. **Smell** something you find pleasing (e.g., coffee, rain, cinnamon, scented lotion, a candle, etc.). As you slowly breathe in the fragrance, notice its characteristics. **Pick up a nearby item** and hold it in your hands. Notice its temperature, texture, shape, and weight. Describe its color(s) and any unique features. **Hold an ice cube.** Notice how it feels in your hands and observe how the sensation changes when it begins to melt.
Mental	**Describe** your surroundings, pretending to be an author portraying a scene. What can you see, hear, smell, taste, feel? Notice details that could interest the reader. **Explain** the process of a routine task (e.g., making coffee, brushing teeth). Pretend you are explaining it to someone with no preconceived ideas about the process. **Pick a category** and list all the items you can (e.g., name different types of birds, move through the alphabet naming birds which start with each letter). **Orient yourself.** Say your full name, age, city, state, date, day, and time. **Count** backwards from 100 by 13. **Recite** lyrics from a song or any text or any words which are meaningful to you.

Category	Actions
Soothing	**Visualize what brings you joy.** Think of as many things as possible, big or small. **Listen to music.** Turn on your favorite song and pretend that you are hearing it for the first time. Listen to positive or calming music. **List your top five** favorite things. For example, you can think about your favorite songs, musicians, actors, movies, foods, restaurants, authors, books, and cities. **Visualize a safe space.** Think back to an environment where you felt peaceful and at ease. Were you inside curled up with a book while it was raining outside? Were you sitting on a beach, listening to waves crashing onto the shore? Mentally return to this space as often as you need. **Comfort yourself physically.** Place a weighted blanket over yourself. Put on your favorite socks, hoodie, or sweatpants. Hug a soft pillow. Pet a furry animal. **Show yourself kindness.** Reflect on your strengths. Acknowledge that you are doing difficult things and trying your best.

EXERCISE: GROUNDING

Looking at the table of grounding techniques, pick three to use when outside your Window of Tolerance. Take a few minutes now to practice these techniques, even if you are not currently dysregulated.

Neurodivergence and Mindfulness

Another factor to keep in mind before engaging with mindfulness exercises is neurodivergence. "Neurodivergent" is defined as, "having or relating to a disorder or condition (such as autism spectrum disorder, attention deficit hyperactivity disorder, dyslexia, or obsessive-compulsive disorder) that impacts the way the brain processes information : exhibiting or characteristic of variations in typical neurological development" (Merriam-Webster, n.d.c). While some research supports the efficacy of mindfulness interventions in supporting the wellbeing of autistic individuals (Cachia et al., 2016), there is reason to examine its efficacy more fully. Rakshit (2023) explores how mindfulness can exacerbate distress and anxiety for autistic individuals and those with ADHD. Hutton (2020) describes a very distressing experience of mindfulness, reported by one autistic person, and advocates for fostering an inclusive approach to mindfulness that recognizes how its impact and value may vary from person to person. Heidle (2020), an autistic individual with PTSD and OCD, describes a personal experience of mindfulness, indicating that it is sometimes helpful and sometimes extremely unhelpful.

Given the wide variety of ways that people's minds work along with the limited research on this topic, we are not able to give a clear-cut answer for how to approach mindfulness if you identify as neurodivergent. Heidle (2020) encourages people to embrace any alternative practice that works for them, such as going to a quiet, dark room, or "stimming." Stimming, also known as self-stimulatory behavior, is defined as "a repetitive action or movement of the body (such as repeatedly tapping on objects or the ears, snapping the fingers, blinking the eyes, rocking from side to side, or grunting)" (Merriam-Webster, n.d.g). Kapp et al. (2019) document the way that stimming is used for self-regulation and emotional processing. Rakshit (2023) notes that movement-based mindfulness, which can include activities such as walking or yoga, can be more inclusive to various groups. If traditional mindfulness is not working for you, you might consider seeking care from a neurodiversity-affirming therapist in order to find tailored strategies for emotional regulation. We encourage you to try different approaches and embrace what helps you process your emotions, even if it does not fit into the most conventional ideas of mindfulness.

MINDFULNESS EXERCISES

The following mindfulness exercises can be used when you are within your Window of Tolerance. The first exercise prompts engagement with external stimuli while the second focuses on internal stimuli.

EXERCISE: DEFAMILIARIZING THE FAMILIAR OBJECT

1. Ground yourself to the present moment by noticing all of the objects in the environment. Use a soft gaze or a soft touch to scan the surroundings and take note of what is nearby. Next, choose an object that feels familiar. Ideally, this will be an object that you use or engage with on a daily basis. Perhaps it is so familiar that it takes time for your brain to even notice it.

2. Set a timer for two minutes. For the next two minutes, notice anything and everything about this object. Behave like a scientist visiting from another planet, as if you have never seen this object before. Use your senses to take note of all of its features, so that you can accurately relay the information to your extraterrestrial peers. Use as much detail as possible, and do

not make any judgments. Remember: you have never seen this before. The object is not good or bad, it just is. Maybe it has an interesting texture, or colors. Notice its weight or how it feels in your hands. Feel free to smell the object (even if you do not think it has a smell). We encourage you to use your own judgment about whether or not to taste it!

3. When the two minutes are up, reflect on this experience. Did it feel different from your typical interactions with the object? Did you find it difficult to engage with the object in this way?

In addition to noticing what's outside yourself, mindfulness allows you to acknowledge the internal experience of emotions and to relate to them before potentially blocking them with attempts to focus on "why" and "how" questions. Along with the mountains of empirical evidence for the benefits of mindfulness, there are also countless strategies to practice and incorporate this form of internal observation. We'll present one strategy that's been especially helpful when working with clients who are engineers.

The goal of this exercise is to allow the emotion to be processed by mindfully maintaining attention toward the physical sensations of the emotion and the breath. The mindful attention toward the body's physical manifestation of emotions can help prevent getting stuck in the emotional loops, which are fueled by interrupting thoughts.

EXERCISE: OBSERVING SENSATIONS OF AN EMOTION

1. Read the following steps, in full, before engaging with the exercise.

2. Find a comfortable position in which you will not fall asleep.

3. Identify one sensation (or a lack of sensation) and where it is arising in the body. Is a particular emotion associated with that sensation? For instance, perhaps you feel a tension in your forehead when experiencing anger. Queasiness in the stomach might arise with feelings of anxiety. Maybe you notice a numbness in your shoulder and are not sure what emotion is present. You might be noticing several sensations and several areas of the body; focus on just one for now.

   • Keep in mind that there are no "right" or "wrong" sensations or emotions. Building awareness of the physical sensations of emotions is a skill to be developed over time, so we will go into more detail about this skill in the following chapter.

4. Next, direct your attention to that location of the body with the identified sensation. Set an alarm for two to five minutes and maintain focus on that part of your body. At the same time, notice your breath. Aim to continue to hold your attention on the part of the body and on the breath simultaneously. It can be helpful to imagine that you are directing your breath toward that

part of your body, giving it oxygen. Notice sensations, lack of sensations, size, temperature, and other characteristics of the physical experience that are arising. Use phrases such as "I'm noticing..." before taking note of the sensations (e.g., "I'm noticing my shoulders are holding tension").

5. During the two- to five-minute period, notice if or how the sensations change. The brain will likely produce other thoughts ("This feels silly," "Am I doing this right?" or "What do I need to get done today?"). Simply notice the thoughts and then redirect your attention toward the body sensations and the breath, saying, "I'm noticing I'm having the thought...." and then finish the sentence with the thought that popped up. This back-and-forth between thoughts and noticing the body/breath will likely occur multiple times during the two- to five-minute exercise.

6. Reflect on this experience. What was it like? What did you notice? What was hard about it? At this point, perhaps the emotion or sensation will ease. Perhaps the emotion or sensation will feel more acute. Whatever you are experiencing, it is valid. As we mentioned previously, if you feel dysregulated, please consider talking to a trusted person about the experience and use grounding skills to return to your Window of Tolerance.

Summary of the Steps in Observing Sensations of an Emotion Exercise:

- Read through the exercise.
- Find a comfortable position.
- Identify a sensation (or lack of sensation) arising, possibly related to an emotion, and where it is located in the body.
- For two to five minutes, mindfully notice that area of the body with the sensation.
    - Notice your breath.
    - Notice any changes to the sensation.
    - Notice thoughts that arise, then redirect your attention toward the body part and breath.
- Reflect on the experience.

SUMMARY

Mindfulness is the foundation of decompiling your emotions. The next two chapters will apply mindfulness as a stepping stone to identifying language to describe emotional experiences. With practice, mindfulness allows us to identify patterns of internal experiences. After building up pattern recognition, ascribing language to those patterns is possible.

CHAPTER 5

IDENTIFYING EMOTIONS USING LANGUAGE AND PHYSICAL SENSATIONS

WHAT THERAPIST HAS *NEVER* ASKED, "HOW DOES THAT make you feel?" In fact, even if you have not set foot in a therapist's office, you have probably heard this caricature of the therapeutic experience in the media. This question can elicit discomfort, nervous laughter, and even eye-rolls…But therapists do not ask this question to embody that cartoonesque version of mental health professionals. Instead, research shows that naming emotions literally changes the brain.

LANGUAGE

Brain imaging studies demonstrate how putting words to feelings can make emotions such as sadness, anger, and pain less intense (Lieberman et al., 2007). Verbalizing emotions activates the prefrontal region of the brain, associated with higher cognitive functions like reasoning, problem-solving, comprehension, creativity, and impulse control. It also reduces the involvement of the amygdalae, those previously-discussed brain structures that focus on emotions, motivations, and safety responses.

Of course, this is not to say that naming emotions eliminates them. Naming simply changes the brain's response, which reduces emotional intensity and helps foster more balance.

You might be wondering, "Didn't we just learn about how we should not jump to our prefrontal cortex by automatically responding to emotions by asking 'why' and 'how'?" Very good! We did! While jumping to the prefrontal cortex by analyzing and interpreting cuts off access to the emotional experience, intentionally naming the felt emotion allows a more clarifying experience of the emotion. Asking "why" and "how" questions temporarily blocks access to the emotion. On the other hand, noticing "what" you are feeling, helps the brain stay present with the emotion while still being anchored to the prefrontal cortex.

Naming emotions and noticing them when they arise are skills that on the surface may sound easy but are actually quite challenging. Many people are not taught to tune in to internal experiences, let alone given the language to describe those experiences. You likely can sense when you feel "bad" or "off," but discerning when that "bad" feeling is related to regret, frustration, hurt, or some combination of these requires an additional step that is often overlooked.

Sometimes the step of noticing an emotion is skipped entirely, for the sake of intellectually understanding the "why" behind it, or to look for a solution to resolve the "bad" feeling. Instead of jumping to "Why am I feeling this way?" and "How do I fix this?", we can begin by scanning our internal environment and collecting data about *what* we are feeling. This scan gives us the best chance of accurately interpreting and managing those emotions. Of course, gathering internal data will be most effective when drawing on the scientific principle of objectivity: looking for the truth without making personal judgments towards the self or the experience. As an analogy, imagine encountering unexpected behaviors in a new piece of software. It would be important to carefully and objectively document the full range of faulty behaviors before making conclusions about where these behaviors came from or how to fix them. "Isolate the bug," as they say, before tinkering and trying to fix the code.

Remember that no emotions are good or bad; they just *are*. Emotions are chemical states in the brain and body; their presence is not moral or immoral, any more than blood oxygen or vitamin D levels. Instead of attaching morality to emotions, think of them as sensations that direct attention and orient the individual to what's important.

Two practical strategies can increase emotional awareness: 1) improve the emotional vocabulary, and 2) learn how physical sensations, thoughts, and behaviors pair with emotional experiences. Here, we provide concrete strategies, concepts, and tools to make the process of noticing and identifying emotions more accessible. We also encourage reading about each approach and actively engaging with all of the exercises in this chapter. Keep in mind that one strategy is not superior to another, and there is usually value in using multiple approaches. All of these strategies are designed to reach the destination of identifying feelings.

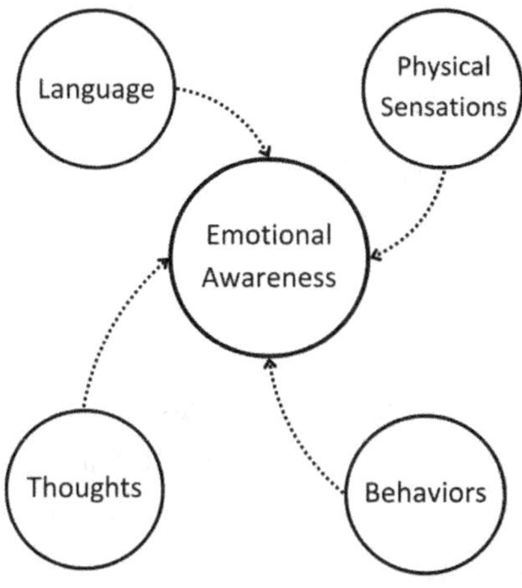

The Feeling Wheel

Emotions are nuanced and, at times, can be difficult to identify. The Feeling Wheel, created by Gloria Wilcox in 1982, is a commonly-used tool, one that many engineers say they find helpful in enhancing their emotional language. The inner part of the Feeling Wheel contains the emotions "mad", "scared", "joyful", "powerful", "peaceful", and "sad." The complexity grows from there as more nuanced emotions radiate from the center.

The Feeling Wheel

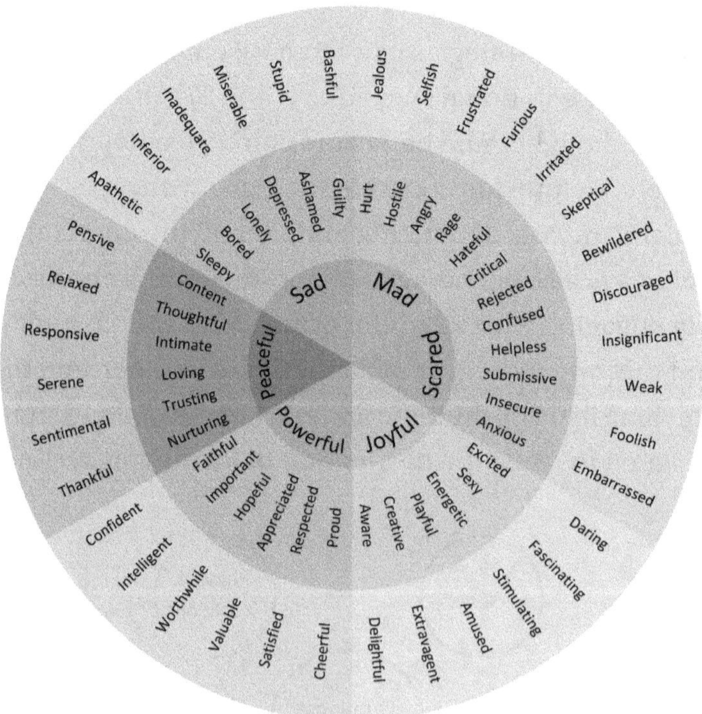

For access to enlarged, color images, go to appliedwellnessinitiatives.com.

The Feeling Wheel, Gloria Wilcox, Transactional Analysis Journal, copyright © International Transactional Analysis Association, reprinted by permission of Taylor & Francis Ltd, https://www.tandfonline.com on behalf of International Transactional Analysis Association.

EXERCISE: EXPANDING EMOTIONAL VOCABULARY

Use the following steps to add new terms to describe your feelings.

1. Think of a time you felt one or two of the six center emotions on the Feeling Wheel. What was happening at that time? When approaching this exercise for the first time, pick an experience that is not highly upsetting or emotionally charged. On a scale from one to ten, with "10" being an experience that was extremely distressing, identify an experience that is rated between "2" and "4."

2. Next, work your way towards the outer layers of the circle, considering each emotion that shares the color of the chosen basic emotion. Could you have been feeling each of these more nuanced emotions? Were you able to access these emotions at that time? Can you feel them now?

3. Finally, if you were able to identify additional emotions connected with your experience, do any of these emotions surprise you? Are there any emotions **not** on the wheel that you would like to add? Does a more nuanced understanding of these emotions shape the way you recall the original experience?

VIGNETTE

Idris examines the six emotions in the center of the Feeling Wheel. The word "powerful" stands out. Idris remembers feeling powerful this morning when a colleague had consulted with him, knowing that he specializes in robotics. Idris examines the next layer of emotions outside of "powerful," realizing that he also felt, and continues to feel, "appreciated." He has only been with this company for four months and is still adjusting. Until this morning, he had not received much positive feedback and was beginning to worry about what he had to offer the company. He branches even further out on the circle and identifies "valuable." Idris did not have the words for this feeling earlier this morning, but reflecting on it today helps him realize that the feeling of "power" extended from feeling valued.

Idris is not particularly surprised by the emotions he identifies. However, he is surprised by how illuminating this exercise is. He could have left this morning's experience in its unexamined, simplest form, knowing that he had experienced a general, positive emotion after a "good" morning. But there was more than that and digging deeper helped him identify the nuances of his feelings, to understand and appreciate the full range of his experience.

The Emotions Map

The Feeling Wheel has been a staple for many therapists over the past several decades, displayed on anything from posters, to pillows, to stickers. While we have personally found it to be useful, we have also noticed limitations. As stated earlier in the chapter, the wheel is not large enough to capture and include the vast number of emotions humans are capable of experiencing.

With a desire to expand on emotional vocabulary and awareness, we created an "Emotions Map," which includes a wide variety of both broad and nuanced emotions.

The map is divided by six different categories of emotions: angry, disgusted, sad, surprised, happy, and fearful. These categories, however, are not neatly separated; the same words can be found in different categories. For example, the emotion "humiliated" is in both the sad and fearful categories. And the map is not based strictly on research and science. Instead, we explored how emotional language can be stretched. For example, imagine feeling the type of humiliation that emerges from a place of sadness as compared to that which comes from a place of fear. Some of the words we include are (arguably) not technically "emotions," such as "frozen," "hollow," and "shaken up." And yet, they are frequently used to describe emotional experiences, so we included them.

You might disagree with some of the choices we have made regarding the categories or wording. Or maybe important or useful terms from your first language are missing. If so, we encourage you to draw your own version of the Emotions Map, including all of the details that are meaningful to you. Both the Feeling Wheel and the Emotions Map are valuable tools to expand the language of emotions, so please use whichever tool(s) feels most helpful.

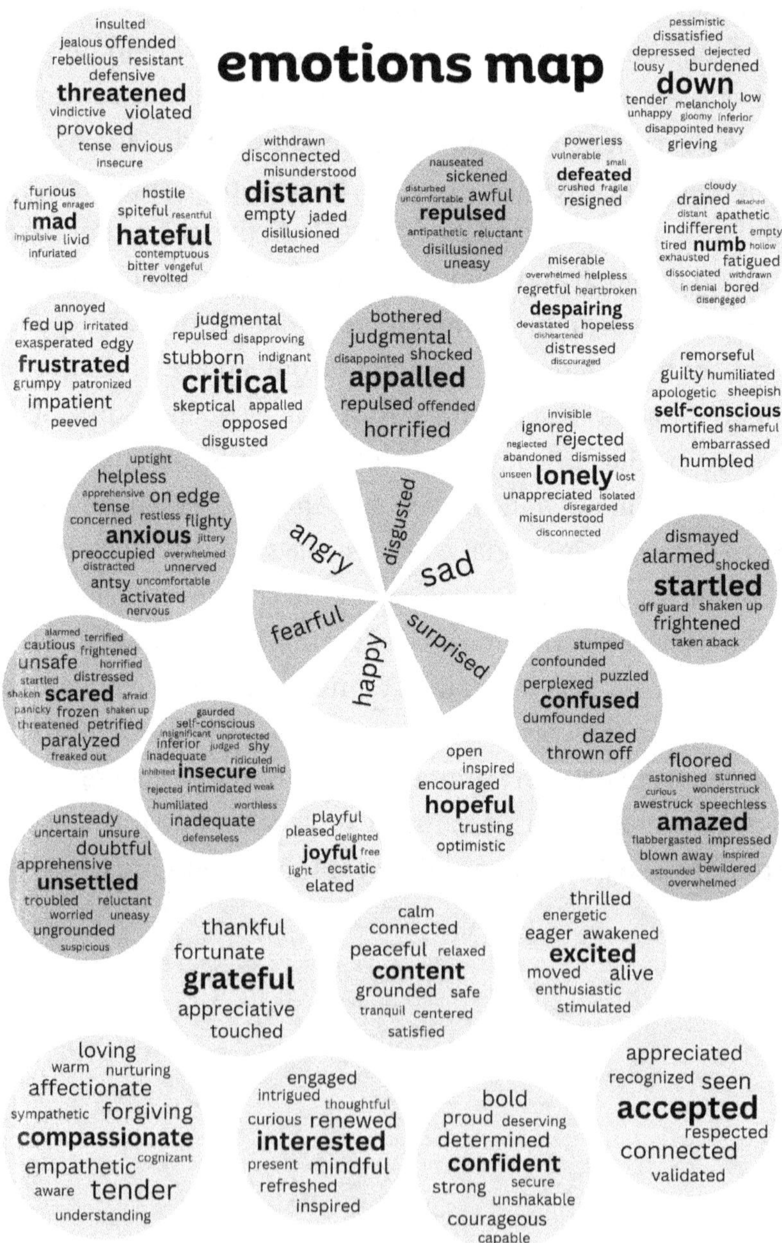

For access to enlarged, color images, go to appliedwellnessinitiatives.com.

PHYSICAL SENSATIONS

While emotion might feel like an abstract experience stuck in the brain, it is actually a physical, whole-body experience. Emotions engage with cardiovascular, skeletomuscular, neuroendocrine, and autonomic nervous systems to help meet life's challenges (Levenson, 2003). The autonomic nervous system is an essential component that prepares the body for actions such as "fighting, fleeing, freezing, comforting, bonding, and expelling, each of which requires somewhat different configurations of physiological support" (Levenson, 2003, p. 350). In response to certain emotions, one's heart rate will increase in order to take blood where it is needed the most. When feeling scared, blood rushes to the legs and arms, allowing one to run quickly. Fear can also lead to quickened breath, which helps the bloodstream carry oxygen to the arms, legs, and lungs. This physiological response is the body preparing for actions that can help maintain safety. However, additional bodily changes might accompany this preparation, such as chest pain, dizziness, and breathlessness.

While the body is trying to be helpful in these situations, these additional sensations can feel strange, uncomfortable, and even threatening. Recall that the body processes emotional pain and physical pain in similar ways. To the conscious self, these sensations are often a shock. It can be confusing at best and terrifying at worst to find the body's deep ancestral instincts preparing for a fight with a saber-toothed tiger if in fact you are merely standing in a conference room taking pointed questions from your boss. Understanding how the body responds to emotionally charged experiences, we can explore these physiological sensations with curiosity and integrate them into the overall emotional experience.

Is It an Emotion, or Hunger?

While emotions are physiological experiences, not all physiological experiences indicate emotions. For example, fatigue and hunger are accompanied by physiological mechanisms, yet these signals are not caused by emotion. Unfortunately, people can misinterpret these cues and perceive them as emotional reactions rather than unmet biological needs. For instance, at some point, you have likely felt "hanger," that irritability or anger arising due to hunger. While this experience might be interpreted as anger or annoyance, the relief that comes after having a bite to eat clarifies that it was indeed hunger that you were experiencing.

It can be confusing to discern when a physiological cue reflects a biological need or an emotion. To add to this complexity, indicators of a biological need can also amplify existing emotions. Watching someone take the last available item in a store, listening to your partner loudly chew their gum, or noticing a colleague tapping their pen against their desk while you are trying to concentrate: these are all experiences that would likely bring up minor annoyance or frustration. But if you are depleted and in need of food or sleep, these experiences can lead to intense emotions. Suddenly, that minor annoyance might present as anger or even rage. An unmet biological need can magnify the intensity of existing emotions.

We are more likely to interpret hunger cues as strong emotional reactions to our environment, or the people around us, when our present circumstances are substandard (MacCormack & Lindquist, 2019). But this does not mean that we are destined to feel hangry whenever our surroundings are challenging. The ability to tune into our body's signals increases the chances that we will recognize our hunger's impact on our mood and regulate accordingly. While there are times when it is useful to explore the depths of our anger and irritability in a way that builds insight into our psychological needs and values, at other times, we just need to eat lunch, or to attend to some other biological need (like sleep, thirst, or rest).

In addition, the overlap between physiological sensations reflecting biological needs and those reflecting psychological needs can impact individuals inequitably. Without resources to meet basic biological needs (sufficient sleep, food, or water), emotions can feel more intense. Said differently, the capacity to process emotions requires a baseline of fulfilled biological needs. When these needs are consistently unmet, the impact goes beyond feeling hangry, as the individuals are less psychologically equipped for emotional processing work. Instead, the brain powers down to save its energy. Individuals who work multiple jobs, for instance, might miss the sleep necessary to do this emotional exploration. Thus, as people have inequitable options to meet their biological needs, they might also have inequitable resources to meet their psychological needs.

Emotions Are Personal

Do humans all experience the same physiological responses for each emotion, every time? If only it were that simple! The complexity and diversity of humanity is undeniable. For years, researchers have been trying to determine if it's possible to develop a standardized metric describing how emotions present in the body. A meta-analysis of more than 200 studies measuring emotional states and corresponding bodily changes points to "No" (Siegel et al., 2018). This research reveals variation in physical changes between different people during emotion, challenging the idea that each emotion has a universal physical "fingerprint." Not only can the experience of an emotion, such as sadness, differ from person to person, one's own physiological response to sadness may vary depending on the context. While these findings have supported the presence of patterns among humans within a range of shared bodily experiences for various emotions, the reality of what one individual is feeling can only be found with ongoing, intentional examination of both the body and mind.

The complexity and diversity of humanity is undeniable. With variation as the norm, what is the next step? We highlight the study above to underscore the importance of learning and of the art of noticing *your* unique physiology, of noticing how *one's own* body physically communicates anger, joy and other emotions.

Consider: highly sensitive lab equipment comes with a manual intended to describe every mode of operation, yet in practice, it can be more important to learn the quirks and characteristics of each individual device firsthand. This oscilloscope needs the gain knob to be jiggled occasionally for the display to stay on; that pair of calipers works in metric, but the US Customary scale is improperly calibrated. There is no one-size-fits-all approach, and the more the experimenter can tune in to the functioning of the equipment (i.e., the emotional process), the more they can deepen their understanding of the data (that is, the awareness of the emotional experience).

The following exercise provides practice tuning into one's internal experience. The "body scan" is a highly-utilized practice in therapy offices, with many variations. In the mindfulness segment, we asked you to notice physical sensations related to an emotion. In this exercise, we are exploring physiological experiences more broadly. As with mindfulness, this exercise should be approached cautiously by those who identify as neurodivergent. For some, noticing internal somatic sensations can be substantially challenging, distressing, or ineffective. Continue to pay attention to the Window of Tolerance. If you can engage in this exercise from within your window, please proceed. If you are concerned or unsure about how the following exercise might impact you, remember that you can always revisit this exercise at a future time and/or with a licensed mental health therapist. The following table can help to generate ideas for describing physical sensations. This table is not comprehensive but a starting place to identify possible sensations that might arise.

Physical Sensations

Area	Language
Toes/Feet/Legs	Curled, clenched, sweaty or clammy, tightness, tingling sensation, cramping, hot, cold, shaking, trembling, pain, tired, loose, relaxed
Pelvis	Tightness, clenched, loose, relaxed, centered, shifted
Stomach	Nauseous, sick, tension, tightness, pain in the pit of the stomach, cramping, fluttering, butterflies, hollow, sinking feeling, heavy, light, airy
Fingers/Hands/Arms	Curled, clenched, sweaty or clammy, tightness, tingling sensation, cramping, hot, cold, shaking, trembling, pain, tired, loose, relaxed
Chest	Tightness, tension, pain, loose, hollow, sunken, increased heart rate, decreased heart rate, fluttering heart
Shoulders	Tension, tightness, pain, shoulders positioned high in hunched position or low in relaxed position, loose

Area	Language
Neck/Airway	Quickening of breath, breathlessness, slowing of breath, deep breaths, lump in throat, dryness in throat, difficulty swallowing, choking sensation, pain or tension in neck muscles
Head/Face	Clenched teeth, tight or relaxed jaw, headache, furrowed brow, feeling your face flush or get hot, cold, tearfulness, feeling faint, dizziness, dryness in mouth, trembling lips, tingling sensation
Body	Feeling rigid, tense, frozen, energetic, activated, slow, low energy, cold, hot, heavy, light, relaxed, calm, jittery, sweaty, clammy, closed-off, shrinking, open, expansive, having goosebumps, tingling sensation

EXERCISE: BODY SCAN

Follow these steps to complete a body scan.

1. Enter this exercise with curiosity, letting go of any judgments (what you think you need to be feeling, trying to change what you are feeling, questions of whether or not you're doing the exercise "right" or "wrong", etc.). Instead, tap into the spirit of inquiry, like a scientist or engineer holding on to curiosity without an agenda. Avoid evaluative terms such as "good" or "bad" (even if experiencing mild physical discomfort). Instead, see if you can describe the pain in concrete terms (e.g., "I notice a burning or a sharp sensation"). If judgments

arise, that is okay; rather than trying to "get rid" of the judgments, simply notice them and refocus attention on the experience in the present moment.

2. Find a comfortable position and take three deep breaths. Next, bring your attention to your toes, feet, and legs. Make note of any sensations. Also note if there is a lack of sensation or numbness. Resist the urge to change anything; simply notice your internal experience. Then, shift attention to the pelvis and stomach and repeat the practice above. Continue to work your way up the body, bringing attention to your fingers/hands/arms, your chest, your shoulders, your neck/airway, and your head/face. After scanning each individual part, observe how your body is feeling altogether.

3. Next, notice if any sensations demand your attention more than the others. What might these sensations be trying to communicate? Are any emotions present? Is there any context that is important when observing these emotions?

4. Consider: did you notice any emotions while scanning the body? If so, it might be helpful to create your own reference guide to identify any future physical manifestations of those emotions. This following guide can be used to display the emotions and their corresponding physical sensations.

Sensations Reference Guide

Sensations	Emotion	Context
List the sensations you noticed. Where did you experience this sensation or lack of sensation in the body?	*List the corresponding emotions that arose during the activity, associated with the sensations. If helpful, refer to the Feeling Wheel or the Emotions Map (provided earlier in the book) to help identify language that describes the emotions you experienced.*	*List any recent events that could be influencing this emotion and the corresponding physical sensations.*

VIGNETTE

Chen readies themself to enter the exercise as a scientist would, feeling curious and open. They accept that judgments will likely arise and prepare themselves to center their attention back onto their physical sensations as needed.

Chen finds a comfortable spot under a tree outside and taking three deep breaths, they start the body scan by tuning in to their toes. Immediately, they notice that their toes are not flat in their shoes, but instead they are in a curled position. This surprises Chen; they thought their body would be more relaxed while on their lunch break; their next class does not even start until 3 p.m. Still, they make a conscious effort not to judge their experience and shift their attention to the whole foot. They notice that their feet feel tired. Their attention moves up their body until they reach their stomach. They observe a trace of a fluttering feeling, almost as if there are butterflies in there. They also note a slight hint of nausea. When Chen's body scan reaches their chest, they realize their heart is beating at a fast rate. Chen notices the thought "I need to relax," and quickly realizes that this is a judgment. They choose to let this judgment pass and to bring awareness to the movements of their heart just as they are. When Chen reaches their head, they notice their jaw is tight, as if they are bracing themselves for something. When they scan their entire body, they detect mild tension.

Of all the physical sensations, their quick heart rate feels most present. This sensation reminds them of times when they had felt nervous, and also times when they had felt excited. Chen connects with both of these emotions as they reflect on what happened earlier today, right before they sat down to do this body scan.

They had been preparing some slides. Chen had been feeling both excited to present their hard work and nervous about speaking in public. Chen thinks back to the other sensations they felt, and to the curled toes, the nausea, and tight jaw... this all feels like nervousness to Chen. Chen interpreted the fluttering in their stomach as excitement, as if they were on a rollercoaster.

When they complete the exercise, they realize that even though they went to lunch and had mentally moved on from working on the slides, their body continued to process the emotions outside of their cognitive awareness. Chen documents their experience in their Sensations Reference Guide.

Chen's Sensations Reference Guide

Sensations	Emotion	Context
List the sensations you noticed. Where did you experience this sensation or lack of sensation in the body?	*List the corresponding emotions that arose during the activity, associated with the sensations. If helpful, refer to the Feeling Wheel or the Emotions Map to help you identify language that describes the emotions you experienced.*	*List any recent events that could be influencing this emotion and the corresponding physical sensations.*
Increased heart rate, curled toes, nausea, tight jaw, tension in body	Nervous	Preparing for a presentation that requires public speaking
Increased heart rate, fluttering in stomach	Excited	Preparing for a presentation that requires public speaking

Reflection

Asking, "Where do you feel that emotion in your body?" (odd as it may sound) connects the mind and body to better understand the self. The previous exercise is designed to create more awareness of the body and, in time, connect the physical sensations to emotions. The reverse can be done as well. When mentally identifying an emotion, complete a brief body scan in order to find the correlation between the two experiences (mental and physical). Of course, correlation is not causation. Yet over time, observing from both perspectives, the various emotions and physical states that co-occur are likely to accurately reflect the nature of your personal mind-body connection.

When Chen completed this exercise, they discovered that while they were able to distinguish differences in their physical manifestations of nervousness and excitement, there was also some overlap, as their fast heart rate and fluttering in their stomach felt connected to both emotions. As you become more familiar with how the body expresses emotions, you will likely notice overlap as well. Remember, there is no "right" or "wrong" here. A simple guess at what you are feeling will bring you one step closer to the truth, even if your guess is destined to be updated later if you discover that another more nuanced emotion is more accurate. If unsure of what that tingling sensation in the hand means, or where an emotion such as jealousy occurs in the body, you can simply take note of this and remain open to finding the answers at a later time. This process is a journey, not a destination.

SUMMARY

Using the skills of mindfulness can help you identify the various physiological sensations that arise. Over time, you can detect patterns and associate them with various emotions. By also expanding your emotional vocabulary, you can have more categories of emotions within which to code these sensory patterns. You can even learn to perceive these sensory patterns with more precision and accuracy. Bringing language to these patterns is another step in the process of decompiling emotions, in order to understand the underlying needs and values and respond accordingly.

CHAPTER 6

IDENTIFYING EMOTIONS: THOUGHTS AND ACTIONS

Many of our clients enter counseling having had difficulty distinguishing thoughts from emotions. When asked to name their emotions, they say things such as, "I feel like things aren't working out for me," or "I feel like no one's on my side." While this certainly paints a picture of what is going on, it is not the *complete* picture, as these statements reflect *thoughts* but not the underlying *emotions* (e.g., defeated, frustrated, lonely, unsupported) that accompany them. Ultimately, the two are interrelated but distinct, which is why we devote separate sections of this chapter to thoughts and emotions.

THOUGHTS

Good news: identifying thoughts can actually help us to identify emotions. This approach might be especially helpful for people who tend to rely on "thinking" versus "feeling" as a means of processing information. In order to do this identification, however, it is important to denote the difference between the two.

As a review, we've seen that emotions are complex psychological states that involve a subjective experience, a physiological response, and a behavioral or expressive response. Emotions are internal reactions to internal and external cues. Emotions include feelings, such as happiness, sadness, anger, fear, and disgust. Thoughts consist of opinions, ideas, beliefs and perspectives, and are sometimes the product of reasoning or conscious consideration. Thoughts can be verbal (e.g., internal dialogue or self-talk) or visual (e.g., mental imagery). They can be about the past, present, or future, and they can be factual or imaginative.

Thoughts and emotions are closely intertwined. When we experience an emotion, it is accompanied by various thoughts, often related to the situation that prompted the emotion, our interpretation of the situation, or our beliefs about ourselves and the world. The next exercise is designed to distinguish between emotions and thoughts and to deepen understanding of one's internal experiences.

EXERCISE: THOUGHTS AS AN INDICATOR OF EMOTIONS

1. Identify a life stressor, mindfully noticing thoughts that arise while thinking about that stressor (such as "I worked really hard today," "I'm so bad at this!", "I can't believe it's only Monday."). Say the thoughts out loud or write them down. Avoid judging these unbidden thoughts; simply notice them. Try to write down several thoughts before moving on to Step 2.

2. Identify what emotions arise while thinking about the stressor, using tools such as the Feeling Wheel to help with this process. If no emotion-related words fit, write down any sensations in the body (such as "racing

heart" or "tense shoulders") or even metaphors ("I feel like the walls are caving in"). There are no limits while putting words to the experiences. It might take time to fully work out the feelings, and that is okay!

3. Reviewing the list of thoughts, work to pair the emotions with each thought. Over time, using this guide will help with recognizing patterns in the emotional process.

Thought Reference Guide

Thoughts	Emotions
Thoughts you noticed:	*Emotion(s) that correspond with each thought:*

VIGNETTE

Christina is a fourth-year engineering graduate student preparing for a conference where she will share her research findings. This conference has been a long time coming; she has worked long and hard to prepare for this moment. During a one-on-one meeting, her advisor expresses his excitement as both discuss the details of the trip. Her advisor believes Christina's research is cutting-edge and will lead to many opportunities. He continues to discuss Christina's abilities and "natural talent" as an engineer and researcher. He notices that Christina is not matching his energy, so he asks Christina how she is feeling. She automatically says, "Great!" but as soon as her answer comes out of her mouth, she notices herself squirm in her seat as her palms start to sweat. Her response feels incongruent…and this confuses her. The success of her research, this conference, and these accolades from her advisor are everything Christina has ever wanted. She also feels excited to showcase her work for colleagues from across the globe. Yet, something feels "off", and she cannot quite place her finger on it.

When the meeting ends, Christina leaves her supervisor's office and heads outside to get some fresh air, hoping to brush off whatever this "off" feeling is. On her way out, she passes Kyle, a first-year graduate student who is "struggling." Rumor has it that, at the recommendation of his advisor, Kyle has been working with an academic coach in order to improve his time-management and study skills. Christina notices a thought: "I wish that were me." This thought stops her in her tracks. On the surface, it does not make much sense! As a first-generation college student, she has spent years fighting her way through difficult courses and failed research attempts. She has come so far and has accomplished more than she ever thought possible. She is finally on her way to seeing the fruits of her labor. And yet…she is thinking about what it might be like to be struggling through her first year again, what it might be like to be Kyle.

Christina makes her way to her favorite bench outside and gets out a pen and some paper. She floods her notebook with all of the thoughts that come to her mind:

"I wish I were Kyle."

"No one expects anything from Kyle."

"He doesn't know how good he has it right now…he has years before he'll experience the pressure I'm experiencing."

"I'm feeling so much pressure."

"My supervisor thinks I'm a natural at all of this."

"No one understands how hard it's been...or how hard it is!"

"I haven't had the privileges others have had. I have to work twice as hard."

Christina takes a look at the thoughts on the page, realizing the "off" feeling she experienced in the meeting was not trivial. Seeing her stream of thoughts helps her piece together what she might be feeling. Christina takes a deep breath and opens herself up for self-exploration. With the help of the Feeling Wheel, Christina reflects on what emotions are arising:

"I wish I were Kyle; no one expects anything from Kyle" **Envious**

"He doesn't know how good he has it right now...he has years before he'll experience the pressure I'm experiencing." **Envious, Annoyed**

"I'm feeling so much pressure." **I feel like a balloon that's about to burst.**

"My supervisor thinks I'm a natural at all of this." **Unseen, Proud, Sweaty Palms**

"No one understands how hard it's been...or how hard it is!" **Unseen, Frustrated, Lonely, Overwhelmed**

"I haven't had the privilege others have had. I have to work twice as hard." **Angry, Sad, Exhausted**

"I'm not good enough." **Shame**

"How am I going to continue to produce results like this?" **Pressure in chest, racing heart**

Next, Christina observes the emotions, physical sensations and metaphors she paired with her thoughts. She found it exhausting to complete the exercise, as she is new at exploring her emotions. She decides to create a Thought Reference Guide to help identify her emotions (through her thoughts) more quickly in the future. Christina does this by grouping her thoughts under each "emotion category":

Christina's Thought Reference Guide

Thoughts *List the thoughts you noticed.*	**Emotions** *Emotion(s) that correspond with each thought.*
I wish I were someone else, I wish I had their experience	*Envy*
I'm feeling so much pressure	*Stress, Overwhelmed*
My experience is not understood by others	*Lonely, Disconnected, Unseen*
Life has been unfair to me	*Anger, Frustration*
How am I going to continue to produce results like this?	*Anxiety, Restlessness, Pressure*
I'm not good enough	*Shame*

Epilogue: *A few weeks later, Christina noticed additional thoughts arise after interacting with Kyle. Christina was curious to see if the arising emotions were similar to her previous experience with Kyle or if any changes occurred. In her Thought Reference Guide, she noticed similar thoughts including, "I'm feeling so much pressure," but she also noticed the new thought, "I hope Kyle is doing okay." Reflecting on these* *thoughts, Christina realized that while her interactions with Kyle continue to bring up stress (they remind her of the work she needs to complete), she has also grown in her curiosity and compassion for Kyle and his experience. Based on her awareness of the compassion she feels, Christina makes the decision to offer to work with Kyle to help him troubleshoot a research issue. With a newfound ability to recognize her internal experiences, Christina sees that she is more able to connect with others in emotionally stressful circumstances.*

Reflection

You might notice that, in her Thoughts Reference Guide, Christina changes and broadens some of her thoughts. Instead of writing the thoughts *"I wish I were Kyle; no one expects anything from Kyle,"* Christina writes *"I wish I were someone else"* under the Envious Thoughts category. Under that same category, instead of writing *"Kyle doesn't know how good he has it right now...he has years before he'll experience the pressure I'm experiencing,"* Christina writes *"I wish I had his experience."*

In this exercise, writing more general, less specific thoughts serves two purposes: 1) it allows one to dig deeper into the emotion and/or core of the thoughts, and 2) it makes the Thought Reference Guide accessible across different situations. This generalization, of course, is optional. Write the exact thoughts under the Emotion Categories or write a "bigger picture" version of them.

Christina also assigns multiple feelings to some of her thoughts in Step 2 of the previous exercise, and then decides to put her thoughts under only one Emotion Category. This is also a matter of preference. When completing that exercise, feel free to assign the same thought under multiple Emotion Categories, or to assign the thought under the emotion that feels strongest. One thought can induce several emotions. Remember to consider the big picture: the purpose of this exercise is to assist in identifying emotions, so create a Thoughts Reference Guide that will help to achieve this goal.

One challenge for Christina in accessing her emotions is the thought "I shouldn't be feeling this way." From Christina's perspective, her emotions seem to be at odds with what she believes was "supposed" to be her experience; her emotions feel unacceptable. Thoughts and judgments such as this not only serve as a barrier to exploring a whole range of emotions but can also exacerbate the situation by leading to feelings of shame and the feedback loops that we mentioned earlier in the book. Judgments about emotions can fuel "feelings about our feelings" and distract from the crux of the internal experience. We will dive deeper into this topic later, when we discuss primary and secondary emotions.

We cannot overemphasize that there is no "right" or "wrong" when it comes to feelings; **all emotions are valid as they are. In other words, all emotions are valid simply because a person feels them.** As discussed earlier in this book, not only does denying emotional experiences fail to make them go away, but attempting to do so can intensify them.

ACTIONS

Have you ever been surprised by your own behavior, perhaps to the point of regretting it? Maybe this looks like blurting out an uncharacteristically passive-aggressive comment toward a friend, or perhaps unintentionally oversharing a personal detail with colleagues. This can feel very unsettling. As humans, the desire for control over one's surroundings and actions is normal. Impulsive behaviors, or actions that are performed hastily without forethought or consideration of the consequences, are considered to be the instantaneous results of emotion (Strack & Deustch, 2004).

Think back to the discussion on the function of emotions and the question: "What is this emotion trying to do for you?" Emotions provide you with a drive to try to meet your needs in the moment. In a work meeting where you feel undervalued, your anger might motivate you to attack in order to feel more secure in the situation, and a passive-aggressive comment may spill out. If you are feeling isolated, your loneliness might attempt to help you start a conversation by sharing a piece of gossip that you are not sure should be shared.

It is not inevitable to act impulsively when feeling strong emotions; it is possible to pause, notice the internal experience, and proceed to make conscious decisions. However, the risk of acting impulsively is increased when emotional awareness is lacking.

EXERCISE: ACTIONS AS INDICATORS OF EMOTIONS

1. Think about a recent situation where you felt surprised by or regretful for your actions. Maybe you interrupted someone during a conversation, ate a whole bag of chips when you were not hungry, or spent too much money on something you did not need. Write down this behavior.

2. Next, write down what was happening just before the behavior occurred. How about when the behavior occurred? Who were you with? What was happening? How were you feeling physically? Include as many details as possible.

3. Given the behavior and context, try to identify any emotions you were experiencing at that time of the behavior. Were you feeling anxious? Angry? Excited? Lonely? It is possible you were feeling multiple emotions at once. Write them down.

4. Now that you have identified the impulsive behavior, the context, and the emotions, reflect on how these elements are all connected. What do you think your emotions were trying to do for you? What underlying need was related to this emotion? How was the behavior trying to meet that need? How effective was the behavior in meeting that underlying need? Remember, the purpose of this activity is not to judge or criticize yourself, but to better understand your emotional responses and impulsive behaviors. The more you understand these patterns, the more control you will have over future responses.

5. Group the behaviors that share emotions by using the following Actions Reference Guide. Over time, you will be able to refer to this guide and recognize patterns to help understand your emotional processes.

Actions Reference Guide

Action	Emotion	Function of Emotion
Impulsive behaviors that occurred	*Emotion experienced before or during an impulsive behavior*	*What is this emotion trying to do for you? What need of yours is it trying to meet?*

VIGNETTE

Hari, a software engineer, excitedly pushes a batch of new code as an update to his company's internal tools, promising a collection of great new features. But because he was running up against other deadlines, his work was hasty, and the buggy code resulted in irretrievable data loss. Another engineer quickly spots the problem and sends a patch, so the harm done is limited.

But that afternoon, when a separate group asks about his availability to take on additional job responsibility on an unrelated project, Hari finds himself quickly agreeing, even though the extra work comes without pay and affects his work-life balance. In addition, Hari suspects that his hasty work on the flawed code is because he is struggling to focus on so many projects at a time and has not been getting enough sleep.

A few days later, Hari's therapist checks in about progress towards his goal of improving work-life balance. Hari reflects on his recent difficulty setting boundaries in the workplace, recalling how he impulsively agreed to take on extra work without extra pay. Hari, exhausted from the late hours he has been putting in over the last few days, expresses both confusion and frustration with himself for agreeing to this extra work. In the session, Hari tells his therapist he wants to understand the reasons behind this impulsive decision to add more work to his plate.

Hari tells his therapist about his experiences earlier that day: the way he rushed through his code, the data loss, his colleague spotting his error which minimized the impact of Hari's mistake, and the way he later swiftly took on more responsibilities. Hari says, "My heart was pounding out of my chest when I realized there was a bug...my stomach was in knots." He notes that his stomach also felt upset when he later agreed to a new project that afternoon, knowing that he lacked the bandwidth to take on more work. Hari says when he quickly agreed to the additional work, he remembers speaking fast, almost eager to convey his reliability to the team.

Hari understands that he had been feeling anxious and guilty at the time he was approached by the second group to take on additional work. Hari and his therapist process his feelings surrounding the data loss. He expresses that he had been feeling anxious all day because he had not been giving the code his full attention. Hari discusses with his therapist how his feelings of guilt, including the physiological sensations in his chest and stomach, functioned as a means of attempting to mend his relationships with his co-workers after his mistake. His experiences from earlier that day had been weighing heavily on his mind.

Unfortunately, Hari's guilt found no clear course of action, as he could not remedy the impact of the bug. Hari reflects on how he was presented with a new work opportunity and how he had been unaware of the intensity of his lingering feelings of guilt when he reactively agreed to the new project. Similarly, he had not realized how much his anxiety had compounded. He feared he might let people down once again and had an urge to take action in order to feel in control.

Reflecting on these events, it became clear that a conscious decision would have afforded Hari the chance to reflect on his work schedule and clearly see that he did not have time for a new undertaking. In fact, the pressure Hari was under to meet several deadlines led to his hasty work in the first place. Also, if Hari had proactively taken a pause instead of immediately reacting to his environment, he might have realized that he was attempting to "fix" a circumstance by focusing on an entirely different one. In the end, the decisions made based on his impulsive urge did not effectively address the underlying emotion of guilt. Hari creates an Actions Reference Guide in order to be able to recognize any ongoing patterns and identify his emotions more quickly in the future.

Hari's Actions Reference Guide

Action	Emotion	Function of Emotion
Impulsive behaviors that occurred	*Emotion experienced before or during an impulsive behavior*	*What is this emotion trying to do for you? What need of yours is it trying to meet?*
Overextending self	*Guilt*	*Mend relationships, connection*
	Anxiety	*Repair, reach safety*

Reflection

Hari impulsively took on more work out of guilt and the motivation to fix possible damage to his relationships with his co-workers and to prevent further damage. This behavior was misguided and actively diverged from his efforts to improve his work-life balance. If Hari had been able to slow down and process his feelings of guilt and discern what this emotion was urging him to do, it is possible he could have found a more effective means of repairing the relationships without compromising his goals. For example, Hari could have repaired his relationships with the team members who lost data by providing them with an apology. Depending on the work setting, he could have called a meeting to discuss strategies to bolster communication and support among team members in order to reduce errors.

Ultimately, actions are not bound to the impulsive reactions of emotions. Another option Hari had was to notice the urge to make up for his mistake to come and go without taking any action at all. He could have simply recognized his emotion and what it was trying to do for him and used this insight to determine that he was not ready to take any actions at this time.

As we've mentioned, feelings are neither good nor bad but exist for survival. The modern world is different from that of the hunter-gatherers, and the concept of "survival" has become more complex and nuanced. In that context, guilt could be data that Hari values his relationships and that working to repair these relationships is important. However, the automatic behavior tied to guilt was not effective. While an impulsive reaction to the emotion of guilt might have been necessary for the survival of early humans, the modern world affords and even demands a pause to reflect on a more effective response to the needs beneath that emotion. And with an awareness of our needs, we are one step closer to making decisions aligned with our values and goals.

SUMMARY

For some, it is easier to notice thoughts or actions than to notice physiological sensations. Mindfully noticing thoughts and actions, finding patterns in these experiences, and then associating these experiences with emotions is another way to expand the awareness of emotions. Many roads lead to emotional awareness, so start with the road that is easiest for you. Over time, gradually building an awareness of thoughts, actions, or physiological sensations can give a clearer sense of emotions and how you experience them.

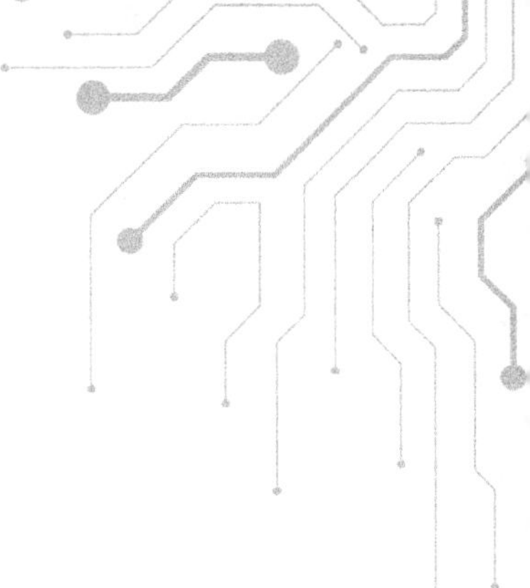

CHAPTER 7

UNDERSTANDING EMOTIONS 2.0

AT THIS POINT IN YOUR READING, YOU MAY BE AWARE that decompiling emotions requires both effort and intentionality. There are a myriad of emotions, and each serves a distinct function(s) to help you get your needs met. While these skills can take years to hone, perfection is not a prerequisite for reaping the benefits. For instance, even if you do not notice each time you feel guilty, noticing guilt even some of the time can slow your automatic reactions and improve the outcome of your decisions.

Slowing down automatic responses and making decisions more aligned with the needs conveyed by the emotion can create positive ripple effects. One decision can contribute to a series of beneficial circumstances. In the previous chapter's example, if Hari had slowed down enough to notice his guilt, he might have decided to apologize for his mistake while still maintaining his boundaries for work-life balance. This decision could position Hari to be more rested and perform more effectively at work, reducing future mistakes. Even if there were other emotions that Hari did not recognize, noticing this one moment of guilt could have allowed him to make a decision that improved his overall circumstances.

The ability to hone effective responses to emotions can be enhanced beyond just a general awareness. By building emotional awareness and understanding the connection between emotions to needs, we can then understand how *beliefs* about emotions impact the emotions themselves. To recap: emotions are shaped by beliefs, associations, and instincts to protect us from painful experiences. Compared to other animals, humans have a more developed prefrontal cortex that provides the ability to create narratives, perspectives, and judgments. While these capacities are helpful in many contexts, when the narratives intersect with emotions, the result can be a confused haze of overlapping emotions and thoughts, making priorities unclear.

For instance, someone may hold the belief that the emotion of sadness is an indicator of "weakness." Perhaps there were subtle or not-so-subtle messages received during their upbringing that suggested this belief. In US culture, direct and indirect messages convey not to cry, but to smile instead (as the saying goes, "Laugh and the world laughs with you. Cry, and you cry alone."). While these messages often come from a place of compassion—or perhaps, discomfort at witnessing another's pain—they often contribute to deeply held beliefs that sadness is not okay. Given these messages, hiding sadness is somewhat adaptive, as it prevents criticism in these social contexts.

Over time, though, these messages can compound into core beliefs that are often outside of conscious awareness. These beliefs, and the conscious and unconscious attempts to avoid the emotion can alter the experiences of sadness, leading sadness to become intertwined with other psychological concerns such as social rejection.

EXERCISE: BELIEFS ABOUT EMOTIONS

At this time, review the following list of emotions and reflect on your beliefs about each one. Is the emotion socially acceptable? What direct or indirect messages did you receive about each emotion? We might logically know that sadness, for instance, is important and human. At the same time, we might hold deeply rooted, negative beliefs about expressing sadness, leading us to perceive it more negatively. These beliefs may be more challenging to notice than the feelings themselves.

For the purposes of this exercise, simply be curious about the deeper, learned beliefs. Additionally, take some time to reflect on typical responses to each emotion. For instance, is this an emotion that you embrace and warmly accept? Do you fight with that emotion and try to avoid it? After filling out the table, reflect on any insights gained during the process.

Beliefs About Emotions

Emotion	Beliefs About the Emotion	Typical Response to the Emotion
Sadness	*It shows weakness, and I need to project strength.*	*Avoid at all costs; I judge myself for feeling sadness.*
Happiness		
Regret		

Emotion	Beliefs About the Emotion	Typical Response to the Emotion
Fear		
Anger		
Sadness		
Other:		
Other:		

Examining deeply held beliefs about emotions is important, as it can highlight the emotions that you are subconsciously prone to avoid. When unhelpful beliefs are not challenged, the mind remains extremely creative in finding methods to avoid these "unacceptable" emotions. For instance, someone who fears sadness but is experiencing sadness may lean on avoidance strategies such as substance use, video games, working long hours, and an endless variety of other behaviors. The mind can come up with narratives to justify those avoidance behaviors, allowing the protective systems to persist even when they are creating problems. This cycle can sometimes be difficult to catch, because the mind is flexible and can quickly adapt and find other ways to avoid emotions.

VIGNETTE

Growing up, Jacob learns that sadness is a problematic emotion. Bullies in his school tease boys for crying and call them names such as "girly" or "weak." Jacob often becomes tearful after getting hurt or getting in a fight with his sister. His family responds with comments such as "Don't cry!" or "You're okay," without acknowledging his sadness.

Over the years, Jacob learns to hide his sadness. When something is bothersome, Jacob unconsciously distracts himself with alcohol and video games. Jacob tells himself narratives like, "It is healthy to have a few drinks with dinner," or "It is important to decompress with video games."

After realizing that the drinking and video games are impacting his work performance, Jacob works hard to change his behaviors and rely less on drinking and video games. While on the surface this appears to be a positive adjustment, Jacob continues to avoid his sadness by working long hours and neglecting time with his family and other relationships. The emotions do not go away.

CLINGING TO SAFER EMOTIONS

The mind can also creatively combat uncomfortable emotions by clinging to other emotions that are perceived as "safer." For instance, some may perceive anger as more acceptable or "safe" than sadness. Rather than giving the sadness space, then, the brain quickly responds with anger. This transition can happen so quickly that the person does not even know that they initially experienced sadness! Without this awareness, they may then feel justified in their anger, making quick decisions based on that emotion, rather than recognizing that sadness more accurately reflects their underlying needs.

Even though anger may not feel good, if the beliefs around anger are more accepting, or if the emotion feels more familiar, it can generate a sense of comfort. In our work, we have observed that the "safer" or "more comfortable" emotions can differ from person to person. For some, sadness may be easier to access. For others, it may be easiest to cling to guilt. Let's revisit Jacob's story:

Jacob learns the gender-based messages that sadness is "weak" and "feminine," and anger is "masculine" and "strong." Even though anger leads Jacob to feel a tightness in his body and a mental preoccupation about upsetting things, Jacob is unconsciously motivated to hold on to anger as a way to avoid feelings of sadness. For instance, in response to being rejected by a colleague, Jacob experiences strong feelings of anger. If Jacob were to spend time to reflect on the situation and notice his emotions, he likely would notice that underneath the anger is a sense of sadness in response to being denied an opportunity for belonging and acceptance.

Safer Emotions in the Engineering Field

The discussion of so-called safer emotions would be incomplete without further considering the impact of culture. Studies have found the concepts of "difficulty" and "struggle" to be ever-present in engineering circles; one survey reported that the "theme of 'Hardness' seemed to permeate the conversations of faculty and students, conveying worth and status" (Godfrey & Parker, 2010). In their 2023 article "Undergraduate student perceptions of stress and mental health in engineering culture," Jensen et al. (2023) propose that such themes "may contribute to expectations of high stress and poor mental health as necessary in engineering programs" (p. 2). Rigorous college courses are badges of honor as "toughness" and "resiliency" are part of student norms and values. Instead of acting as warning signs, stress and poor mental health are accepted as indications of a successful engineering experience.

The research also shows that engineering culture, which values a heavy workload, serves as one of the barriers for individuals seeking help and support (Jensen et al., 2023). Many engineering students delay coming to therapy, beginning sessions only after stress, anxiety and feelings of being overwhelmed have impacted their lives in a dire way. What is striking is that despite their clear discomfort, some of our clients have become attached to these difficult feelings. In fact, these emotions are so widely experienced and accepted among their peers, faculty, and staff that *not* feeling stressed, anxious or overwhelmed could be perceived as a sign that they are doing something wrong.

We witness clients struggling with internal battles surrounding their identity, grappling with implied questions such as: "Without high levels of stress, am I really an engineer?", "If I don't feel overly anxious, does that just mean I'm missing something?", and "If I'm not feeling overwhelmed, am I not pushing myself hard enough?" The constant pressure and activation an engineering student might feel during a difficult semester is not pleasant, but it is familiar. And what is familiar can feel safe.

The Impact of the Engineer's Identity on Emotional Safety

It's "normal" for engineers to be stressed, in the sense that so many feel that way. And not all engineers experience the same type and level of stress. Yet engineers with identities that are not highly represented in their cohort may experience added stress and pressure due to prejudice within the system.

A 2020 study examined the ways in which science, technology, engineering, and mathematics (STEM) programs affect the mental health of female graduates. The participants of the study identified as Black, African American, LatinX, and White/Caucasian, and either completed STEM doctoral degrees or chose to leave their programs prior to completion (Arnold et al., 2020). The study included 33 women, and the data presented in the report focused on the experiences of six. The six participants highlighted experiences of receiving derogatory and dismissive remarks, microaggressions, and pressure to "represent" their race and/or gender. While qualitative studies such as these are not intended to yield causal connections, they do provide insight into what some students are experiencing that might otherwise go unheard. Insights gained from such studies can then be used to investigate trends more broadly.

One participant who identified as LatinX discussed how one of her supervisors was known for stopping non-native English speakers in the middle of their presentations to correct the pronunciation of words, thereby informing them they needed to improve their English (Arnold et al., 2020). Another participant who identifies as a Black woman discussed how someone in her cohort "jokingly" told her she only got into her program due to these held identities. When she later failed an exam, she struggled deeply with the narrative that she did not belong. Some of the participants in the study reported they did not discuss mental health concerns in the academic setting out of fears of how others would respond or perceive them. Others in the study "avoided discussing these concerns with certain individuals whom they perceived as arrogant, aggressive, or disingenuous, or with whom they did not have shared racial, gender, or cultural identities" (p. 16-17). In this environment, experiences such as these built on what were already extremely rigorous academic demands.

Unfortunately, in some cases these experiences can lead to talented and capable students leaving their programs. The danger of a culture which celebrates continuous struggle is that it can fail to recognize how the additional struggles related to identity can compound the stress of being an engineer. It is imperative that the unique struggles and barriers faced by underrepresented individuals are recognized and addressed so that instances of sexism, racism, and discrimination are not dismissed as just another challenge in a program which prides itself on difficulty.

If someone experiences stress, anxiety, and a sense of being overwhelmed as "safer" emotions, a natural response might be, "Safer than what?" What resides underneath, and how could it be any more uncomfortable than these challenging emotions? The answer is not simple, as it depends on the individual. In the next segment, we will discuss how emotions naturally stack on top of each other and how to build insight into this process.

PRIMARY AND SECONDARY EMOTIONS

Psychology recognizes the phenomenon by which emotions can be quickly covered by a different emotion; these are often referred to as primary and secondary emotions. Primary emotions include the initial, often subtle, emotional responses to a stimulus. For instance, the emotions of sadness and grief after a breakup are likely primary emotions; they are directly tied to the need for connection and belonging. Primary emotions are indicators that accurately reflect the core needs in a given situation.

Secondary emotions are generated by *the mind's* response to primary emotions. Influenced by beliefs, experiences, and thoughts about emotions, secondary emotions arise to respond to and to block the sensitivity of primary emotions. When an emotion does not feel "acceptable," or feels particularly vulnerable, the secondary emotions step in. They are often learned and habitual, occurring quickly and reflexively. In other words, secondary emotions are "feelings about feelings."

Any emotion can be either a primary or secondary emotion. Depending on personal history and beliefs about various emotions, one may be more disposed to experience certain emotions as secondary emotions. (In the earlier scenario, Jacob's primary emotion was sadness, and his secondary emotion was anger.) Often, the primary emotion passes very quickly, whereas the secondary emotion is louder and more sustained because it feels more familiar or has been more socially acceptable. The secondary emotion is often the *first* emotion that clients consciously access and describe. As a result, secondary emotions can make understanding needs very challenging, as they misdirect attention away from the primary emotion.

In our example, Jacob will likely recognize and articulate his anger more quickly than his sadness. If he quickly reacts to meet the needs indicated by his anger, he may neglect the deeper needs indicated by sadness. Jacob may also decide to set boundaries at work to protect himself and create distance from others, when the sadness is actually indicating his need for connection and support. The more that decisions are driven by secondary emotions, without understanding the primary emotions underneath, the more those decisions can misdirect us from the underlying needs.

EXERCISE: ACCEPTANCE LEVEL OF EMOTIONS

Fill out the table to help identify your common secondary emotions.

Emotion	On a scale 1-10, how acceptable is it to feel this emotion?	Reflecting on your experiences, which emotions are likely common secondary emotions (because they are more acceptable)?
Sadness		
Anger		
Guilt		
Happiness		
Fear		
Other:		
Other:		
Other:		

A few other methods can also help shed insight into whether an arising emotion is primary or secondary. It is not necessary to follow the listed methods in order; choose one or a few of these methods to practice at different times.

1. Reflect: When you became aware of an emotion, was there a moment of experiencing a different emotion before the initially identified emotion jumped in? This can be difficult to detect. Practicing mindfulness, over time, can help you recognize the subtle presence of primary emotions.

2. Refer to the table where you identified your acceptance level for each emotion. Consider whether the presenting emotion feels safer. If it is a safer emotion, there may be a higher probability that the emotion was experienced as secondary.

3. Review the Feeling Wheel in Chapter 5. Do other emotions resonate as you review the Wheel? If so, this could suggest the presence of a different primary emotion.

4. Talk it out or journal. Bringing language and curiosity can slow down the emotional experience and offer perspective. Just as talking to a trusted friend or a therapist can help us uncover what might be underneath the emotion, journaling with reflection and curiosity can help you slow down and understand your emotional experiences. Keep in mind that there is a difference between venting or ranting and reflection or curiosity. Repeating the same comments to prove a point or justify an emotion is probably venting. When you catch yourself venting, consider taking a break before continuing the conversation or journaling.

5. Questions to explore include: What circumstances led to the emotions? Were other emotions also present? What beliefs were being activated before and during

the emotional experience? What did you wish would happen? How would you have felt if the situation happened differently? What did you need in that situation?

SELF-COMPASSION

Building the ability to identify secondary emotions can promote faster recognition of primary emotions, and, in turn, comprehension of the needs reflected by those emotions. When paying more attention to the primary, often uncomfortable, emotions, tolerating that discomfort is key. One way to help build this ability is the capacity for self-compassion.

In our work, helping clients foster self-compassion is foundational to the efficacy of therapy. Our experiences are supported by research which underscores the benefits of self-compassion, including higher levels of happiness, curiosity, optimism, and wisdom (Neff et al., 2007); and lower levels of anxiety, depression, self-criticism, and rumination (Neff, 2003). In *Self-Compassion: The Proven Power of Being Kind to Yourself,* Kristin Neff explores this concept, along with tangible strategies to incorporate more self-compassion into one's worldview (Neff, 2011). The three tenets of self-compassion are mindfulness, common humanity, and self-kindness.

Let's start by defining these terms. "Mindfulness" was described in a previous chapter and is the practice of directing attention to the present moment with kindness and non-judgment. "Common humanity" is acceptance of pain as part of the human experience, knowing that emotional pain can be a reminder that, in fact, we are all human. Often the response to emotional pain is a sense of shame or isolation: "I am the only one who doesn't get it," or "I am weak and strange." By contrast, common humanity is a way to normalize difficult emotional experiences. Normalizing these experiences can reduce the shame or loneliness of pain. When the primary emotion is normalized, escaping to a secondary emotion is not as necessary. Finally, "self-kindness" means responding to pain with empathy and softness, the way that one might respond to a friend who is experiencing a challenge. Examples of self-kindness might be a statement such as "It's okay to feel frustrated for making a mistake and scared about what will happen," or "I know I can learn from this experience." Simple actions such as enjoying a warm cup of tea or hot chocolate can also be an expression of self-kindness.

Reading these examples of self-kindness, you might notice discomfort arising, or perhaps embarrassment. It can feel really uncomfortable to respond to emotions in this way, especially if the typical inner dialogue is critical. For many people, the automatic thoughts that arise in response to emotions and pain can be quite harsh and judgmental.

Our clients often defend their self-criticism, believing that this "tough love" is what allows them to feel motivated and to persevere, or fearing that being kinder towards themselves will lead to complacency or laziness. While this intuitively makes some sense, research actually shows the opposite effect. Research suggests that self-compassion is related to *increases* in motivation (Breines & Chen, 2012). Self-criticism, on the other hand, is negatively associated with intrinsic motivation and goal progress (Powers et al., 2007). Instead, self-criticism is associated with side effects such as depressive symptoms, social anxiety, and interpersonal problems (Werner et al., 2019). Self-criticism in response to failure trains the brain to associate failing with pain rather than an opportunity to learn. When failure results in the pain of self-criticism, the brain can then learn to avoid that outcome, not by succeeding, but rather by avoiding the task altogether. Self-compassion, on the other hand, is restorative and conserves mental and emotional energy that can be then used to take further action.

As authors of this book, we can attest to the value of self-compassion in maintaining our motivation. As with anyone pusuing a long-term goal, we experienced stress, anxiety, and discomfort throughout the writing process. At times, we realized that some of the content we worked on was no longer necessary, and we had to delete several pages at a time. In those moments, emotions of frustration, regret, and anxiety arose. Responding to ourselves with self-compassion allowed us to recover more quickly and to move away from self-criticism; it prevented us from getting stuck in shame or rumination about our past decisions and the accompanying emotions.

After tending to these emotions, we were then able to reorient ourselves to the next step in the writing process. While self-criticism was tempting (as we too have received erroneous messages that this self-criticism is necessary to feel motivated), it ultimately would have prolonged our stress response and depleted our energy. Self-compassion instead allowed us to be agile in the midst of inevitable challenges and mistakes and to move forward in a way that better served our goals.

EXERCISE: SELF-COMPASSION BREAK

The website self-compassion.org offers a number of guided practices and self-compassion exercises. One exercise from this website is to create a self-compassion break. This includes choosing a series of statements that address the three tenets of self-compassion, in order to use these statements during moments of stress or emotional pain. Here is a version of that exercise:

Pick one statement that resonates with you, to encourage mindfulness:

- I am experiencing distress.
- This is painful.
- I am noticing tension in my body.
- I am noticing this moment of suffering.

Pick one statement that resonates with you, to encourage common humanity:

- We all suffer.
- This pain reminds me that I am human.
- I am connected to others in this pain.
- Pain is a part of the human experience.

Pick one statement that resonates with you, to encourage self-kindness:

- May I love myself.
- May I offer myself compassion.
- May I be curious about what I am needing right now.
- May I be a friend to myself.

Write the selected three statements somewhere you can easily access them during times of emotional pain.

VIGNETTE

Jamal is an engineer who recently went through a break up of a long-term relationship. After reading the decompiling emotions section of this book, he decided to create a self-compassion break. On a Notes app in his phone, he writes three statements from the list above that resonate with him: "I am noticing this moment of suffering. This pain reminds me that I am human. May I be a friend to myself."

The next time Jamal feels sad when thinking about the break up, he pulls out his Notes tab and reads the statements to himself. Jamal reads the statements slowly while taking deep breaths. After a few moments of taking this break, Jamal goes back to the engineering task he was previously working on. While the sadness is still present, Jamal is able to respond to the sadness with self-compassion. He experiences relief from the self-criticism and shame he was previously experiencing alongside the sadness.

SUMMARY

Although this book contains a decompiling emotions section and a decompiling thoughts section, thoughts and emotions are closely intertwined. As this chapter relates, beliefs about emotions can impact how they are experienced. Family history, culture, workplace norms, and other environmental expectations can all impact perceptions of emotions. When certain emotions are believed to be "unacceptable," secondary emotions arise. When decompiling an emotion, it is necessary to uncover the primary emotion, in order to confirm the underlying needs that created the emotional response to the situation, rather than getting stuck in the secondary emotional response to the emotion.

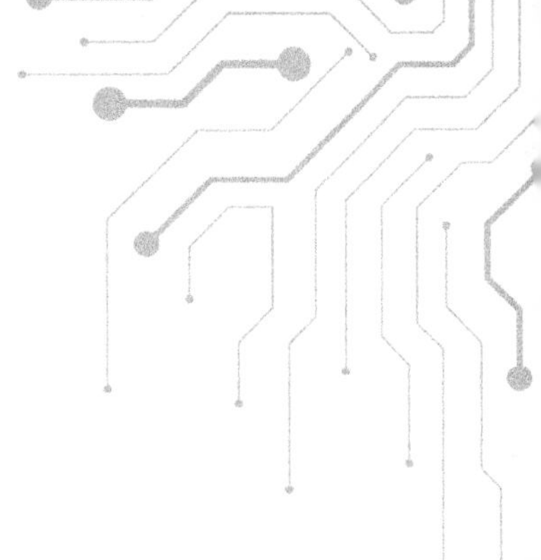

CHAPTER 8

LIVING YOUR VALUES THROUGH EMOTIONS

AT THIS POINT YOU MIGHT BE THINKING "DECOMpiling emotions is a lot of work!" You may even be questioning whether to make the effort. Or you may feel that your current way of relating to yourself and to your emotions is working "well enough." Perhaps there is some fear arising about facing certain emotions ... or, maybe your reaction is something entirely different. You might also feel hopeful about the new opportunities to experience life in a more fulfilling way. No matter what your response might be, it is valid and makes sense in your unique context.

Understanding emotions is like learning a new language with new rules. And as soon as you think you understand your emotions, you may find that there is a whole other level of awareness to explore. We offer the following exercise as a way to work through whatever feelings crop up as you learn this new material.

EXERCISE: IDENTIFYING EMOTIONS WHILE READING

1. What emotions arose as you read the decompiling emotions section so far? Try to identify the emotions, without adding judgment, perhaps referring to the Feeling Wheel.

2. Reviewing the Function of Emotions table, what do you think each identified emotion has been trying to do for you?

3. What feelings come up as you consider making changes to how you respond and relate to emotions?

After checking in with yourself and noticing the arising emotions, review the list below to remind yourself that relating to your emotions effectively can be beneficial. Then, consider whether or not you are ready to make changes to your responses to emotions. If you are not ready at this point, feel free to step away from the book and revisit this section when you're ready:

- **Reducing the side effects that can arise from suppressing emotions or intellectualizing.** As discussed, avoiding emotions can lead to worsening symptoms of intensified emotions, anxiety, depression, weakened immune systems, and other physical health symptoms.

- **Taking away the power of the "negative" emotions.** When consciously or unconsciously fearful of experiencing certain emotions, we give them a lot of power. People often unknowingly modify their behavior to avoid experiencing those emotions. In doing so, their decisions are being driven by avoidance rather than moving toward the things they care about.

- **Improving the ability to meet your needs and make better decisions.** Understanding emotions (primary and secondary) leads to a more accurate understanding of our needs and, in turn, decisions are informed by that insight.

- **Increasing the ability for meaningful and fulfilling relationships.** Relating to emotions effectively informs how we show up in relationships and communications.

VALUES

Effective emotional regulation involves responding and relating to emotions in a way that aligns with values. A core philosophy of Acceptance and Commitment Therapy (ACT), an evidence-based therapeutic model, entails learning to make decisions that move toward those values, rather than focusing our attention on moving away from pain. According to ACT, avoidance of uncomfortable internal experiences is the cause of cognitive distress. Rather than thinking about what path will be less distressing, ACT posits that a more meaningful question is "What discomfort am I willing to experience in order to move in the direction of my values?"

Welcoming all internal experiences is the "acceptance" part of Acceptance and Commitment Therapy. The "commitment" part of ACT refers to committing to actions that are concordant with our values. In this context, the term "values" describes what we want life to be about. A few examples of values include community, advocacy, honesty, adventure, and learning.

Throughout this section, we have explored how decompiling emotions builds insight into underlying needs. Decompiling your emotions can also shed light on your values. Values are similar to, yet different from, needs. Values reflect what we want to bring to the world, whereas needs are what is necessary to sustain our biological and psychological systems. Clarity about values facilitates decisions that contribute to a more fulfilling life. Additionally, this clarity supports our understanding of needs and how to access them.

One psychological human need is "purpose" or "meaning." Awareness of values points to purpose, and therefore to the actions that meet the need for purpose. Values are often broad and cannot be checked off a to-do list. Pursuing our values is a lifelong endeavor. Distinct from a goal with a clearly defined outcome, a value is direction that does not end. New actions that represent a value can occur at any time.

According to ACT, it is useful to be curious about how your values might link to attempts to reduce negative thoughts or emotions. Additionally, aiming to meet others' expectations can be a motivation to set certain values. Though these influences are not unusual, we ask clients to search beyond these influences, fears, and expectations.

For instance, consider "peace" as a value to move toward. A value of peace might motivate behaviors including taking a conflict resolution course or protesting a violent war abroad. While these actions might create short-term discomfort, committing to these actions is a way to move toward the value of peace.

Alternatively, consider peace as a means of pleasing someone else or moving away from uncomfortable conflict. This might look like avoiding a disagreement by subordinating one's own needs or opinions. Values driven from a need to please others or to avoid pain or discomfort are "pseudo-values." A helpful question to ask is, "If I were to get rid of these fears and expectations, what would I want to focus on?" This answer is a value.

Being willing to experience discomfort allows the pursuit of a value-centered life. It can be helpful to use the ACT metaphor for values: a compass. Picture this compass orienting you to what you find important and what you want your life to be about. In reality, this path might guide you through some rough terrain. Being unwilling to experience the terrain, however, means missing an opportunity to move toward your values and fulfillment.

As we've said, identifying our values likely will not be achieved in one sitting. Especially if you have not considered your values before, we encourage you to use the next exercise to plant a seed for reflection. If you already have a clear sense of your values—genuine values and not attempts to please others or avoid discomfort—we encourage you to use this activity to reaffirm or revise those values.

EXERCISE: IDENTIFY YOUR VALUES

Follow these steps to better identify your values:

1. Review the full list of values below, adapted from The Personal Values Card Sort resource (Miller et al., 2001).

2. Put a check next to all values that resonate with you.

3. This list is not exhaustive, so add any of your values that are not on the list.

4. Of the checked values, work to identify your five most important values.

5. For each of the five values, ask:

   - Am I drawn to this value primarily as a way to avoid discomfort? If yes, how so?

- Am I drawn to this value primarily to meet expectations of others? If yes, how so?

- Am I unwilling to experience discomfort in pursuit of this value?

6. If the answer to any of these questions is "yes," go back to the list and identify other values to replace those, then ask the same questions again. Repeat this process until all five values on your list are not informed by wanting to avoid discomfort or to meet the expectations of others.

Values List

Achievement	Equity	Innovation	Tradition
Adventure	Fairness	Learning	Transparency
Autonomy	Faith	Love	Wellness
Accountability	Friendship	Mindfulness	(Other)
Beauty	Generosity	Nature	(Other)
Collaboration	Hard Work	Peace	(Other)
Compassion	Integrity	Responsibility	(Other)
Competence	Kindness	Safety	(Other)
Cooperation	Honesty	Service	(Other)
Creativity	Humor	Stability	(Other)
Diversity	Inclusion	Sustainability	(Other)

In addition to engaging in this exercise, decompiling emotions and thoughts can also help build insight into values. Experiencing thoughts and emotions and then unpacking their deeper meaning can point to what is most important. Typically, what causes a person the most distress is related, directly or indirectly, to what is important to them. Getting nervous before a job interview, for instance, indicates that something about that experience reflects one's values. While the values might vary from person to person (e.g., achievement, competence, stability, learning), the tension is a signal to be curious about what feels most important about this experience.

SUMMARY

Decompiling emotions can take work, and hesitancy to engage in this work is natural. Even if skills within the decompiling process are not done perfectly or fluently, though, the benefits still occur. Gradually relating to emotions in a way that reduces the side effects of emotional avoidance can also allow insight to decisions that will be consistent with our needs and values. The process of developing these skills is cyclical and expanding. Insight into values enhances the ability to regulate and decompile emotions. In turn, regulating and decompiling emotions increases insight into personal values. Practicing one skill broadens the capacity for the other skills.

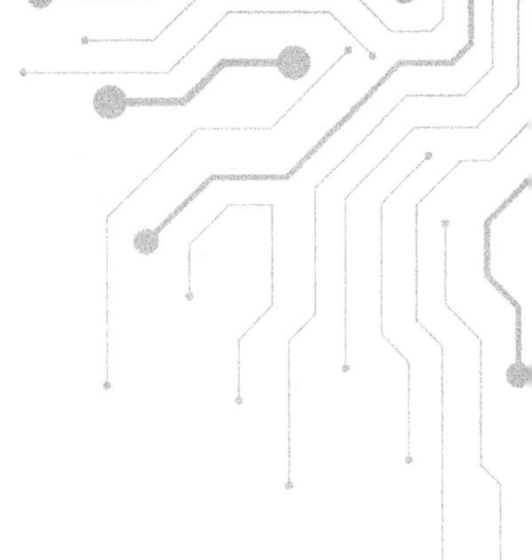

CHAPTER 9

PUTTING IT ALL TOGETHER: THE EMOTION DECOMPILER

WE'VE COVERED MANY SKILLS RELATED TO IMPROVING your relationship with emotions. In the following segment, we will summarize and organize the skills we have covered in a step-by-step process to follow when emotions arise.

Note that we are providing one avenue for experiencing and understanding emotions. This process takes a linear, concrete style, informed by a Western, individualistic lens. Other cultures and communities offer several other methods for emotional processing. While we are describing one approach, there are other ways to effectively respond to emotions. In addition, these skills can be challenging to implement, despite the linear process.

Making habits of these skills, and not just having an intellectual understanding, requires repetition. We encourage you to read this section as a starting place, and from there, deepen your learning about these skills through reflection, discussion with others, and practice. At the end of this chapter, we will offer an exercise to identify tangible next steps to support the gradual habit formation of these skills.

Here is an overview of the linear process for decompiling emotions. If you notice yourself outside of your Window of Tolerance, at any point in the process, pause and engage in a grounding exercise. Only return to the Emotion Decompiler if you can continue the process while in your window.

The Emotion Decompiler

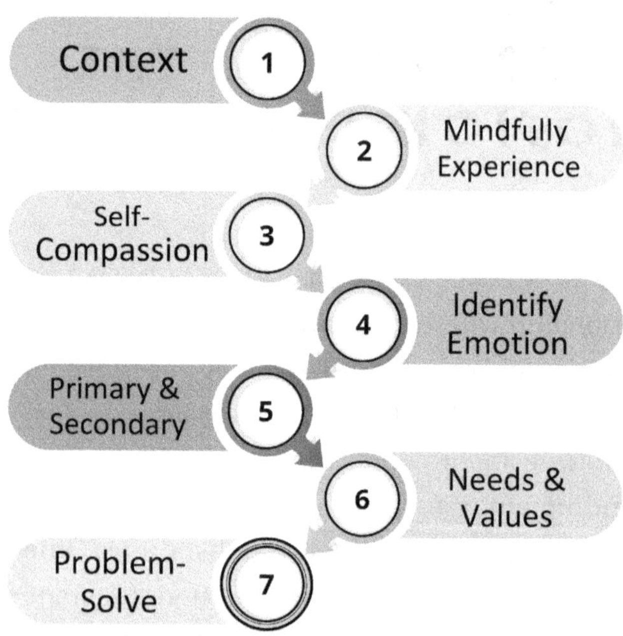

STEP ONE: CONSIDER THE CONTEXT.

Considering the context is an important step in decompiling emotions. Responses to arising emotions will likely be dependent on the surroundings, personal responsibilities, and the people nearby. For instance, is this a space to safely embrace emotions? Do you have the mental and emotional capacity? Are you able to stay within the Window of Tolerance to experience and explore the emotion? Would addressing a physiological need, such as food or sleep, effectively address the emotional need? Is there an imminent danger that requires automatic action?

Often, depending on the context, taking time to mindfully experience your emotions and reflect is not effective or even possible. It can be helpful to consider the places that are safe to decompile emotions as well as the contexts in which it's better to defer the process. While avoiding emotions in some contexts is strategic, it is still important that space is later provided to acknowledge the emotions. For instance, during a rough day at work, if one does not feel comfortable showing sadness or frustration to others, they might plan to take a walk later in the evening in order to process.

Some questions about context include:

1. Would expressing my emotions likely be received with respect and compassion by the surrounding people?

2. Do I have the cognitive capacity to process the emotion at this time (i.e., do I need to focus my energy on other urgent tasks instead)?

3. Am I able to remain within my Window of Tolerance?

4. Am I reasonably rested and nourished in order to be able to have the energy required to process emotions?

5. Identify two places that are likely effective and helpful to decompile my emotions (e.g., at home, on a walk, at a friend's home, while taking a bath, while sitting outside, etc.).

STEP TWO: MINDFULLY EXPERIENCE A PHYSICAL SENSATION.

Mindfully notice your experience of a sensation (or lack thereof) arising in an area of the body. Notice the breath and any changes to the sensation over the next two to five minutes. Notice thoughts that arise and redirect your attention to the body and the breath. Remember to refrain from judgment. If judgment arises, mindfully notice that thought as well. At this point, you may or may not have language to describe the emotion(s) that accompany the sensation.

For assistance, refer to the exercise titled *Observing Sensations of an Emotion: Noticing Your Internal Experience* in Chapter 4. Remember to use the grounding exercises if you're outside of your Window of Tolerance. Pause or refrain from the rest of the decompiling process while outside that window. If you find that mindfully noticing sensations does not work well for you, consider an alternative action at this step, such as stimming, exercise, or movement-based mindfulness.

STEP THREE: RESPOND TO THE SENSATION WITH SELF-COMPASSION.

Implement the three aspects of self-compassion in response to the arising sensation: mindfulness, self-kindness, and common humanity. This is a good time to use the Self-Compassion Break exercise in Chapter 7.

STEP FOUR: IDENTIFY THE EMOTION.

Take time to identify the language that most accurately describes one emotion that you are experiencing. If you already have a sense of what emotion(s) are arising, consider whether there is more precise language to clarify them. When experiencing several emotions, identify one that is most noticeable. Refer to resources such as the Feeling Wheel and Emotions Map (in Chapter 5) to identify language that describes this emotional experience. You can identify the emotion by noticing thoughts, actions, and/or physiological sensations.

STEP FIVE: BE CURIOUS ABOUT PRIMARY AND SECONDARY EMOTIONS.

As a reminder, primary emotions are the mind's authentic, aligned emotional reaction to a presenting stimulus. Secondary emotions are the emotional reaction to the primary emotion itself. Secondary emotions often appear in response to primary emotions that are perceived as less acceptable based on one's belief systems. Refer to the skills to distinguish between primary and secondary emotions in Chapter 7.

If feeling a *secondary* emotion, recognize that the arising emotion is trying to protect you from experiencing what is an "unacceptable" emotion, based on your internalized belief system. Keep in mind that this process of secondary emotions is very common and human. Next, consider what primary emotion is underneath the secondary emotion. Whether or not you can put language to the primary emotion, return to Step Two to mindfully experience the sensations that arise as you are curious about the primary emotion. Proceed with the steps from there, paying attention to the internal experience tied to the primary emotion.

STEP SIX: IDENTIFY UNDERLYING NEEDS AND VALUES.

If the emotion being experienced is a *primary* emotion, consider the function of the emotion. What needs and values are reflected by this emotion? Refer to the Function of Emotions table (Chapter 3), Identifying Needs table (Chapter 3), and Values List (Chapter 8) in order to identify the need(s) and value(s) underlying the emotion.

STEP SEVEN: PROBLEM-SOLVE TO MEET NEEDS AND MOVE TOWARD VALUES.

Having decompiled the emotion, you can move to problem-solving, leveraging engineering-related, creative problem-solving skills.

It's important to note that, while it may be tempting to jump to problem-solving (as it can feel more straightforward and solution-focused), we've learned how the prior steps allow the body to experience the emotion first, in order to prevent side effects from suppressing those emotions. Without giving space for the first six steps, one might commit to solving a problem before accurately clarifying the underlying need or value.

This is similar to trying to repair a faulty circuit board. First, you would need to make a careful assessment of which circuit elements were connected to power in order to avoid hurting yourself, damaging your tools, or damaging the circuit itself. Without this precaution, a hasty intervention might end up frying an IC or blowing a diode. Then, you might measure some voltages and inspect some circuit elements before soldering new connections. You could waste a lot of time and risk further damage if you believe a whole segment needs to be replaced, when in fact the only error is, for example, an LED that has been installed backward.

VIGNETTE

*Following a work event, Bella notices that she feels distressed and upset. Given the rise of emotion, she decides to refer to the Emotion Decompiler. Because she was not able to process her emotion in a work **context,** Bella practices **mindfully noticing** sensations that are arising when she gets home. After offering herself **compassion,** she **identifies the emotion** as sadness. Bella takes a few minutes to journal about her experience and* *determines that sadness is a **primary emotion.** She identifies that this sadness is **representing a need** for connection. Bella is expected to work in a very isolated context. Additionally, she does not feel very supported by her supervisor. In addition to needing connection, Bella reflects that connection is also a personal **value.***

As she reflects on strategies to problem-solve, Bella realizes that, in part, she needs to work toward acceptance that her current position will likely not meet her social needs. This acknowledgement and acceptance allows her to offer herself compassion, given that the loneliness of the position is painful. She can also notice when the sadness arises and comfort herself by validating her feelings of loneliness and recognizing these emotions as a reasonable response to the circumstances.

*Additionally, Bella **problem-solves** to find other creative ways to fulfill her need for connection. For instance, she asks a few coworkers to lunch. She also realizes the importance of prioritizing social connection outside of work. Bella decides to join a kickball league in the evenings and reaches out to friends to make plans for the weekend. Finally, Bella uses this insight to advocate for more collaborative work opportunities.*

Decompiling her reaction to a work event allowed her to accurately identify her underlying needs and values. With this data, Bella was able to problem-solve accordingly.

IDENTIFYING NEXT STEPS

As discussed earlier, integrating these decompiling skills so that they become a more automatic response to emotional discomfort takes time and practice. Consciously implementing the new pattern of behavior through repetition is necessary for the brain to form new robust neural networks. New behaviors become more automatic the more they are repeated (Lally et al., 2009).

Imagine that your neural networks are a familiar hiking trail (B. Salazar, personal communication, September 2018). With an established, well-practiced way of responding to emotions, you don't need to put much thought into the experience. The hiking path is well-groomed and has clear signs. Creating a new way of responding to emotions, in contrast, is like the process of forging a new trail. Initially, the new path might look more like an unmarked forest. The first several times using this new path might feel unpleasant and require avoiding trees and rocks. You might lose the path or miss the cue to make a turn. You might need to lean on additional resources the first several times out, such as a shovel or a chainsaw.

The good news, however, is that each time you traverse the new path, it becomes clearer. Footprints appear, the entrance of the trail also becomes more apparent, and eventually, you can make the hike with less preparation or support. Having this new trail does not mean that you will never go down older trails. The other trails will still be there. However, as the new path gradually becomes more appealing and automatic, the other trails become less necessary.

To help you feel more supported while gradually forming this new path, we offer a resource to plan in a way that feels more manageable and specific to your needs.

EXERCISE: IDENTIFYING NEXT STEPS

1. Fill out the Integrating Skills Planning Activity to assess each skill.

Integrating Skills Planning Activity

Skills	For each statement, rate your confidence level.	Confidence level: 1 (not confident) - 4 (very confident)	Learning tools and resources to develop this skill
Mindfulness	*I am able to notice my internal and external experiences on purpose, in the present moment, and non-judgmentally.*		*Mindfulness apps; mindfulness retreats; mindfulness-based therapy*
Identifying Emotions	*I have a large vocabulary of the emotions that I can identify within myself.*		*Feeling Wheel; Emotion Map; therapy; creating personal reference guides described in earlier chapters*
Considering the Context	*I am aware of the spaces where I can express my emotions effectively and with respect and support by others. I am aware of the environmental barriers that create hurdles in being effectively resourced to decompile my emotions.*		*Step One of the Emotion Decompiler*
Somatic awareness	*I am able to notice the physical sensations that arise as I experience emotions.*		*Mindfulness apps; somatic therapy; body scan exercises*

Skills	For each statement, rate your confidence level.	Confidence level: 1 (not confident) - 4 (very confident)	Learning tools and resources to develop this skill
Awareness of the Window of Tolerance	*I am able to identify when I am within or outside of my Window of Tolerance. I am able to use grounding skills when outside of my window.*		*Window of Tolerance Table; trauma therapy; Grounding Techniques Table; Grounding Practice Exercise*
Self-Compassion	*I am able to respond to my pain with self-kindness. I am able to remind myself that my pain is human and worthy of compassion.*		*Books and articles by Kristin Neff, PhD and Chris Germer, PhD; https://self-compassion.org; Self-Compassion Break*
Values Clarification	*I am able to describe my values and what is most important to me. I am willing to endure discomfort and face my fears in order to pursue these identified values.*		*Acceptance and Commitment Therapy books and videos; Personal Values Card Sort (Miller et al., 2001)*

2. Based on this review of the identified skills, list one or two skills that you are most motivated to work on.

3. Brainstorm a list of actions to take to foster that skill(s). Do not commit to any one action yet. The more ideas the better.

4. Identify one action on the list that you are most drawn to.

5. Frame the identified action to meet the characteristics of a SMART goal: Specific, Measurable, Attainable, Relevant, and Timely (Doran, 1981).

    - Specific (e.g., "use a mindfulness tool like the Headspace app" versus "learn mindfulness")

    - Measurable (e.g., "use the mindfulness tool three times a week")

    - Attainable (e.g., "use the mindfulness tool three times a week for ten minutes")

    - Relevant (e.g., "use the mindfulness tool to develop skills to better regulate my emotions")

    - Timely (e.g., "start using the mindfulness tool today at 5 p.m.")

6. Compose the identified action into a succinct SMART goal.(e.g., "I will use Headspace app three times per week for ten minutes at a time to help me build skills for emotion regulation. I will start this practice today at 5 p.m.").

SUMMARY

Congratulations on completing the decompiling emotions section! We hope that you now feel more confident with navigating emotions. Building these skills into habits takes time and patience.

Questions, uncertainty, and mistakes are inherent to the learning process.

Knowledge of emotions will serve as a foundation for the next section on decompiling thoughts. Emotions and thoughts are different processes, but they impact one another in important ways. Gradually building the skill to decompile emotions will, in turn, enhance your ability to decompile thoughts, and vice versa!

In the upcoming sections, some material might elicit strong emotions. We encourage you to draw upon the emotional insight you have gained and the skills you have developed to respond to those emotions. As always, remember that you are still in the driver's seat and can take a break when needed.

DECOMPILING THOUGHTS

CHAPTER 10

WHAT IS A THOUGHT?

WHAT IS A THOUGHT? PERHAPS THE ANSWER SEEMS obvious. You might say, "I experience thoughts all day long, so I should know what they are!" A straightforward definition of thoughts is offered by the American Psychological Association: "an idea, image, opinion, or other product of thinking" (American Psychological Association, n.d.g).

Humans *do* experience a lot of thoughts, with some research suggesting more than 6,000 per day (Tseng & Poppenk, 2020). On the surface, thoughts might seem intelligible. Thoughts are an ever-present soundtrack in the background, or sometimes the foreground, of the human experience. This pervasiveness might lead one to assume a level of mastery. This same pervasiveness, however, can make it challenging to differentiate between thoughts, the self, and the physical world. Just like a fish in water, humans can struggle to understand their thoughts as they swim in them all day long. Let's start this section by reviewing a few reasons why thoughts are more complicated than initially assumed.

HUMANS HAVE LIMITED CONTROL OVER THEIR THOUGHTS

The human brain's capacity for associations is powerful, but difficult to appreciate because it operates so naturally. For instance, as a child, you may have learned to associate the word "cow" with the sound "moo." You also may have learned to associate "cow" with a large black and white animal. If you learned these associations, not only did you develop the association between "cow" and "moo" and then between "cow" and "the large black and white animal," but you also associated "the large black and white animal" with the sound "moo." This collection of associations, based on Acceptance and Commitment Therapy's Relational Frame Theory, is depicted in the triangle below (Hayes, 2004).

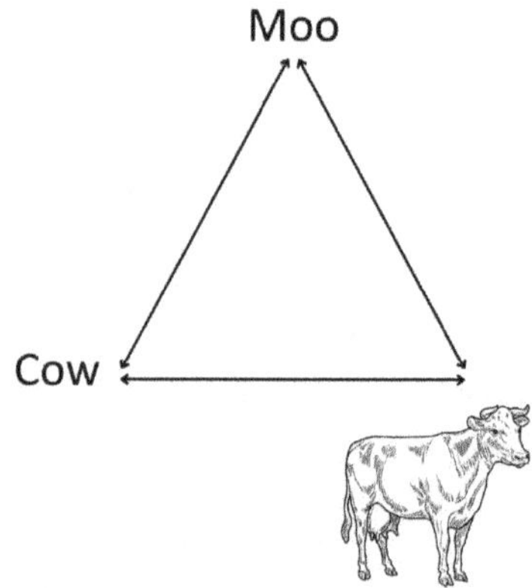

Over time, this triangle connected with other triangles. For instance, perhaps you then associated "cow" with "pig" as they are both farm animals. "Pig" has its own triangle of association, possibly connecting to "oink" and "pink medium-sized animal with a flat snout." These connected symbols continually expand over the course of our lifetime, creating a mosaic of connected triangles.

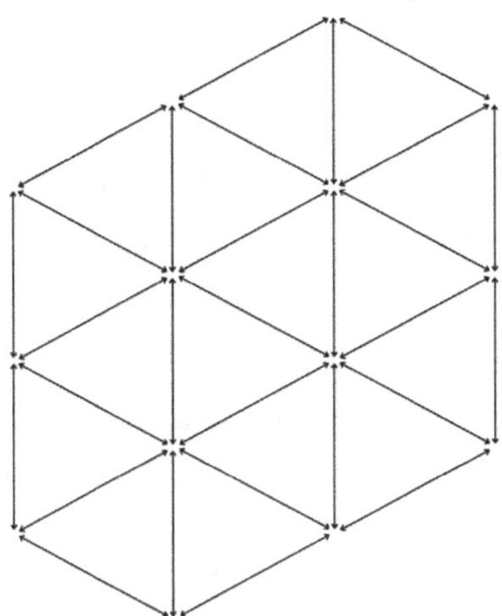

As it turns out, emotional experiences are also webbed together in similar networks. For instance, perhaps you got into an argument with a friend during a school field trip to the local farm. This experience is then added to this network of association. Now, not only do you associate farm animals (cows, pigs, etc.), but these words are also tied to the sadness and anger you felt that day. Because of this association, driving past a farm may now elicit those emotions, even years after that trip.

This emotional association is also possible with positive experiences. Maybe you remember having delicious ice cream during that field trip to the farm. Now when you drive by a farm, you experience a sudden excitement for that sweet, creamy treat. Driving by a farm is not necessary to cue these associations, but merely thinking "farm" can generate these visceral reactions.

Given that you do not choose what the English language calls those black and white animals and that you cannot control how that friend from fifth grade spoke to you during the trip to the farm, the associations that arise do so automatically. Each person has a unique web of associations which build upon themselves over the course of their lives, based on lived experiences. So much in life is outside of our control, and our learned associations are not an exception.

As we navigate the world with these systems of associations, then, some of the thoughts that pop into our mind can feel random and out of place. Imagine going for a walk and having the thought, "I wonder what I'll eat for lunch at work tomorrow." The next thought that pops up is a memory of the time you accidentally dumped a plate of lasagna on your lap in front of all of your coworkers. All of a sudden, your cheeks feel hot and turn red, your heart rate increases, and your jaw tightens. There you are, outside walking your dog, embarrassed about something that happened six months ago, simply by imagining how it could happen again. You might start brainstorming ways to package a messy meal more safely, or you might say, "I'll never bring lasagna to work again."

Given the complicated nature of association networks, the mind can quickly generate a thought which appears to be completely detached from the environment. These seemingly random firings of the brain are known as "spontaneous thoughts." Just as you did not choose to think of that embarrassing lasagna spill, these spontaneous thoughts demonstrate the limited control humans have over their thoughts.

THOUGHTS DO NOT ALWAYS ACCURATELY REPRESENT DESIRES OR ETHICS

Not only do humans not have full control over thoughts, but thoughts can also inaccurately reflect our true desires. Imagine walking your dog, when all of a sudden you say to yourself, "I could push my dog in front of this moving car." Before you begin to question our ethics and morals (or worry about the dark turn this book just took), consider this: we simply described a thought—not what is going to happen or what we want to happen, but a thought. The thought about your dog is just as much of a thought as "I wonder what I should eat for lunch at work tomorrow," "It's hot outside today!" or "I need to cancel my free trial for that subscription service." While none of these thoughts can be controlled, humans tend to notice the uncontrollable, *upsetting* thoughts more than the uncontrollable, *innocuous* ones. This can be even more confusing and distressing if we are unaware of what associations led to these distressing thoughts.

Maybe you are familiar with the uninvited, disruptive, strange, or even disturbing kind of thought. It would actually be quite rare never to have had such an experience. Most people–an estimated 94%–experience what are called "intrusive thoughts" (Radomsky et al., 2014). The APA defines intrusive thoughts as "mental events that interrupt the flow of task-related thoughts in spite of efforts to avoid them" (American Psychological Association, n.d.d).

In reality, our brains will accumulate countless webs of associations throughout a lifetime. At some point, everything will be a reminder of something, and these associations can cause imaginations to run free in a process outside of human control. The brain can, and will, elicit thoughts that do not align with one's actual desires, morals, or ethics.

THOUGHTS ARE NOT ALWAYS ACCURATE REPRESENTATIONS OF THE EXTERNAL WORLD

Thoughts do not have direct contact with the outside world. And while experiences of the physical world inform thoughts, this process is not a direct exchange of information. Instead, humans make sense of the world through the brain's *interpretations*. In

The Brain: The Story of You, author and neuroscientist David Eagleman states:

> The brain has no access to the world outside. Sealed within the dark, silent chamber of your skull, your brain has never directly experienced the external world, and it never will. Instead, there's only one way that information from out there gets into the brain…Everything you experience—every sight, sound, smell—rather than being a direct experience, is an electrochemical rendition in a dark theater (Eagleman, 2017, pp. 41-42).

Whether you are smelling a flower, looking at a picture, or having a thought, your brain automatically and instantaneously assigns meaning. Naturally, this means that individual experiences of the world are quite subjective. What, we might ask, is reality? Is there a reality? It depends on who you ask. Some philosophers say that the world is as real as the ideas of the mind. In contrast, science relies on objective facts every day, helping us generate new technologies and navigate the world and beyond.

And while the focus on objective facts works in science, the brain's indirect access to the physical world leaves room for an altered perspective of the truth. Just as a bent or discolored mirror will impact the reflection presented, humans also perceive the world in a way that is impacted by the filters of the mind.

One category of mental filter is called "cognitive biases," defined as "systematic but purportedly flawed patterns of responses to judgment and decision problems" (Wilke & Mata, 2017, p. 1). These processes can be subtle, flying under the radar of the conscious mind. "Confirmation bias," a specific type of cognitive bias, captures the human tendency to process information by looking for, interpreting, and favoring information in a way which supports preexisting beliefs. This also includes overlooking information which contradicts those beliefs. We notice all the details that confirm why our favorite actor is so great, while overlooking his movie that flopped.

Another example of a cognitive bias is the "hindsight bias," which demonstrates the tendency for humans to feel as though they "knew it all along," overestimating the ability to have predicted an outcome of an event after learning the results. For example, imagine that after building a failed prototype of a design, an engineer experiences the thought, "I should have known that it wouldn't work!" This thought would likely evoke self-criticism and anger. However, if they were somehow able to look into the past, it would likely be clear to them that their decisions for the design were reasonable given the available information.

Cognitive biases, including the hindsight bias and confirmation bias, show how human thought does not always accurately represent the physical world. While it is tempting to think that we might be exceptions to this rule, we might be experiencing another type of bias, one which highlights the tendency to view oneself as less susceptible to bias than others. Biases do not suggest a lack of knowledge or logic. Instead, they serve as a reminder of our humanity and the power of perception.

"Cognitive distortions" are another type of mental filter which comes up in many of our therapy sessions. Similar to cognitive biases, cognitive distortions impact how the mind perceives the external world. Cognitive distortions are a principle conception of the legendary Dr. Aaron Beck's Cognitive Behavioral Therapy (CBT), a therapeutic approach that focuses on how thinking influences emotions and actions. While cognitive biases are mental filters that impact *judgment,* cognitive distortions are thought patterns that impact *mood.*

One example of a cognitive distortion is referred to as "fortune telling," or the tendency to predict a negative outcome based on little to no evidence. Take the thought "I am going to fail," for example. While there could be some evidence that we are not prepared for an exam, such as being unable to explain a concept or pass a practice exam, it is also inaccurate that we *know* whether we will pass or fail. Another common cognitive distortion is "black-or-white thinking." This is the tendency to view the world in extremes, either all good or all bad. The thought "This is going to be miserable" when thinking about an upcoming visit to our in-laws is one example. While there might be aspects of the visit that will be unpleasant, this pattern of thinking ignores the possibility of more positive aspects also existing. We might consider that it is unpleasant to sleep in an unfamiliar bed and to engage in disagreements while enjoying spending time at the lake and eating the cookies our in-laws made.

Just as it is human nature to have thoughts impacted by cognitive bias, the same is true for cognitive distortions. These mental filters impact how the external world is interpreted and can lead to perceptions that are not fully accurate. To emphasize how many types of cognitive distortions exist and how they impact your view of the world, please take some time to complete the following exercise.

EXERCISE: BUILDING INSIGHT REGARDING COGNITIVE DISTORTIONS

Building insight into cognitive distortions is a challenging task requiring extensive self-awareness, feedback from others, self-compassion, and mindful noticing of thoughts. Later on in this section, we will offer more information and exercises about thinking patterns. For now, take some time to review the following table of cognitive distortions.

Identify the distortions that you might be prone to. Then consider examples of how these thought patterns have shown up over the past two weeks.

Cognitive Distortions

Cognitive Distortions	On a scale of 1 (never) to 5 (frequently), indicate how often you experience each of these distortions.	Write an example of how these distortions have shown up.
Magnification and Minimization: *Exaggerating or minimizing the importance of events.*		*"Getting accepted into that conference wasn't that big of a deal."*
Catastrophizing: *Seeing only the worst possible outcomes of a situation.*		*"My head hurts… I should get an MRI to check for a brain tumor."*
Disqualifying the Positive: *Recognizing only the negative aspects of a situation while ignoring the positive.*		*"It was so cold and miserable at the party."*
Overgeneralization: *making broad interpretations from a single or few events.*		*"I am always awkward, and no one likes me."*
Magical Thinking: *the belief that thoughts or actions will influence unrelated situations.*		*"If I wear my favorite jacket, I will perform well in the interview."*

Cognitive Distortions	On a scale of 1 (never) to 5 (frequently), indicate how often you experience each of these distortions.	Write an example of how these distortions have shown up.
Personalization: the belief that one is responsible for events outside of their own control		*"They quit their job because I didn't ask for their feedback on a work assignment."*
Jumping to Conclusions: interpreting the meaning of a situation with little or no evidence.		*"They lost the client— the company must be planning for layoffs."*
Mind Reading: interpreting the thoughts and beliefs of others without adequate evidence.		*"They must hate me because they didn't offer me a drink."*
Fortune Telling: predicting outcomes (usually negative) of events.		*"This conference is going to be miserable."*
Emotional Reasoning: the assumption that emotions reflect the way things really are.		*"I am awful at exams because taking them makes me feel anxious."*
"Should" Statements: the belief that things should be a certain way.		*"I should be a faster reader."*
Black-or-White Thinking: thinking in absolutes such as "always," "never," or "every."*		*"People always disappoint me."*

VIGNETTE

Raina realized how often the cognitive distortion of "should" shows up in her thoughts. In the last few weeks, Raina thought about the statement that she "should" exercise more and how she "should" spend more time on a work assignment. Raina reflects on how she feels shame in response to these thoughts. After this exercise, Raina also questions how much her mood is impacted by these cognitive distortions.

SUMMARY

Engineers rely on thoughts to do quality work. On the surface, they might feel like an "expert of thoughts." After all, they experience them all day long and are known for logical, precise thinking. Their skills of logic and reasoning bring comfort, too, providing a sense of control and confidence in how they interact with the world. So, it can be discomforting to face the faults that inevitably come with human thinking and unsettling to recognize that: (1) humans do not have full control of their thoughts, (2) thoughts do not always accurately reflect their desires or ethics, and (3) thoughts are not always accurate representations of the self or the external world.

In the coming chapters, we will provide an overview of the landscape of thoughts, the function of these imprecise thinking patterns, and how to effectively respond to thoughts that contribute to distress. As we unpack the messiness of thoughts, some emotions and discomfort might arise. Reframing the understanding of thoughts and how to relate to them might even evoke temporary destabilization. If so, please use the skills reviewed in the Decompiling Emotions section, including mindfulness, grounding, identifying emotions, somatic awareness, self-compassion, and values, referring also to the Emotion Decompiler for assistance.

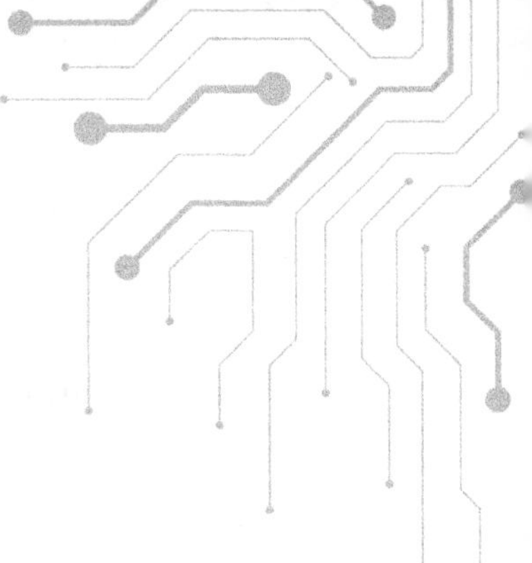

CHAPTER 11

MAKING SENSE OF SENSELESS THINKING

AS ESTABLISHED IN THE PREVIOUS CHAPTER, THE MIND can be...messy. Given the convoluted nature of thoughts, researchers have been eager to understand how they operate and why. And while there are still many unknowns, psychologists have come to agree upon a particular framing and structure for thinking operations. This framing helps researchers and therapists find clarity in a system of thinking that can feel chaotic. Building on research dating back to the late nineteenth century (James, 1890), psychologists have separated thought processes into two categories: those which rely on intuition (automatic) and those which rely on reasoning (controlled) (Schneider & Shiffrin, 1977).

The types of thoughts we have covered thus far (associations, spontaneous thoughts, intrusive thoughts, cognitive biases, and cognitive distortions) are examples of "automatic processing." Humans and other animals are not in control of automatic processing. This process is quick, effortless, highly efficient, and embedded in long-term memory. It is very difficult to alter.

Automatic processing helps people navigate their surroundings without expending a lot of mental energy. This energy is saved

163

for what is called "controlled processing." Controlled processing is conscious, slow, and typically follows a series of steps. It demands energy, effort, and attention and aids the process of reasoning and analysis. This form of processing is flexible and can be readily altered; it is used when facing novel or complex situations (Schneider & Shiffrin, 1977). These two forms of processing work together in tandem to support the brain's demands.

THE FUNCTION OF AUTOMATIC AND CONTROLLED PROCESSING

As you can imagine, our human ancestors relied heavily on automatic processing for survival. Day in and day out, associations, spontaneous thoughts, cognitive biases, and distortions helped them to navigate life's urgent demands. These thoughts, although inexact and out of their control, provided speed and efficiency. In order to hunt and protect their community, early humans could not afford to think of the "best" approach or plan during crucial moments when they had to make significant decisions, determining whether or not an approaching stranger is a threat. They did not have the time or energy to deliberate. When they successfully met the demands of the present moment, they lived to see a new day.

Of course, human ancestors were no strangers to controlled processing. This separated them from the animals around them. They were able to plan and coordinate, make decisions regarding how much food to eat versus how much to save for the future, to create tools and clothing that helped in situations yet to come, and even to depict past events. When they had the time, safety, and mental energy to do so, early humans' insight and innovations made long-term survival possible.

What do these thought systems look like today? In *Thinking*

Fast and Slow, author Daniel Kahneman presents a picture of a woman who looks angry and discusses how human minds immediately make inferences about her mood, tone of voice, and predictions of what she might do next (Kahneman, 2011). The response to the picture of the woman showcases our automatic processing, which Kahenman refers to as "System 1." This system is instantaneous and outside of human control. Other examples that might be automated activities familiar to engineers include doing simple math, logging into a computer, and navigating a familiar office building. Kanheman even posits that finding a strong move in chess can be an automatic process—for a chess master, that is.

In contrast, Kanheman demonstrates how controlled processing, or "System 2," operates by presenting the math problem "17 × 24 = y." Unless you have memorized the multiplication tables all the way through 24, you likely are not able to use automatic processing to solve this problem. Controlled processing will kick in when recalling how to solve multiplication problems, orienting your attention to the numerical values and the operations required. Whether you do this math problem on paper or in your head, it likely requires effort. This slow thinking is also deliberate and orderly. Other examples of effortful activities, which, as Kahneman puts it, "require attention and are disrupted when attention is drawn away" (Kahneman, 2011, p.22), include brainstorming research ideas, reading a new equipment manual, and writing a design proposal.

While some of the activities that make up automatic processing are innate and oriented toward animal survival, others become automatic through repeated experience. For instance, the math just presented required controlled processing; but which type of processing is involved when solving the problem "y = 3 + 3"? At three or four years old, adding two threes together was like walking through rough terrain: unfamiliar, effortful, and strategic. But as an adult? Probably very little processing is required. The answer pops up before we even have a chance to consciously consider the problem. This is precisely why the chess master does not need to be completely mentally present to win a match.

EXERCISE: AUTOMATIC AND CONTROLLED PROCESSING

Take some time to reflect on how automatic and controlled processing show up in daily life. List ways that you engaged with each type of thinking over the past 24 hours.

Automatic Processing	Controlled Processing
E.g. getting ready for the day, preparing a familiar meal, driving to work	*E.g. collaborating during a work meeting, trying a new recipe, interviewing for a job*

WHEN LESS IS MORE

Drawing on experience and pattern recognition, automatic processing is efficient and frees the mind from a taxing cognitive load. Conscious knowledge is not even required for automatic processing to operate. Modern humans primarily use automatic processing to make daily decisions, as schedules are made up of familiar situations such as putting on socks and eating a meal. Accurate predictions of how these habits will play out can usually be made. But because automatic processing is driven by habit, associative memory, and emotions, this mode of thinking is not

100% accurate. Instead, it relies on mental shortcuts and heuristics for a quick response. In other words, it is "good enough."

Many of our engineering clients really struggle with the idea of "good enough," as they pride themselves on being analytical thinkers and can identify with the controlled thinking process. This makes sense! Controlled thinking clearly has its upsides. It allows for a thoughtful response when something out of the ordinary happens, disrupting habitual thought patterns and our understanding of the world. Engineers can step into moments of uncertainty with problem-solving, processing, purposeful decisions, calculations, concentration, and orderliness, all enabled by their controlled processing.

Shortcuts and inaccuracy typically are *not* celebrated in the engineering profession, so it might be tempting to think of automatic processing as "bad" and controlled processing as "good." Engineers appreciate hard data and control over variables. Instead of heuristics or "best guesses," they prefer to think of thoughts as formulaic, with predictable, reliable outcomes. Also, automatic processing only feeds fragments of reality. But what if there were such a thing as "too much information?" What if being thorough could have dire consequences?

A research study from the early 2000s highlights the limits of controlled processes. In their paper *Smart Strategies for Doctors and Doctors-in-Training: Heuristics in Medicine,* authors Wegwarth et al. (2009) share the results of their research on heuristics in a medical environment. In the study, the researchers considered some of the urgent, high-stakes decisions that doctors must make, including whether to assign patients with chest pain to special coronary care units or regular hospital beds. If the patient is in danger of a heart attack, the coronary unit is by far the best place to be. But if they are not, it is an unnecessary expense and takes up a precious bed space.

To help doctors make this decision, the medical community developed an elaborate chart to predict the best course of action based on some 50 different data points. But as the research showed, a much simpler, three-question checklist called a "fast-and-frugal tree" was better than *both* the doctor's instincts and the 50-point checklist: it was half as likely to produce a "false alarm" as intuition alone, and yet 20% better than the highly-detailed prediction scheme at identifying patients who really needed coronary care!

In other words, the researchers found that less information did not necessarily negatively impact accuracy. In the cases they considered, it actually led to even better decision-making. Similarly, navigating thoughts sometimes requires knowing when to rely on intuition, when to employ the maximum rational powers of the conscious mind, and when to find a balance between those extremes.

THE FUNCTION OF COGNITIVE DISTORTIONS

"Cognitive distortions"—often experienced as familiar, automatic thoughts—are strategies for self-preservation, not errors in brain functioning. In his article "The Evolved Basis and Adaptive Functions of Cognitive Distortions," Paul Gilbert (1988) explores how common cognitive distortions served human ancestors. Gilbert explains that these thought patterns stem from cognitive biases, and in their simplest form, work as defenses against threats of death and reproductive failures. They promote quick action, trading accuracy for efficiency.

Let's take another look at black-or-white thinking. As much as political parties would like to convince us otherwise, life is full of complexities and gray areas. These complexities can be exhausting, time-consuming, and even confusing! Organizing and simplifying thoughts into categorical terms such as "good or bad" or "right or wrong" can be advantageous in some ways: it requires less mental energy, supports quick decision-making, and can even reduce risks of making mistakes.

Consider, for example, the gatherers, our ancestors who lived their days relying on absolutes. These foragers developed skills to find safe, edible plants with high nutritional value. At the same time, plants—also in survival mode—evolved protections from preying animals, including toxic defenses. Through experience and learning, gatherers were able to recognize the bitterness associated with the toxins found in these deadly plants. The bitter taste often signaled danger, and the hungry humans were able to make quick, life-saving decisions to spit the plant out before the digestive process began.

Of course, there were exceptions: *some* plants contained harmless compounds that gave off a bitter taste. Was it worth the risk to find the exceptions? Probably not. What if the bitter, yet innocuous crops were not even that nutritious or tasty? Why spend time and energy on the exceptions to a rule? Instead, adhering to the rule of "no bitterness is safe" and "bitterness is dangerous" helped them pave the way forward for their tribes. As a result, there is a reason some small children will not eat anything except familiar, high-carb, high-fat macaroni and cheese (this is Alison, speaking from experience as a mom of two small children). Some children are genetically wired to avoid bitter foods as they have heightened sensitivity to bitterness.

Like other cognitive distortions, black-or-white thinking tends to occur when we are stressed or facing a threat of some kind. Gilbert (1988) uses the example of failure. The thought "I'm a complete failure" might pop into someone's head when experiencing stress, functioning as a safeguard against making mistakes. Judging oneself in this way could be a variation of the thought "I can't afford to take the risk of thinking my behavior is adequate when it's not." Overestimating one's abilities can have grave consequences, while lack of confidence often leads to complacency or inaction.

As we've seen, over millennia, human brains have learned to find safety in the rigid binaries of automatic processes. This tool became less useful as the world grew more complicated. With agricultural systems and food safety regulatory boards in place, relying on oneself is no longer as necessary in order to detect poison in food. In some ways, more complexity is freeing; it allows the bitterness of a drink of frosty ale, for example, to be enjoyable. On the other hand, complexity can lead to uncomfortable feelings while grappling with the intricacies of the world.

After numerous compliments on a project or evaluation, have you ever fixated on the single piece of negative feedback? This phenomenon, part of the cognitive distortions discussed earlier, is called "disqualifying the positives," and involves acknowledging only the negative aspects of a situation. When this type of cognitive distortion occurs, individuals insist that certain positive experiences do not count, justifying why the positive aspects are not valid. From an outsider's point of view, these reasons may not appear logical. But to the individual who is disqualifying the positives, it all *feels* valid.

Disqualifying the positives is another conservative, better-safe-than-sorry strategy to protect oneself against harm. Historically, focusing on the negative by staying on the lookout for predators was prioritized over focusing on the positive of finding food. Noticing and avoiding danger allowed humans to survive and pass down their genes. Today, receiving positive feedback could lead someone to assume they can successfully achieve a task, riskier than the assumption that they *cannot* achieve it.

The first promotes action (and therefore risk) while the second promotes inaction and the safety of the familiar.

This strategy also has its negative consequences. Disqualifying the positives can have a profound impact internally, fueling self-criticism, low self-esteem, and a negative mood. In certain contexts, this could be a sensible tradeoff to becoming aware of potential new harms. Eons ago, letting one's guard down simply was not worth it much of the time. Gilbert underscores the research of Driscoll (1989), who was interested in the adaptive functions of self-criticism. Some of these adaptive functions include "reducing the expectations of others, avoiding envious attacks from others, avoiding complacency, and by personally drawing attention to one's inadequacies, one may avoid attacks from others, or even elicit their help/support" (Gilbert, 1998, p. 455).

SUMMARY

The messiness of human thought can be organized using the framework of automatic and controlled processes (Kahneman's System 1 and System 2). While it is tempting to view this framework using the dichotomy of "good" and "bad," it is not that clear. Automatic thinking, for instance, has the capacity for error while also increasing efficiency. Controlled thinking, on the other hand, is often more precise but is energy-intensive.

The human errors in thinking are not as straightforward as the errors in a computer program. When a computer produces incorrect information, the computer is not functioning in the way in which it is intended to function. Decompiling the code allows the programmer to identify the error and find a solution. In contrast, in the process of decompiling the mind, we cannot assume that thinking errors are design errors. Rather, when the mind produces inaccurate thoughts, it is functioning exactly how it is meant to, invoking the brain's processes as purposeful mechanisms for survival. Understanding the function of the brain's operations, however, increases our capacity to make sense of this thinking and the underlying needs it represents.

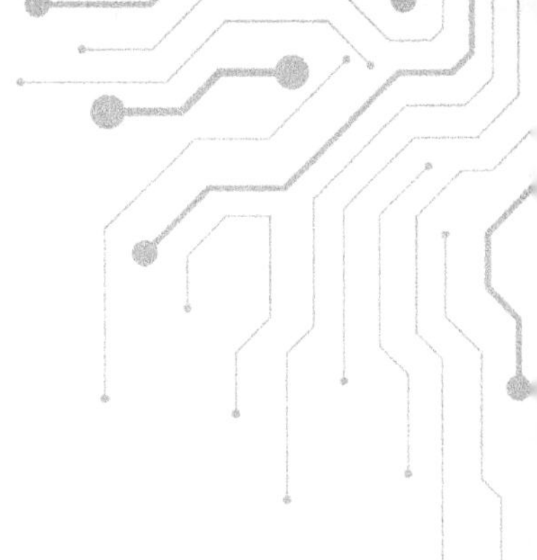

CHAPTER 12

ATTEMPTING TO MANAGE DISTRESSING THOUGHTS

THUS FAR WE HAVE ESTABLISHED THAT HUMAN thoughts are, by nature, convoluted. To add to their complexity, certain thoughts and thought patterns are closely tied to emotional pain. Associations connect inevitable painful experiences to one's understanding of the world, thus interweaving pain within human thought. Intrusive thoughts, spontaneous thoughts, and cognitive distortions bring opportunity for discomfort.

Naturally, humans have adopted various methods to cope with the pain and discomfort tied to distressing thoughts. In this chapter, we will explore the limitations of the coping methods we see most often in our work with engineers. Then, we will offer an alternative approach to managing challenging thoughts–an approach that will allow you to meet your needs and move toward your values.

THOUGHT SUPPRESSION

A common response to painful thoughts is to attempt to control or stop them. Thought suppression, or attempts to avoid certain thoughts, can manifest in several ways. Often, distracting behaviors are used to avoid thoughts that are associated with emotional pain. Some people might fixate on work to avoid painful thoughts about their relationships, others might scroll on their phone. While this tendency is common for everyone, not just engineers, engineers' capacity for problem-solving could allow them to continue to generate new methods of avoidance.

While you might relate to the impulse to grab your phone and briefly scroll through the latest posts whenever the circumstances and conversations around you turn stressful, challenging, or un-comfortable, at its core this is an attempt to escape the stress by fixating on something more superficial. And the escape, however helpful in the moment, does not keep the thoughts from returning. Similar to emotion suppression, efforts to avoid unwanted thoughts can increase the distressing nature and number of unwanted thoughts (Marcks & Woods, 2005). Additionally, researchers have found a positive correlation between obsessive thinking tendencies and efforts to avoid thoughts.

Associations of thoughts help explain how suppressing thoughts leads to increased obsessive thinking. Imagine that web of triangles that connects our lived experience of associations and learning. Now imagine that there is a part of that network that is associated with a painful thought or experience. Attempts to block off the sections of that network might temporarily protect us from expe-riencing those thoughts. However, because our brains understand the world through those associations, the blocked-off thoughts find new channels to integrate within the network. After all, the thought is not "gone"—only one pathway has been cut off.

The brain will not allow a significant thought to just evaporate without a fight, and if one channel is blocked, others will strength-en. For instance, rather than only one or two paired associations, the thought will now have three or four. By blocking those other associations as well, the thought will then continue to find even more associations in order to be integrated within the web of associations. Slaying these thoughts has the same success rate as slaying the mythical Hydra. Attempting to behead this creature will only result in the growth of additional heads, ultimately strengthening it. See if you can spot the new heads growing in the next story.

VIGNETTE

Kai is a PhD engineering student. Kai has always really cared about their work and has dedicated years to achieving their career goals. They have had several successes, including publishing research and passing their comprehensive preliminary exams. Despite these successes, Kai finds themselves experiencing the thought "I'm going to fail." The thought of failing feels really scary and painful given Kai's investment in their goals.

Kai is concerned by this thought and assumes there is truth to it. Kai tells themself that they cannot have that thought, as they worry that the thought itself could contribute to a self-fulfilling prophecy. With hopes of avoiding this thought in the future, Kai works even harder in preparing for their upcoming exam. Although Kai could have likely passed the exam with 20 hours of preparation, Kai spends 30 hours preparing to increase their confidence. Kai is pleased to have passed the exam and has relief from the thought "I am going to fail."

A few weeks later, Kai is accepted to speak at a conference. Kai notices the thought arising again: "I am going to fail." Similar to the last time, Kai works to prevent that thought by preparing more than necessary. In preparation for the presentation, Kai meets with their advisor. As they work through the details of Kai's work, Kai starts to feel pressure to get it right. In that conversation, Kai worries that his advisor doubts their abilities, and Kai's concerns of failure reemerge. The discomfort Kai feels in the meeting with their advisor leads to Kai avoiding these meetings altogether.

Later, Kai attends the conference and receives praise for their work. Again, Kai feels relieved and has a break from the threat of thinking about failure. Over time, Kai develops a pattern of consistently overpreparing and avoiding interactions that have previously been associated with thoughts of failure. Gradually, the number of contexts that are associated with the thought "I am going to fail" increases. Ironically, Kai's attempts to not think "I am going to fail" puts more pressure on that thought, and it actually leads Kai to be more likely to experience that thought in the future.

When we abide by the belief that a particular thought is unacceptable, the brain is given an impossible task. As a challenge, do your best to read the rest of this paragraph without once thinking of a bear riding a unicycle. Do not under any circumstances consider the way the bear might extend his arms for balance or recall the distinctive way that a unicycle tends to sway slightly back and forth as it is being ridden. Ignore the temptation to decide if it is a black bear or a grizzly bear or something more novel like a panda. And of course, forbid yourself from considering the various kinds of hats the bear might wear in the event that he was riding the unicycle at a circus...

You'll likely find that you are unable to successfully complete this challenge. This is because the directions we have created include a vivid description of what we are asking you not to think about –the bear– thereby evoking all of the associations that you were attempting to avoid.

Given the painful quality of certain thoughts, it is natural to want to avoid them and the contexts where they arose. However, the more they are avoided, the more these thoughts appear in new contexts. Over time, avoiding all of the ways painful thoughts can show up can feel like getting stuck in a pattern of mental gymnastics.

Given engineers' predilections for determination and ingenuity, we have observed how they can apply these traits to the goal of avoiding distressing thoughts. They persist in efforts to find a solution to painful thoughts and creatively generate endless possible solutions. While these tendencies are extremely beneficial in engineering work, when applied to attempts to suppress painful thoughts, the distress can be exacerbated. Much energy can be expended via these avoidance tactics, energy which could otherwise be applied to activities more aligned with their values and meeting their needs. And like the bear, the more effort that goes into avoiding thoughts, the more they show up.

OVERTHINKING

Human brains have evolved to learn from past mistakes, solve problems, and plan ahead. These skills are clearly helpful to an extent, but sometimes their appealing, rational veneer disguises the fact that in many cases, this reasoning becomes counterproductive. Sometimes, rather than suppressing painful thoughts, our clients will go to the other extreme and overthink their concerns, attempting to find resolution. Thinking about something over and over again, from every angle you can imagine, may even feel productive. But the results are unsatisfying when the problem is unsolvable. Here we are referring to "overthinking," a pattern that typically does more harm than good.

Overthinking refers to putting "too much time into thinking

about or analyzing [something] in a way that is more harmful than helpful" (Merriam-Webster, n.d.e). The two forms of overthinking we will explore in this chapter are rumination and worry. "Rumination" can be defined as "recurrent and repetitive thinking on symptoms, feelings, problems, upsetting events, and negative aspects of the self, typically with a focus on their causes, circumstances, meanings, and implications" (American Psychological Association, n.d.f). Rumination is extremely time-consuming and often involves asking questions that cannot be answered, such as, "Why did this happen to me and not others?"

While rumination focuses on past events, "worry" focuses on the future as "an attempt to engage in mental problem-solving on an issue whose outcome is uncertain but contains the possibility of one or more negative outcomes"(American Psychological Association, n.d.i). Worry can start with the question "What if…?"; it is sometimes preceded by imagining and problem-solving several made-up scenarios and problems—like picturing the rush to the exit in the extremely unlikely event that the plane crashes during takeoff. Many times, worrying is done in hopes of guaranteeing future safety. Many people hold the belief that worry can reduce the chance of negative outcomes and painful emotions, while increasing the chance of finding improved solutions (Freeston et al., 1994). Humans do not like uncertainty and the act of worry can be perceived as an influential antidote.

The problems that rumination and worry try to solve, however, are typically unsolvable. You might replay and analyze a past social interaction after having the thought, "I was so awkward," in order to gain clarity on whether or not others like you. But if the prior interactions were not clear to begin with, reshuffling old data won't prove anything. What starts out as an attempt to find resolution of an uncomfortable thought can quickly turn into a frustrating battle with the brain. One might also respond to the thought "What if I'm awkward again?" with worry. This could include imagining different social scenarios in the future, in hopes of predicting and preparing for what might go wrong... only to later discover that the predictions of the nearly infinite possible futures were incorrect.

With colorful, innate imaginations, and the intricate web of associations, humans can analyze thoughts from many angles and create countless possible scenarios. With rumination and worry, these thoughts play on a loop and usually have no satisfying end. And predictably, the scenarios do not completely remove anxious thoughts or the anxious feelings that come with them. Instead, we are simply left with less time, less energy, and even more discomfort.

VIGNETTE

Julia had an interview last week for an exciting new job opportunity. She had to answer questions and give a presentation about her research as part of the interview process. As she waits for a response, Julia is consumed with rumination about the interview, replaying the questions and her responses over and over again. She is absorbed in thoughts about how she could have responded better and worries about whether or not the organization will offer her the job. She also worries about her capacity to perform well at the job and how she would respond if they made an offer. These thoughts are distressing to Julia, and she does not want to have them.

Julia is intellectually aware that she cannot change the past. However, she is also driven to find control in a situation that is, at this point, largely outside of her control. Unconsciously, Julia believes that if she reflects on the interview long enough, she can find a solution to the puzzle of whether she will receive an offer and how to prevent future mistakes, by being able to anticipate what will happen. Given the stress of uncertainty, Julia's mind attempts to cope by finding a solution.

While it is indeed understandable that Julia is driven to find a solution and relief from her uncertainty, it is also clear that the rumination and worry are not helping. Not only is she experiencing anxiety, regret, and uncertainty related to the interview, now she is also experiencing the added pressure and exhaustion that accompanies the rumination and worry.

Rumination and worry are understandable reactions to the stressful uncertainties of life. These forms of thinking can function as attempts to prevent future distress, either by trying to remove uncertainty or by anticipating and preparing for potential negative outcomes. While it is natural to want to avoid future distress, these patterns of thinking typically exacerbate the concerns.

We observe how highly analytical engineers are particularly likely to engage in these types of analyses due to their drive to solve problems and discover the unknown. The processes involved in this approach mirror aspects of the previously discussed controlled processing. It takes energy and effort to analyze the past and search for solutions. This can make rumination and worry *feel* productive and engaging, as though you are on the cusp of figuring something out or accomplishing something important. But that fleeting sense of control, preparedness, or certainty pales in comparison to the ultimately unknowable and unsolvable nature of many of life's stressors. Worse, while the detail-oriented nature of controlled processing usually leads to more accuracy, worry and rumination can inject biased and distorted thinking into the processing cycle–leading to biased and distorted results.

Take the "negativity bias," for example. This tendency for the human brain to register negative stimuli more readily than positive impacts the way events are remembered. This bias makes it easier to recall negative feedback, even when positive feedback is more abundant. Then, as controlled processing is used to analyze past experiences it draws from a disproportionately negative pool of memories; this analysis is a setup for biased results before the rumination even begins.

Consider an employee fixating on the one critical comment in an otherwise glowing performance evaluation. They can easily justify this fixation as a rational drive to constantly improve, without realizing that they have not absorbed the all-important positive feedback as well. Another example could involve a belief such as "Things never go my way." This thought is an example of "black or white thinking," a well-known cognitive distortion. If someone regularly experiences this automatic thought, it can influence the way they engage with their worry. They may attempt to create potential scenarios consistent with the idea that things are likely to go poorly, in a sense justifying the need to prepare for any and every possibility (and consider the assumption that underlies this: the superstitious premise that one "always has bad luck" or is in some sense "cursed.")

Rational planning skills have limited effectiveness if the premise itself is irrational. One cannot engage in a fair analysis of situations based on a foundation of personal fears, insecurities, and challenges. An engineer would not attempt to make essential decisions based on data that is inherently faulty or systematically skewed, right? So, in order to get an accurate reading, we must get to the source, to know where this information is coming from, and what sorts of biases it contains.

SUMMARY

The sophisticated human mind comes with the potential for inner pain. Ultimately, attempts to cope with painful thoughts can be fruitless and self-defeating. An engineer's determination and problem-solving skills work well professionally and academically. However, when these same skills are used to avoid and overthink, the consequences of these coping strategies can be amplified. That said, there are indeed times when problem-solving is an effective response to thoughts. In the following chapter, we provide guidance on discerning when thoughts call for problem-solving vs. an alternative approach. A full discussion of what this alternative approach looks like follows in Chapter 14.

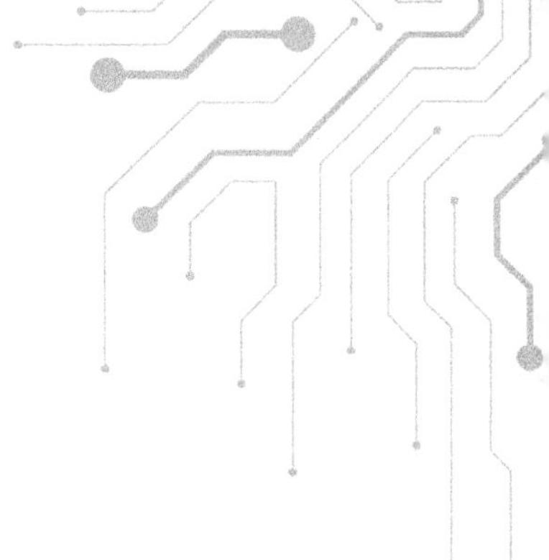

CHAPTER 13

WHEN DOES PROBLEM-SOLVING HELP?

ASSERTING THAT PROBLEM-SOLVING DOES NOT ALWAYS work can be confusing because often, problem-solving is extremely helpful. Engineers are hired *because* of their particular problem-solving skills. Attempts to "solve" the problem of painful thoughts, however, can include suppression tactics (to avoid current thoughts) and overthinking (to prevent future thoughts).

While all humans, regardless of profession, are susceptible to coping strategies, we notice that engineers frequently have difficulty releasing these approaches. Their capacity for perseverance and problem-solving often makes it hard to accept that these skills are not serving them. The perseverance that allows them to be resilient in their engineering work can lead them down rabbit holes of unproductive attempts to "fix" their thoughts.

In this chapter, we will provide guidelines to help determine when problem-solving is effective, when it is not, and what to do if you are not sure. In the following chapter, we will present specific skills for how to respond to painful thoughts when problem-solving does not work.

OUTSIDE WORLD VERSUS INTERNAL EXPERIENCES

When it comes to responding to distressing thoughts, assessing whether the thought is related to the outside world or internal experiences is key in determining whether or not problem-solving is helpful (Hayes, 2022). This is the first step of the Thought Decompiler, which will be depicted in full at the end of this section.

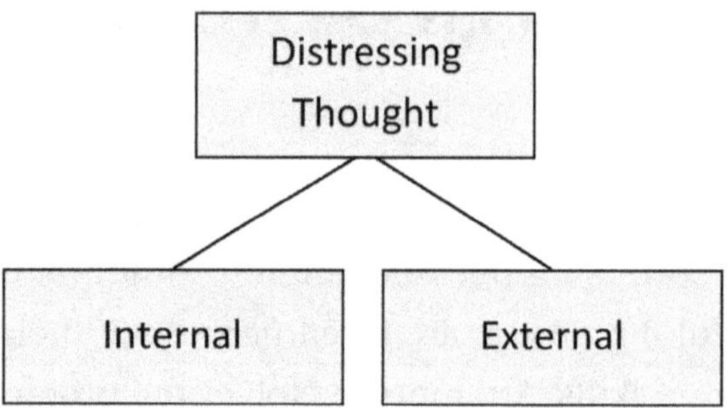

Distressing thoughts regarding the outside world relate to external problems, such as a broken pipe, a canceled flight, or a debt. These thoughts can typically be objectively assessed. In other words, another person would likely perceive the thought in a similar way. When it comes to problems of the outside world, problem-solving works very well. This is typically where the strengths of engineers really shine.

Examples of distressing thoughts relating to difficult internal experiences include rumination about a past mistake, thoughts of worthlessness, and thoughts of failure. These thoughts are more difficult to assess objectively. Often, these thoughts are filtered by cognitive distortions, such as "mind reading," "fortune telling," or "'should statements." When it comes to the internal experience, the typical problem-solving approach no longer works. That said, the most effective way to relate to the thought depends on whether it is related to the outside world or one's internal experience.

External Versus Internal Thoughts

Thoughts about the External World	Thoughts about Internal Experiences
• Content is typically not about self (e.g., the car, job, assignment) • Objective assessment is possible (e.g., the door is jammed) • Others would likely perceive the concern in a similar way	• Content of thought is often self-focused (e.g., I am a likable person) • Objective assessment is difficult or impossible • Linked to cognitive distortions

EXERCISE: IDENTIFYING EXTERNAL VERSUS INTERNAL THOUGHTS

Determine whether each thought listed below is about the outside world or internal experiences. An answer key is provided after this exercise.

Thought	Check to indicate whether the thought is regarding the outside world or an internal experience.	
	Outside World	**Internal Experience**
I never get what I want.		
It is storming outside.		

Thought		
I am a loser.		
I will never pass this exam.		
I am running late.		
I should work harder.		

Answer Key

Thought	Outside World	Internal Experience	Explanation
I never get what I want.		x	*This is an example of the cognitive distortion, overgeneralizing. There are probably several times when this person did get what they wanted.*
It is storming outside.	x		*This is a reflection of what is occurring in the external world that can be objectively assessed. Other people would likely perceive the situation in a similar way.*
I am a loser.		x	*This is a self-critical thought, and it cannot be objectively assessed. Different people would likely define "loser" differently.*
I will never pass this exam.		x	*This is an example of the cognitive distortion called fortune telling. While the person may sense they are not prepared for the exam, they do not actually know that they will not pass.*

Thought	Outside World	Internal Experience	Explanation
I am running late.	x		*If there was a scheduled meeting time, and it is past the time selected, it can be objectively assessed that this person is running late. If it is not past the selected time, but there is a reasonable estimation for how long it will take to arrive, that can also be assessed objectively.*
I should work harder.		x	*This thought includes the word "should," which is an example of a cognitive distortion. There is no universally established understanding of what working "hard enough" means.*

VIGNETTE

After completing the previous exercise, Anand realizes how often he experiences thoughts that are not able to be objectively assessed and are related to a cognitive distortion. Many of his thoughts are related to his internal experience rather than about the external world. While Anand is praised for his logic and reasoning by his friends and co-workers, he realizes that even he is not immune to experiencing thoughts that are filtered by distortion.

WHEN DISTINGUISHING IS MORE CHALLENGING

While it can be difficult to differentiate thoughts regarding the outside world or an internal experience, sometimes it is easy. "The dishwasher is not working," for example, can be objectively assessed: does it turn on or not when you press the button? It is easy to determine that this thought reflects an external experience; therefore, problem-solving would be an effective response.

Perhaps a thought regarding an internal experience is also clear, such as "I am stupid." The thought refers to an internal evaluation. Perhaps this is a familiar, habitual thought after making a mistake. You can acknowledge that you know you are not actually stupid, but the thought still shows up. Even though this thought is painful, you might still be able to recognize it as hyperbolic and a reflection of your internal experience rather than about the outside world.

Other times, determining whether a distressing thought is related to the internal or external world is not clear. Consider the thought "I offended my coworker." Is this related to an internal experience of fear, anxiety, and self-doubt or does this thought reflect an accurate interpretation of what happened? The actions in response to this thought would differ greatly depending on the assessment of its accuracy. If you did, in fact, offend your coworker, problem-solving about ways to repair and apologize would be useful. If you did not offend your coworker, and the thought is a reflection of your self-doubt, then apologizing would not be helpful and would likely be confusing to others. When the nature of the thought is unclear, Socratic questioning is useful.

Socratic Questioning

When it is unclear whether a thought reflects something in the outside world or an internal experience, "Socratic questioning" can bring more clarity. This is another element of the Thought Decompiler.

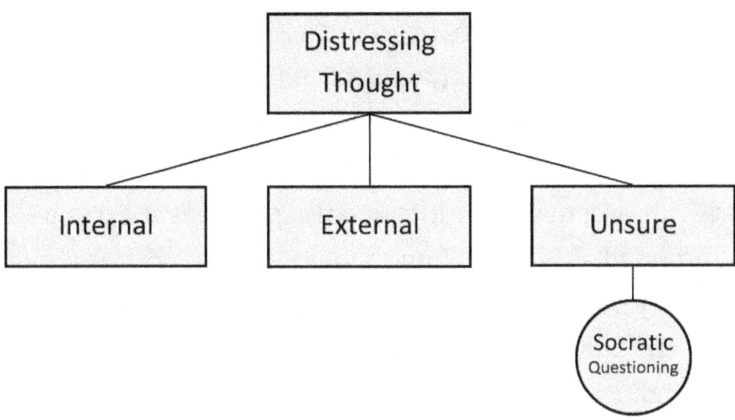

Because unclear thoughts often arise via automatic processing, Socratic questioning incorporates controlled processing to bring a different perspective. Socratic questioning allows an examination of automatic thoughts that are typically overlooked. Because these automatic thoughts show up...well...automatically, it is natural to take them at face value.

After years of perceiving a thought as accurate, it can be difficult to reevaluate the accuracy of that assumption. For some, the automatic thought "It's all my fault" pops up so routinely that it can feel like an obvious fact and becomes integrated into one's sense of identity. Someone who experiences this thought on a regular basis is likely able to point to evidence to support it. In reality, this "evidence" is likely steeped in confirmation bias. In this case, Socratic questioning is a process of examining such a thought and interrogating its veracity from an impartial position.

To set a foundation, let's take a lesson from children, as they usually ask the best questions. Their crucial job is to explore and make sense of the world, a world of which they know very little. Where they lack knowledge and experiences, they also lack assumptions. So, they possess a genuine curiosity that is untouched by societal judgment and expectations. It is not until later that automatic processing takes over, and assumptions based on lived experience shape how their world is perceived.

The other day my (Alison's) three-year-old told me that his head hurt. He appeared to be fairly distressed while he said this and with an urgency that indicated the pain was sharp. I pointed to his forehead, and asked him, "Does it hurt here?" He shook his head "no." I pointed to his temples and repeated my question. Another strikeout. I proceeded to point to all parts of his head until I ran out of parts.

Confused, I decided to proceed by offering comfort. I asked him if he wanted a drink of water. Clearly disgruntled, he said, "No, I don't want to! It feels bad!" It was then that I realized that he had a sore throat. I pointed to his throat and asked him if that was where the pain was. Relieved that I was finally understanding him, he emphatically nodded yes. (I touched my own throat, wondering when we all decided that it was not a part of the head.) Our assumptions about body parts differed.

With age, the skill of asking good questions becomes less intuitive, in part due to the brain's prioritization of efficiency over curiosity. Rather than being a moral failing, these assumptions are actually quite useful in many ways. Returning to the idea of automatic versus controlled processing, remaining in controlled processing by engaging in active, deep thinking is not efficient. If a peer were to tell you that their head hurt, musing to yourself, "What really counts as the head, anyway?" would expend precious time and energy. In this case, it would probably be safe to assume that your peer does not have a sore throat. Sure, you could be wrong, especially if they are from a different cultural background, but this situation does not exactly call for investigative clarification. Instead of going about our days questioning everything that crosses our paths, we can reserve questioning for particular circumstances by using intention and skill.

Skillful questioning dates back to ancient philosophical traditions, some of which stem from Socrates' teachings. Socrates' approach to education was unique in Western civilization at the time. Instead of taking on the role of the expert, he joined his students in seeking answers. This alignment allowed his students to take active ownership of their learning, asking questions designed to challenge implicit assumptions, uncover deeply held beliefs, and bring awareness to contradictions. Used in education, coaching, and counseling, the Socratic method helps individuals learn through dialogue as opposed to simply taking in information. In counseling, Socratic questioning assists in examining thinking patterns. Instead of a mental health professional telling a client, "That thought is irrational," the client is encouraged to examine their own thoughts from all angles to determine whether or not their thinking is logical.

Socratic questioning can be effective when coming from a place of openness and curiosity. The goal of questioning is not emotional relief but opening up to the truth. Approaching the act of Socratic questioning with an open mind as well as the willingness to receive any new data is important, as there is ample risk of confirmation bias.

For example, while determining the accuracy of the thought "I offended my coworker," it might be easy to focus your attention on evidence in support of this belief. While it is possible that the strange look the coworker gave supports the idea that they were offended, it is also possible that the brain is actively looking for (and misinterpreting) the smallest signs of conflict. Perhaps the strange look had more to do with the ketchup stain on your shirt!

This Socratic questioning approach is similar to how an engineer might analyze one of their prototypes, particularly if it is throwing an error code or otherwise not behaving as expected. If a part seems to be broken, could it actually be working well but relying on a malfunctioning system? You have some evidence; even with a hunch about what might be wrong, can the hunch be tested? You might play out the potential consequences of various ideas. Perhaps removing a redundant component would fix the immediate issue, but would it lead to deeper problems elsewhere? *It's okay to ask these questions about thoughts, too.*

Use Socratic Questioning when:

- you are unsure whether a thought pertains to a problem of the "outside world" or the "internal experience,"

- the content of the thought is both related to the self and external to the self (e.g., "I offended the other person"), or

- an objective assessment is challenging, but not impossible (i.e., determining if they were offended or asking if a presentation was well received).

Questions to Ask

Let's dive into what Socratic questioning looks like. First, remember that Socratic questioning is most effective and appropriate when unsure if a thought concerns the outside world or our internal experience, as these questions can help increase clarity. Socratic questioning gathers valuable information in order to make sense of a thought and decide how to respond to that thought. Not all questions are inherently useful, so it is important to understand the types of questions that promote insight.

While there is no standard set of Socratic questions, Socratic questions are clear, neutral, open, and tentative (Sutton, 2020).

To begin, it is assumed that the answer is genuinely unknown, and that there is no correct or preferred answer.

Socratic Question Overview

Type of Question	Examples of Questions	Applying Questions to Specific Thoughts
Thoughts Versus Feelings	Is my concern fear-based? Am I more focused on how I'm feeling instead of the facts?	"I will fail." Is my belief that I will fail the exam based on my fear of failure or based on evidence that I am not prepared?
Evidence	Is it possible to collect evidence to explore this concern? If so, is there evidence that supports my concern? Is there evidence against it?	"I offended them with my joke." Could I ask someone to offer feedback to help me determine whether or not my comment was offensive?
Assumptions	What assumptions am I making? Is it possible I'm misinterpreting the evidence? Is more information needed?	"They didn't make eye contact with me; they must not like me." Am I making assumptions about why others are behaving the way they are? Are there other possible reasons they acted that way that I am not considering?
Nuance	Could my thought be an exaggeration of reality? Am I engaging in "all-or-nothing" thinking, when reality is more nuanced?	"I never know what to say." Do I actually *never* know what to say? Are there instances when I did know what to say?

Type of Question	Examples of Questions	Applying Questions to Specific Thoughts
The Source	Did someone pass this thought or belief to me? How reliable is the source? Did this thought or belief come from someone I trust? Is it possible the source's thought or belief has more to do with them/ their challenges than it has to do with me?	"I should be smarter." What messages did I receive, perhaps in childhood, that might be informing this thought?
Expanding One's Viewpoint	Is there another way of viewing this situation? How might someone else think about what's happening? Is there an alternative explanation?	"The project failed because of me." How might someone else interpret why the project failed?
Expectations	Are my expectations of myself and/or others realistic? How did these expectations come to be? Is there room to reevaluate and/or adjust my expectations?	"I cannot make a mistake." Are my expectations of myself to never make a mistake reasonable? Where did I learn that I can never make a mistake?
Control	How much control do I have in this situation? Is it possible that I'm overestimating what's in my control?	"I need to respond to this email today, so the project does not fail." Am I overestimating how much the project's success is within my control? Am I overestimating how much the timeliness of this email will impact the outcome?

Type of Question	Examples of Questions	Applying Questions to Specific Thoughts
Likelihood	How likely is this thought to be true? Is my brain coming up with worst-case scenarios?	"She will break up with me." How likely is it that this thought is true?
Looking Ahead, Gaining Perspective	What's the worst that could happen if what I fear became true? How might I cope if this were to happen?	"I will be fired." How would I cope if I did get fired?

Considerations

Because the controlled processing involved in Socratic questioning takes time and energy, be thoughtful about when and how to go about it. Rather than diving into Socratic questioning after each thought, reserve the brain's resources to examine thoughts that are distressing and/or in moments when you are unclear about how to proceed. It would likely not be helpful to examine thoughts like "The sky is blue," as presumably that thought causes limited distress and probably does not impact decisions. For these kinds of thoughts, automatic processing is more efficient.

Next, having identified a thought to examine, setting a context that helps engage in this thinking is useful. For instance, journaling about these questions helps slow down our thoughts and observe them more objectively. Talking through these questions with a trusted person or therapist can also be a strategy to examine thoughts at a distance. Setting a time limit might also be a valuable way to contain this questioning, so it does not consume more energy than necessary. For example, set an alarm to examine the thought "No one likes me" for 15 minutes. As this is a distressing thought and controlled processing is a limited resource, setting this time guardrail prevents getting carried away or overwhelmed with hours of questioning. Consider taking a trial-and-error approach to determine the context that is the most helpful.

It's sometimes difficult to jump into Socratic questioning. For example, you might observe a distressing thought while at work and then not have the time or energy to address it. As we've said, Socratic questioning does not always need to be done in the moment. In fact, in an environment that already demands complete attention and/or concentration, we do not suggest trying this approach, as turning inward and away from the present could be counterproductive. Engaging in an important task or connecting with another person are reasons to stay present and delay Socratic questioning. If waiting brings up uncertainty or discomfort, refer back to the skills from the Decompiling Emotions section, including mindfulness and self-compassion, to help tolerate the emotions.

If it's difficult to discern whether a thought reflects the internal or external world, consider that there might be elements of the original thought that reflect the external world, even if the thought as a whole reflects your internal experience. Consider the thought "No one likes me." After examining this thought with Socratic questioning, it might be clear that it reflects an internal experience; it cannot be objectively assessed and is likely an exaggeration of what is true in the external world. However, perhaps there was a time when a co-worker was upset about a specific situation. The thought "My co-worker was upset" at that time was a reflection of the external world, because he expressed his feelings and asked to handle the situation differently moving forward. So, while "No one likes me" reflects an internal experience, "My co-worker was upset" is a related thought that reflects the external world.

Because it relates to the external world, working to problem-solve that portion of the thought about the co-worker will likely be effective, perhaps by means of apologizing and changing future behavior. Problem-solving "No one likes me," however, is less effective.

EXERCISE: PRACTICING SOCRATIC QUESTIONING

Use a recent thought to practice this new skill.

1. Identify a recent distressing thought, one that is difficult to assess in terms of whether it is reflecting the "outside world" or an "internal experience" (e.g., "My coworkers do not like me," "I need to work harder to prevent getting fired," "I should be a better friend or employee," "My partner is going to leave me," "I am not good enough," or "I am a bad student/employee").

2. Identify five relevant questions from the earlier Socratic question table. Take time to journal, reflect, or discuss these questions with a trusted person to build insight to how accurate this thought might be.

3. Review the list of cognitive distortions. Consider whether or not the thought might fit into any of the thinking patterns in the following collection:

Magnification and Minimization: Exaggerating or minimizing the importance of events.	*Disqualifying the Positive: Recognizing* only the negative aspects of a situation while ignoring the positive.	*Jumping to Conclusions:* Interpreting the meaning of a situation with little or no evidence.

Overgeneralization: *Making broad interpretations from a single or few events.*	***Catastrophizing:*** *Seeing only the worst possible outcomes of a situation.*	***"Should" Statements:*** *The belief that things should be a certain way.*
Mind Reading: *Interpreting the thoughts and beliefs of others without adequate evidence.*	***Magical Thinking:*** *The belief that thoughts or actions will influence unrelated situations.*	***Emotional Reasoning:*** *The assumption that emotions reflect the way things really are.*
All-or-Nothing Thinking: *Thinking in absolutes such as "always," "never," or "every."*	***Fortune Telling:*** *Predicting outcomes (usually negative) of events.*	***Personalization:*** *The belief that one is responsible for events outside of their own control.*

4. After considering the thought with this Socratic questioning approach, consider whether it reflects the "outside world" or your "internal experience." If the thought is an example of a cognitive distortion, it likely reflects an internal experience. If the thought cannot be assessed objectively, or if there is a different way to interpret the thought, it also might be related to an internal experience.

VIGNETTE

Shun writes down the thought "I need to work harder to prevent getting fired," as this thought has been recurring. He writes down some relevant Socratic questions to help him identify whether or not this thought is based on the external world (and therefore problem-solving would be helpful).

- *Is it possible to collect evidence to explore this concern?*
  - *Shun recalls that he can read his performance review from last quarter. His supervisor has an open-door policy and has previously been willing to offer feedback on his performance.*

- *What assumptions am I making?*
  - *Shun is assuming that he is not working hard enough and that not working "hard enough" will result in being fired. There is also an assumption that there will not be intermediary steps taken before he would be fired. He is assuming that he would not be given an opportunity to repair his mistakes.*

- *Is there another way of viewing this situation?*
  - *Shun could acknowledge his high expectations for himself and that others do not expect the same level of effort from him.*

- *How did my expectations for myself come to be?*
  - *Shun reflects that a previous boss would often make demeaning comments such as "Stop being so lazy" and "If this doesn't work, it will be your fault." In that work environment, Shun often felt fearful that he would be criticized. He developed a vigilant approach to work and self-criticism to try to avoid being judged or punished. In the new work setting, Shun's boss does not make the same demeaning comments and normalizes making mistakes. Shun realizes that this fear of getting fired likely comes from his previous work environment, and that his brain continues to generate these thoughts out of caution.*

- *How likely is this thought to be true?*
  - *Shun reflects on the satisfactory feedback he received in his latest evaluation report. He also thinks about how, on multiple occasions, his boss has expressed that mistakes are okay and framed them as learning opportunities. Shun comes to the conclusion that his boss would likely give him the opportunity to make changes if it is ever determined that his performance is not satisfactory. A few comments on the evaluation report note ways for Shun to improve, such as responding to emails sooner and asking for help more often. While Shun received some critical feedback, given the other evidence, Shun determines that it is not likely he will be fired.*

Shun notes that the thought that he will be fired is connected to the cognitive distortions of "fortune telling" and "catastrophizing." He also considers that the thought might be related to "disqualifying the positives" as he does not often think of all of the positive feedback or successes he has had at work. Because the thought is related to cognitive distortions, and "working harder" is not clearly defined, Shun determines that the thought is related to his internal experience. Shun took time to problem-solve ways to respond to these concerns. Now when Shun notices the thought "I will get fired if I do not work harder," he can remember that this thought is reflecting an internal experience, and he does not need to problem-solve.

While Shun recognizes that the thought is linked to his internal experience, he also identifies a few related thoughts that are linked to the outside world, such as his boss wanting him to ask for help more often and responding to emails more quickly.

Understanding the nature of these thoughts allows him to focus his problem-solving efforts toward these specific concerns rather than the broader, more elusive aim of "working harder."

CHANGEABILITY OF PROBLEM

Good work! You have now developed skills to distinguish between thoughts reflecting the external world and an internal experience. There is still one variable to assess before determining how to move forward in the decompiling process. For thoughts reflecting the outside world, Hallis et al. (2012) describe the importance of assessing the "changeability" of the problem.

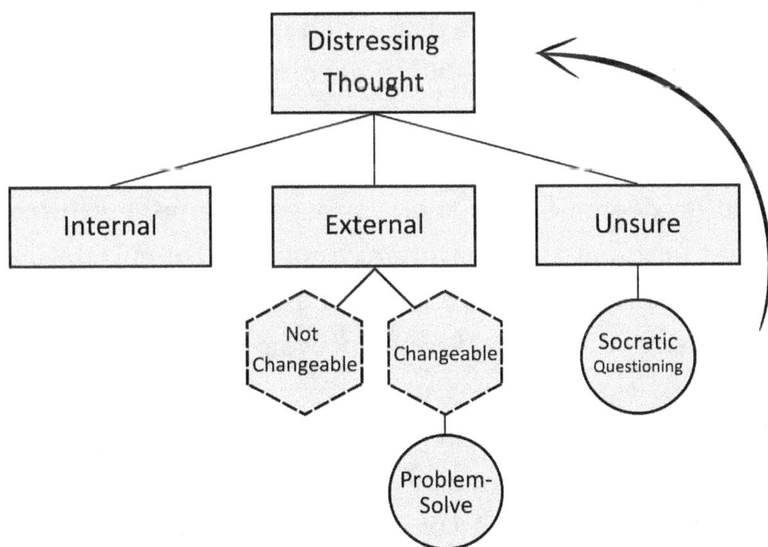

For many problems, change is very possible and problem-solving is appropriate. Returning to our previous example, a broken pipe can be fixed effectively with the use of problem-solving. At other times, problems in the external world are not changeable, and a different approach is more effective. An example includes the death of a loved one. While this pain is related to an external concern, humans do not have the capacity to change the circumstances in full. Of course, problem-solving can help to manage the logistics of a funeral or signing up for therapy, but problem-solving will not be able to bring back the loved one or stop the grief.

Sometimes the changeability of circumstances is difficult to assess. An example of this difficulty is addressing chronic health concerns. Perhaps a distressing thought related to these circumstances arises such as "this pain will last forever". Will problem-solving be effective to address symptoms? It's sometimes unclear. If a solution is possible, problem-solving is important in order to decrease pain and improve functioning. However, constant problem-solving without a solution (or enough data) can cause unnecessary burdens and exhaustion. The stress of this persistent effort could possibly even increase one's stress and exacerbate symptoms.

When you are unsure whether or not a solution to an external problem exists, it can be valuable to problem-solve in a contained way. For instance, let's say a person who was recently diagnosed with a chronic illness commits to attending a scheduled doctor's appointment to learn more about their health and options. They might also decide to research their health condition for a specific amount of time. Outside of that predetermined time for problem-solving, they allow themselves to take a break and apply a different response to the thoughts that arise (an approach reviewed in the next chapter). Overall, when the problem in the external world is not changeable, or when there is uncertainty about its changeability, problem-solving is of limited value, and a different way to relate to those thoughts is necessary.

SUMMARY

In this chapter, we reviewed how to distinguish different types of thoughts and when problem-solving is and is not helpful. We also discussed how Socratic questioning can help when it is unclear whether a thought is tied to an internal or external experience. The Thought Decompiler, which will be summarized at the end of this section, allows insight into when problem-solving skills will be most effective versus when another approach may be warranted. We will review one such new approach in the next chapter.

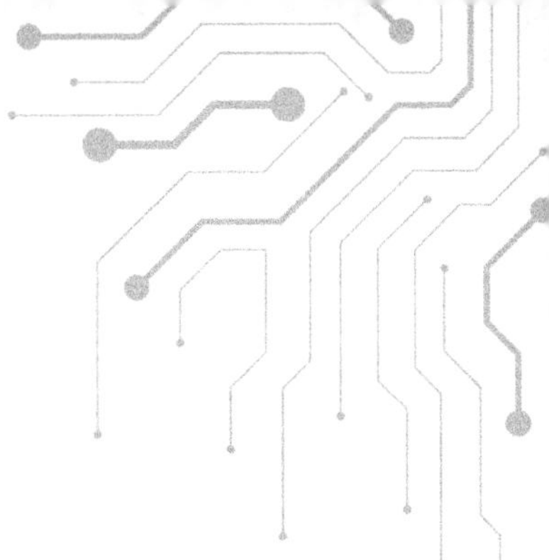

CHAPTER 14

AN ALTERNATIVE RESPONSE TO PROBLEM-SOLVING

WHEN THOUGHTS ARE RELATED TO INTERNAL EXPE-riences, or when there is a lack of changeability, problem-solving is no longer sufficient. In these cases, the Thought Decompiler offers a new way of relating to these painful thoughts. In this chapter, we will review three skills that can help diminish the emotional potency of painful thoughts: willingness (being willing to experience painful thoughts in pursuit of actions that are aligned with values), cognitive defusion (observing thoughts without interpreting them literally), and scheduled worry time (containing the worry by setting aside specific time to worry). Next, we will offer guidance on how to understand the underlying needs and values that are reflected in these thoughts, and offer a way to take actions that are informed by those needs and values.

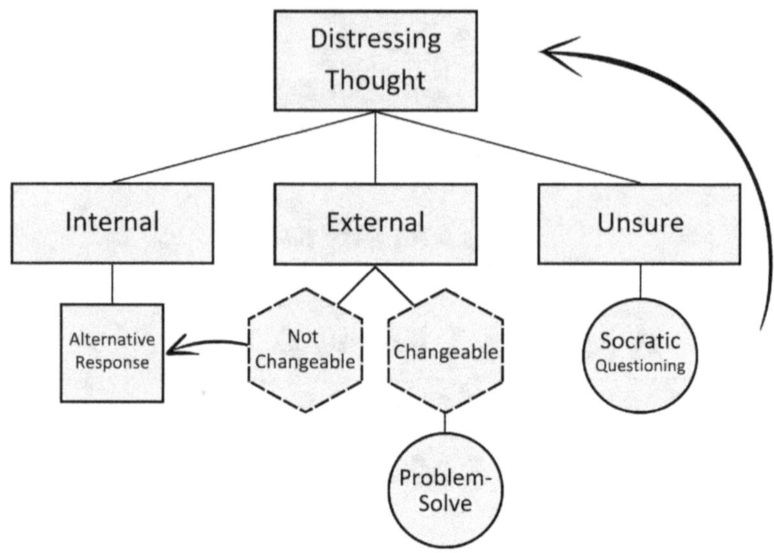

WILLINGNESS

Humans are often drawn to experiential avoidance, or "the phenomenon that occurs when a person is unwilling to remain in contact with particular private experiences (e.g., bodily sensations, emotions, thoughts, memories, images, behavioral predispositions) and takes steps to alter the form or frequency of these experiences or the contexts that occasion them, even when these forms of avoidance cause behavioral harm" (Hayes et al., 1996, p. 1155). Research reveals a positive correlation between experiential avoidance and worry (Santanello & Gardner, 2006), as well as rumination and depression (Cribb et al., 2006).

An alternative response to experiential avoidance is "willingness" (a concept used in Acceptance and Commitment Therapy), which is the practice of accepting and embracing all thoughts and emotions, including those that are uncomfortable. An analogy that elucidates willingness is the use of finger cuffs (Eifert & Forsyth, 2005). For those unfamiliar, finger cuffs are a small tube into which one finger can be inserted on each side. Intuitively, to remove those fingers from the trap, it would make sense to pull them out of the tube. This puzzle is not intuitive, however, in that by pulling harder, the tube gets tighter, which prevents the fingers from going free. Only by lessening that pull does the device become looser. Then, and only then, removing the fingers becomes possible.

Imagine that your uncomfortable thoughts function as finger cuffs. Willingness to experience these thoughts prevents the additional distress that would come with fighting them. Learning the counter-intuitive move of willingness, or resisting the struggle and embracing the experience, prevents you from becoming stuck in a trap.

The truth is, painful thoughts and emotions are parts of a normal, human experience. We all experience uncomfortable emotions and distressing thoughts. Normalizing these experiences supports self-compassion (as presented in the decompiling emotions section) because it highlights the common humanity of these experiences. We are not alone for having these experiences and do not need to fight these experiences in order to be "normal." However, it is one thing to intellectually know that painful thoughts and emotions are challenging, but it is often quite different to *believe* that they are normal. Connecting with others, hearing their experiences, and taking gradual vulnerability risks is necessary in order to internalize the belief that these experiences are common.

The sheer knowledge that distressing thoughts, and the emotions that accompany them, will pass if they are not being fought or denied lays a foundation for willingness. As reviewed in Chapter 4, emotions occur in waves that subside when willingness to mindfully feel them is present. Again, intellectually, one might understand this. It takes the practice of experiencing this discomfort without fighting it to allow *the nervous system* (the system that facilitates the communication between the brain and the body) to learn that these experiences will pass. The body learns this through experience. If this is a new process, working with a therapist can be essential as a way to practice tolerating this distress within the Window of Tolerance.

EXERCISE: INCREASING CAPACITY FOR WILLINGNESS

Reflect on the following questions to build your capacity for willingness.

1. Identify a thought that you tend to resist (e.g., "I am a burden to others" or "They will find out that I am a fraud").

2. What emotions arise alongside this thought (e.g., shame, fear, anxiety, guilt). Check the Feeling Wheel.

3. Consider that you are probably not the only one experiencing a similar thought or emotion. While the thought itself might not be exactly the same, the sense of distress is common.

4. Consider that this experience is temporary, so that your mind and body can learn to ride the wave of the emotion and let that thought pass.

5. Identify one manageable action that you can take to increase your belief in the common humanity of this pain and/or the belief that this distress will pass. Here are some examples:

- Listen to a podcast where people share their personal stories.

- Disclose something about your internal experience to a trusted person.

- Talk with a trusted friend and ask questions to learn about their internal experience.

- Listen to a song that reflects the emotions you are feeling. Allow yourself to feel moved by that song.

- Connect with a therapist who can help shed insight on these experiences and co-create manageable actions.

VIGNETTE

Fiona considered which thoughts are especially painful for her and how she frequently fears that others will perceive her as incompetent. She also worries that she does not belong and perceives herself as an "imposter" in her work setting. For this experience, Fiona identifies the thought "I am not good enough." The emotions associated with this thought include shame and helplessness.

Fiona considers her reading so far, including the idea that these thoughts and emotions are human, and that they will pass. While part of her believes this information, another part of her is skeptical and doubts that anyone could relate to her experience. Despite the skepticism, Fiona decides to help her nervous system learn that these thoughts and emotions will pass and that she is not alone in feeling this distress by trying one of the exercises anyway.

Fiona decides to talk with Maja, a colleague she is close to. They have spent time together outside of work and connected over their love of volleyball. Maja has always been kind and considerate toward Fiona, but they have not spent much time sharing their internal thoughts and emotions. After work one day, as they are driving together to volleyball practice, Fiona shares with Maja that she sometimes doubts her ability and is intimidated by skillful teammates. While Fiona is feeling nervous sharing this, her body quickly relaxes when Maja responds, "I totally know that feeling! Everyone is so smart, and I worry I can't keep up!"

Fiona and Maja are able to connect about their shared experience at work alongside their favorite sport. While Fiona still experiences the thought "I am not good enough" at times, and she sometimes doubts that her experiences are shared and temporary, disclosing this experience to a trusted person who was able to respond empathetically allowed Fiona to challenge these thoughts and know that she is not alone.

YOU ARE NOT YOUR THOUGHTS

As reviewed in the decompiling emotions section, extensive research supports the benefits of mindfulness through "awareness of one's internal states and surroundings" (American Psychological Association, n.d.j). Practicing mindfulness means grounding oneself in the present moment and bringing non-judgmental awareness to what is happening inside or outside of oneself. Taking on the role of an observer without an agenda—curiously and openly making contact with experiences as they arise—is another key aspect of mindfulness. Mindfulness can be practiced in a variety of ways, and whether by focusing on the breath or purposefully tuning into the surroundings, mindfulness helps direct focus toward what is, without evaluating or disconnecting.

In the decompiling emotions section, we explored how mindfulness can also be helpful in noticing and processing emotions. As it turns out, mindfulness is also a great way to build insight into patterns of thought! However, many people find applying mindfulness techniques to thoughts to be more challenging, due to the difficulty of stepping back far enough to see the thoughts as separate from themselves.

Throughout this book, we are building a case that a person is not their thoughts. Think back to the beginning of the decompiling thoughts section where we discussed how humans have limited control over thoughts, that thoughts do not necessarily represent one's desires or ethics, and that thoughts are not always accurate representations of the external world. This being the case, how could thoughts possibly fully represent the self? Instead, thoughts are fleeting *interpretations* of what is happening in the moment. They occur automatically, as a reaction to internal and external cues, and just like any guess, sometimes they are an accurate representation of the external world and sometimes they are not. Yesterday's thought can be followed by a totally contradictory thought today. Thoughts come and go. Yet, the human being experiencing the thoughts remains.

You may be wondering, if a person is not their thoughts, who are they? One way to conceptualize this idea is to consider human senses. A person is not only what they can hear because they are the one hearing it. A person is not only what they can see because they are the one who is seeing it. This same concept can be applied to what goes on in the mind. You are the one who notices a particular thought, not the thought itself. You are the one who can observe rumination, repetition, or spiraling. You are even the one who notices your own self-criticism. All told, you are not what can be observed, because you are *doing the observing.*

Cognitive Fusion

The uncoupling of thoughts from the self is an important skill. Without discerning the two, it is easy to become tangled up in the brain's guesses, ideas, and subjective interpretations, often experiencing them all as accurate representations of what is happening. When this occurs, the experience of distressing thoughts is increasingly painful as it is believed that they are a reflection of the self. In Acceptance and Commitment Therapy (ACT), the state in which a person cannot distinguish between what they are actually experiencing in the external world from the content of their thoughts is called "cognitive fusion."

For thoughts regarding the external world, cognitive fusion can be efficient. For instance, a literal interpretation of the thought "The door is jammed" is likely effective. We can assume this thought is an accurate reflection of reality, take it at face value, and take actions to fix the problem based on interpreting this thought literally.

When thoughts are based on an internal experience, however, interpreting these symbols literally has higher stakes. For instance, the thought "I am worthless" is an example of a thought that reflects an internal experience. Cognitive fusion involves interpreting this thought as a literal reflection of one's self and it comes with increased distress. Furthermore, because this thought is less concrete than "The door is jammed," it is less clear what actions would fix the problem.

Some engineers and non-engineers alike try to "be less worthless" by constantly striving and achieving. Even following those achievements, they still describe experiencing the thought "I am worthless." Their subsequent attempts to fix "worthlessness" are elusive and ineffective. An outsider would likely not perceive them as worthless, but their failed attempts of freeing themselves from this thought frequently cause them to identify with that idea even more.

In addition, interpreting "I am worthless" literally propels confirmation bias. Confirmation bias, in turn, integrates the symbol "I am worthless" even more deeply into their web of learned associations. Unsurprisingly, such cognitive fusion is negatively correlated with well-being (Faustino et al., 2021) and has been shown to be predictive of depressive symptoms (Pinto-Gouveia et al., 2018).

VIGNETTE

Amanda is at work and notices that her co-workers are quiet when she enters the room. In response to noticing this, Amanda thinks "No one likes me." Amanda believes this thought to be true. Interpreting this thought as a literal representation of the external world, Amanda tries to problem-solve to get people to like her, including inviting her co-workers to a happy hour, staying late to help with a work project, and trying to connect with her co-workers by pretending to share their interest in football. While Amanda has spent more time with her co-workers and has developed inside jokes and shared interests, Amanda still experiences the thought "No one likes me."

Experiencing this thought after all of her effort, Amanda now feels even more disappointed in herself. She experiences shame and anxiety related to social interactions, as she tries to avoid the thought "No one likes me" and the emotional pain associated with it. Amanda is quick to interpret her co-workers actions as confirmation that they do not like her and overlooks the

signs that they do enjoy her company. While her co-workers'
initial silence could have been related to a number of factors
(such as being distracted by a challenging work problem or
not hearing her when she entered the room), Amanda's liter-
al interpretation of "No one likes me" as the reason for their
silence amplifies the power of that thought and of Amanda's
negative self-image.

Indicators that suggest you might be fused to a thought or thought pattern (Hayes, 2022):

- Your thoughts include evaluations or comparisons.

- You experience repeating loops of thoughts that are familiar to you.

- You are consumed by thoughts and lose awareness of your physical surroundings.

- Your thoughts are attached to strong emotions, sensations, urges, and memories.

Cognitive fusion is often the automatic response to thoughts. Therefore, it can be very difficult to notice when we are fused to a thought and easy to get confused about where we are among the thoughts that come and go. Keep in mind that it can take time and practice to notice when fusion is occuring, and refer back to the above list as needed.

Cognitive Defusion

Fusion can occur in an instant. Consider a scenario where a supervisor schedules a meeting to discuss your latest evaluation. Based on your unique web of associations, certain emotions or thoughts will arise when seeing or hearing the word "evaluation." Perhaps there is a sinking feeling in the pit of the stomach. While the evaluation is not occurring at this moment, the word "evaluation" can cause the body to experience the same thoughts and emotions that might arise during the actual evaluation. If negative associations are paired with that word, a thought such as "I'm going to fall short" might occur in response. This thought can create a spiral of anxious thoughts and physiological reactions, a chain of thoughts that are at the mercy of what the word "evaluation" means to you.

"Cognitive *de*fusion," on the other hand, is the process of separating thoughts from a literal interpretation of the external world. From a perspective of cognitive defusion, one can observe all of the thoughts that arise in association with ideas or words, with the understanding that the thoughts are not necessarily literal truths. Cognitive defusion allows you to notice what the brain is doing, observing words and thoughts as symbols that may or may not accurately reflect your external reality.

Extensive research supports the efficacy of cognitive defusion. It has been shown to be more effective at decreasing distress than other coping strategies, including thought distraction (Masuda, 2010), and self-affirmations (such as self-talk like "I am worthy of love") (Brandrick et al., 2020). Researchers have also provided evidence that cognitive defusion interventions can reduce the anxiety tied to public speaking (Brandrick et al., 2020).

At this point, you might be thinking, "This sounds great, but *how* do I defuse from my thoughts?" Consider a researcher collecting data. At the point of data collection, the researcher's job is to objectively document what is being observed without investment or judgment about what the data means. It is not until later, when the data as a whole is reviewed, that interpretation or judgment is helpful. Interpreting the results too soon could sway the final conclusion before the whole picture is objectively tracked.

Extending this analogy, the researcher might consider each thought as a data point. The researcher would use cognitive defusion to notice each data point, document it, and then move on to the next measurement. The researcher maintains a disposition of noticing and practicing curiosity without judgment. The researcher is not interpreting each individual data point or measurement as a literal reflection of the phenomenon as a whole, but rather, as one "symbol" to note.

Fusion occurs when attention is focused on a sole data point. The researcher then creates a narrative about what that one measurement says about the overall outcome of the study. The researcher might have an emotional investment in the significance, or lack thereof, of a particular data point. The researcher might be tempted to find other data points that confirm this judgment and dismiss contradictory evidence as an error. Moreover, a more accurate conclusion might be missed, as the focus was narrowed too early, long before a more complete story could be revealed.

It's fair to say that what we have been describing can feel abstract. To make it more concrete, let's change the language. Employing phrases such as "I'm noticing the thought...." and "I'm noticing that I'm experiencing the thought..." can be a powerful way to become an observer. For example, for the thought "I'm so stupid," rephrasing it as "I'm noticing that I'm experiencing the thought 'I'm so stupid,'" highlights the separation between you and the neurons firing in your brain. For many, using these statements can aid the process of looking at the thoughts rather than *through* them.

The following brief exercise offers a sense of what relating to thoughts via cognitive defusion feels like. Please keep in mind that noticing thoughts from a lens of cognitive defusion is not always easy; given the messy nature of thoughts, it is natural to get lost in them. Rather than never getting caught in a thought, the goal of the exercise is to notice when fusion is happening and then return to defusion. The process of getting consumed by a thought, noticing that experience, and then moving back to a defused perspective will likely occur several times during the next exercise.

EXERCISE: MOVIE SCREEN DEFUSION

To make it easier to follow the prompts, read through all of the directions before beginning, or consider asking someone else to read the directions to you or recording yourself reading the directions. When reading the directions out loud, speak slowly and softly, with pauses between the sentences. During the exercise, you do not need to verbally respond to the prompts; just notice what is coming up for you.

1. Set a timer for between two and ten minutes.

2. Find a comfortable position in which you will not fall asleep. Sitting up straight with the feet flat on the ground is often helpful.

3. Close your eyes and imagine that you are sitting in a movie theater, looking at the screen. Imagine the sensations around you. What are you hearing and smelling? Is it cold or warm? What does the sensation of the chair below you feel like?

4. Now, see your thoughts projected onto the movie screen. Notice them as if they were characters in the movie. Perhaps you see words or images, reflecting the thoughts.

5. Notice the thoughts on the screen as they come and go without attachment to any particular thought.

Just as characters in a movie, you cannot control what they do. In your mind, restate each thought using the phrase, "I'm noticing the thought…"

6. Notice the distance between you and the screen. Perhaps you imagine seeing other moviegoers sit in front of you. Maybe you notice dust particles floating in the air, in front of the screen.

7. Notice that you are not the characters on the screen. What does it feel like to notice your thoughts in this way?

8. You might get absorbed into the movie or feel that you are a character in the movie. If this happens, just take a deep breath and then go back to watching the thoughts on the movie screen.

9. After the timer has gone off, take three deep breaths. Slowly move your body, maybe wiggling your fingers or stretching your shoulders. When you are ready, slowly open your eyes.

VIGNETTE

Amanda uses this mindfulness exercise to defuse from her thoughts. In the exercise, she is able to notice the thought "No one likes me" with more distance, as a character on the movie screen. In doing so, Amanda is able to recognize that this thought does not necessarily accurately represent herself or what others think of her. Rather, it is just one of many thoughts that her brain generates during the activity. For instance, Amanda notices that after the thought "No one likes me," she also experiences the thought "I am excited to spend time with my niece," and then, "I think there's a rock in my shoe?" The thought "No one likes me" is understandably distressing. Outside of this exercise, Amanda would typically direct her attention toward the thought and attempt to find a solution. With this exercise, Amanda is able to see that that extra effort of problem-solving was not necessary, as she is separate from the characters on the movie screen. The thought appeared, and then disappeared, from the screen on its own.

SCHEDULED WORRY TIME

In addition to responding to distressing thoughts with willingness and cognitive defusion, many of our clients understandably want other concrete strategies to manage these thoughts. One strategy many of our engineering clients find especially helpful in managing racing thoughts is "scheduled worry time." Worry and rumination are pervasive and can be activated in a wide range of environments and situations. If you typically worry while lying in bed before falling asleep, for example, then over time the simple act of lying in bed can be enough to cue these thought patterns. Or perhaps hearing a certain song on the radio elicits these thought patterns, sending your thoughts into a spiral. The brain's ability to associate the external world with worry can be a powerful one.

Scheduled worry time, also known as "worry postponement," is an evidenced-based intervention which addresses these associations (Dippel et al., 2023). Scheduled worry time does not focus on *how* the worrier relates to their distressing thoughts; instead, the change concerns the *when*. Once a worry-filled thought is identified, the worrier intentionally abstains from exploring that thought more deeply in that moment. Instead, they file it away (mentally or through physical documentation) for later in the day. When their established worry time arrives, they revisit this mental or physical file in a specific environment for a contained amount of time, typically about 30 minutes. Outside of this window of time, the worrier's task is to return their focus to the present moment, engaging in life around them.

Rumination and worry can easily get out of hand, and it can be valuable to contain these thoughts–especially if you need to be fully present. Similar to setting boundaries with a chatty neighbor, setting boundaries with rumination and worry is also possible. You probably would not allow your neighbor to enter your home whenever they want; you would probably request that they ring the doorbell first. You might agree to spend time with them in a planned setting such as a neighborhood barbeque, but you would not miss work just because they wanted to speak with you as you were pulling out of your driveway. Approaching rumination and worry in a similar way can be effective.

Keep in mind that we can make this time our own, deciding on the time of day, the environment, and the duration of time to worry and ruminate. We encourage you to apply a trial-and-error approach to see what works. Examples of times and frequencies include: 30 minutes a day, an hour every other day, or two hours once a week. Setting an alarm can be a helpful tool to signal when the worry time is over. Some people prefer to journal during these times while others prefer to think without writing. There is no one right way these scheduled worry times *should* look—the *right* way is whatever works best for you!

Just as setting boundaries with a neighbor will help them learn when you are open to having a conversation, scheduled worry time can train the mind to know when the worry is welcome and unwelcome. When a worrying thought arises outside of the scheduled worry time, mindfulness skills can be used to notice the thought non-judgmentally, followed by a reminder to revisit the thought at the scheduled time. From there, attention can be redirected to an activity in the present moment, such as a conversation with a friend, a work task, or petting a dog. The worry is acknowledged, with an agreement to revisit it later, so the urgency of the worry can dissipate.

EXERCISE: SCHEDULED WORRY TIME PLAN

Take some time now to individualize a Scheduled Worry Time Plan. This is a starting point, so feel free to change these details later, through a trial-and-error process to find what works best.

1. Identify the length of the worry time (e.g., 20 minutes, 30 minutes, one hour, two hours).

2. Identify the frequency of the worry time (e.g., once a day, once every other day, once a week).

3. Identify the time of day. Please note that it is recommended to not schedule worry time too close to bedtime, to prevent the worries from affecting your sleep routine.

4. Decide where the worry time will take place (e.g., in a specific chair, taking a walk, while taking a shower).

5. If journaling will be part of worry time, determine what resources are available (e.g., a paper journal, a computer, a phone).

6. Choose a signal that your worry time is over (e.g., an alarm).

7. Select an activity to do after worry time to direct attention away from the worry or rumination (e.g., talking to a friend, cleaning, working, watching a show).

VIGNETTE

Jessica builds her scheduled worry time plan. She decides to worry for 20 minutes every day around 4 p.m., while sitting in her chair in the spare room, as she does not often use that space. She plans to bring her paper journal and set an alarm to help her know when the time is over. During this scheduled time, Jessica asks the "what if" questions that worry her. She ruminates on past mistakes and tries to anticipate ways to improve moving forward. When the alarm goes off, Jessica redirects her attention by focusing on preparing dinner.

When a "what if" thought arises outside of this scheduled time, Jessica has learned to use her cognitive defusion skills to notice the thought. She also reminds herself of self-compassion skills, and to be kind to herself in response to the pain that those thoughts bring up. Finally, Jessica agrees to revisit the worry at 4 p.m. the next day.

After a few weeks of incorporating scheduled worry time, Jessica notices that the urgency of the worry does not feel as strong. Her mind has learned to associate the context of the scheduled time with worry. Rather than being consumed with worry and rumination throughout the day, Jessica notices that she is able to let go of the thoughts more quickly.

CONSIDERING THE NEEDS AND VALUES UNDERLYING THE THOUGHT

After choosing an alternate response to a distressing thought, with the support of willingness, cognitive defusion, and scheduled worry time, we can take a step back and incorporate curiosity for the underlying message of that thought. Rather than interpreting the thought literally, we can also be curious about what the underlying needs or values are possibly being reflected by the presence of that thought.

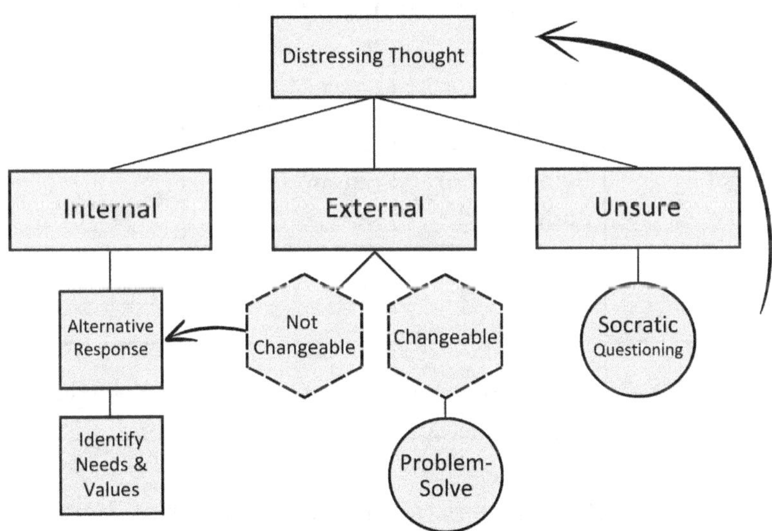

For example, let's say that you have identified the thought "I am going to get fired" as part of your internal experience. Using Socratic questioning, you determine that you are not at risk of being fired and do not need to take action on the literal interpretation of that thought. Instead, the thought itself might present valuable data beyond the literal interpretation. Perhaps decompiling this thought allows you to understand that you deeply value security, including the financial security that comes with the job, as it allows you to support your family. Even if you do not believe that you will be fired, perhaps this thought reveals that you have been feeling less stable or secure lately, thereby revealing a need.

Because decompiling a thought, moving from a literal interpretation to the deeper needs and values underlying that thought, can be abstract and unclear, we've created a list of common human needs. While this list is not comprehensive, we encourage you to refer to it, along with the values list in Chapter 8, while considering your own thoughts.

Common Human Needs

Belonging	Financial security	Physical safety	Power
Sense of identity	Being seen or understood	Emotional safety	Rest
Recognition	Stability	Play	Peace
Connection	Autonomy	Purpose	Knowledge

Please note that there is not a direct translation between a thought and the deeper meaning. Two people might experience the thought "I need to succeed" with different underlying meanings attached. For instance, "I need to succeed" might reflect a need for recognition for one person, while another person might identify the core need as stability. Over time, the underlying need can change for the same person. Willingness and defusion from thoughts allows each person to get to know their own thoughts, with distance, to eventually access the valuable data that comes from them.

EXERCISE: IDENTIFY UNDERLYING NEEDS AND VALUES

Identify a distressing thought, related to your internal experience, that you experience often. After willingly experiencing and observing that thought, consider what underlying needs and values might be reflected by that thought. What is the function of that thought? This reflection process can take time. Activities such as journaling and talking to a trusted person can help access curiosity for the deeper meaning of the thought.

VIGNETTE

Richard often experiences the thought "I am alone." Richard typically attempts to distract himself from this thought as it brings up feelings of shame, loneliness, and despair. When engaging in the first part of the Thought Decompiler, Richard identifies that this thought is primarily a reflection of his internal experience as he has many friends and family members. The evidence in his life is that he is not alone, and in fact, surrounded by others. Following the Thought Decompiler, Richard practices willingness by normalizing the discomfort and reminding himself that this experience will pass. He listens to a podcast to hear others' internal experiences to help him feel more willing to experience this thought. He also incorporates defusion to notice the thought from a distance and see that the thought is separate from himself.

After mindfully experiencing the thought and the associated emotions, Richard considers what might be underneath this thought. He spends time journaling to consider what needs and values might be arising. While the insight is not initially clear, after a few different journaling sessions, Richard identifies that he has a need to be seen. While he is regularly around people and has shared experiences with them, he realizes that he lacks a deeper form of connection that allows him to be seen for his internal experience. Richard resonates with the value, "authenticity", and he sees how this thought reflects the importance of vulnerable, meaningful connection. While he already experiences some level of connection and belonging, decompiling the thought helps Richard realize that there is still room to find ways to incorporate authenticity into his relationships.

COMMITTED ACTION BASED ON NEEDS AND VALUES

After decompiling the thought to understand the need and/or value reflected within it, it's possible to take actions consistent with those needs and/or values. Rather than taking an immediate action in response to the literal interpretation of the thought, the action will be based on the underlying meaning of the thought. This is the final step of the Thought Decompiler. While doing so, discomfort will likely arise. This process of courageously engaging in tasks consistent with the underlying values and needs, while being willing to experience the distress and hurdles that arise, is referred to as "committed action," according to the framework of Acceptance and Commitment Therapy (ACT).

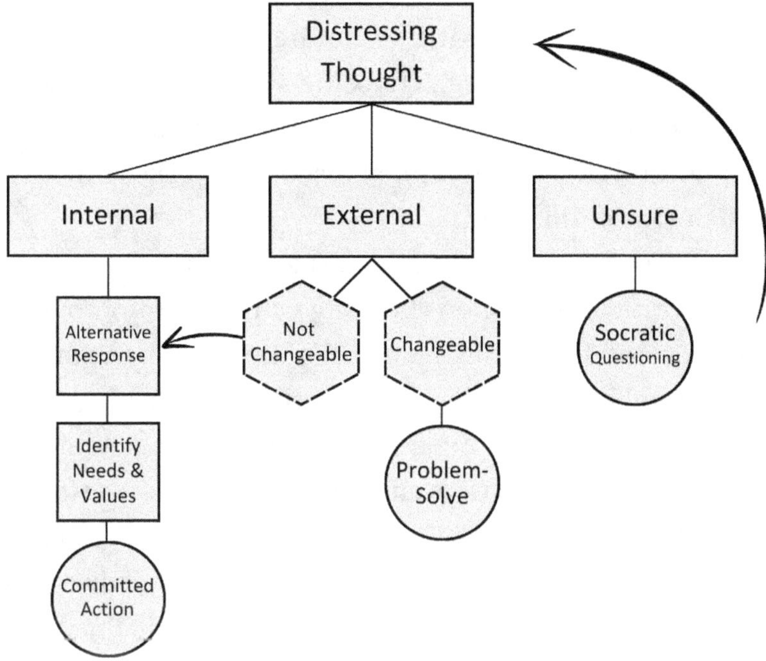

If an underlying value of competence, for instance, is reflected in the thought "I am not good enough," possible actions to move in the direction of that value might open up. For instance, an upcoming opportunity to attend a conference is one way to act consistently with the value. Within this committed action, nerves and self-critical thoughts might arise in the process. However, planning to attend this event is not intended to avoid pain or to meet others' expectations, but rather because competence is a guiding value. It is about committing to the act of attending, no matter if internal discomfort arises.

When you value the work you do and find it important to share with others, the thoughts and emotions around such professional events are often a small part of a much bigger picture. Willingness can help to propel you towards that bigger picture (your values) while experiencing the inevitable fluctuations of your internal experience. It also can help you save energy for what is in your control (e.g., choosing sessions, engaging with colleagues and presenters) instead of fixating on what is outside of your control (that is, emotional discomfort). Discomfort will (or will not) arise on its own.

What does require input and effort are the decisions leading up to the conference. While choosing whether or not to attend a session, clarifying details such as the duration of the talk, the possible number of attendees, and method of delivery, you can consult your values and needs before committing. Again, you cannot choose or control what emotions or thoughts arise (such as excitement, nervousness, self-doubt, or even dread). You cannot control other people's reactions. However, if internal discomfort arises, tapping into the emotional regulation skills in the decompiling emotion section comes into play.

EXERCISE: COMMITTED ACTION PLAN

To help understand willingness and values in context, follow these prompts:

1. Refer to your reflections in the previous exercise, Identify Underlying Needs and Values. Pick one need or value that was reflected in the thought explored in that exercise.

2. Write down activities that are associated with that value or need (e.g., traveling, presenting, starting unfamiliar tasks, asking for help).

3. Circle one activity to start with, then brainstorm about upcoming opportunities to engage with the identified activity.

4. Now, pick one opportunity from the brainstormed list and commit to it. Identify the aspects of the activity you can control and the aspects of the activity outside your control. For instance, perhaps you are willing to ask your partner for help with the travel planning. Your partner's reaction and the thoughts/emotions that arise are not things that you can choose.

5. To hold yourself accountable, setting clear parameters is important. Answer the following questions to create specific expectations:

- What is the activity?
- What day and time will I engage with the activity?
- How long will I engage in the activity?
- Where will I be?
- Who else will be involved?

VIGNETTE

Richard identified that the underlying value that he decompiled from the thought "I am alone" is "authenticity." He considers actions that are aligned with authenticity including expressing vulnerability toward others, creating expressive art, and offering support to others when they are struggling. Richard decides that he would like to start with creating artwork as an avenue for his value. He considers ideas such as taking an art class, going to an art exhibit, and starting up his painting hobby again. Richard commits to start painting again. He considers that he can decide what, when, and how to paint. He can commit to being authentic to himself and his internal experiences as he paints. He cannot, however, control whether or not others offer validation for his work. He cannot control whether self-doubting thoughts or other emotions (such as anxiety or shame) arise.

To help hold himself accountable as he commits to this action, Richard sets a plan. He will paint on Saturday in the morning in his backyard for two hours. Tonight, he will get out his old painting materials and consider if he needs to go to the craft store before Saturday. In order to stay true to the value of authenticity, he will mindfully notice his emotions and paint in a way that expresses those feelings.

His spouse may or may not be around to see what he is painting. He will accept that he cannot control how they respond to his art. On Saturday, Richard does experience self-doubt and some anxiety about whether or not his work will be "good," and has thoughts like "I hope people like what I create." Richard acknowledges that these thoughts and feelings are human, and he is willing to experience them. Richard also feels a sense of fulfillment as he sees that he is taking an action aligned with his values.

SUMMARY

When a distressing thought reflects something about an internal experience or something outside our control, the automatic response of problem-solving to get rid of the thought does not fully work. And, tactics to suppress the thought or to prevent future distress by overthinking tend to exacerbate the symptoms. In these cases, relating to the thought with willingness and cognitive defusion are more effective approaches.

Additionally, incorporating scheduled worry time can be a helpful way to compartmentalize and contain the overwhelming feelings that can accompany worry and rumination. Willingness to experience distressing thoughts in new ways creates opportunities for new data and insights about your needs and values. In turn, this allows you to make decisions based on what you care about, rather than the level of distress you experience. Ultimately, taking more actions based on authentic needs and values gradually contributes to a more fulfilling life.

CHAPTER 15

PUTTING IT ALL TOGETHER: THE THOUGHT DECOMPILER

WE INVITE YOU TO PAUSE AND REFLECT ON HOW MUCH you have already learned! As a human, it is natural to see thoughts as an integral part of yourself, so it can feel unsettling to imagine an alternative way of understanding and relating to those thoughts. Building these skills takes time, and to ease any sense of being overwhelmed, we'll summarize the skills reviewed in earlier chapters by presenting the Thought Decompiler, in full. We will then offer a guide to tangible next steps for gradually practicing and integrating these skills, allowing you to form new habits.

The Thought Decompiler

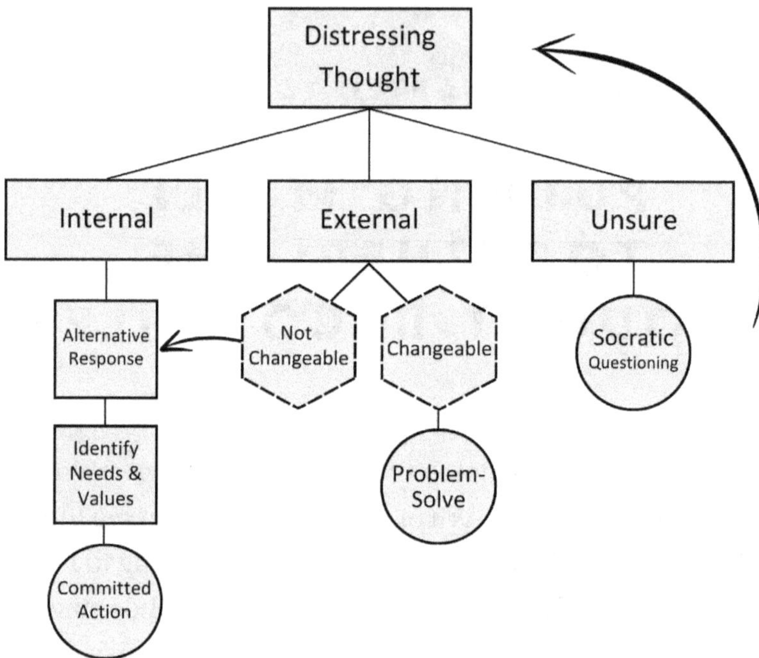

STEP 1: IDENTIFY A DISTRESSING THOUGHT.

Unless the thought is about a life-threatening emergency (not including intrusive thoughts, which can describe imaginary life-threatening scenarios that are at odds with what you desire), immediate action may not be necessary. We advise that the Thought Decompiler not be used for unwanted thoughts experienced in an environment which requires your undivided attention (e.g., a party, meeting, or dinner date), as it will impact your ability to engage with your surroundings. Rather, in these situations you can take note of the thought and revisit it when there is time and capacity for reflection and assessment. Additionally, it is not necessary to decompile every distressing thought. Instead, focus these efforts on decompiling a few thoughts that bring particular distress or confusion.

STEP 2: DETERMINE IF THE THOUGHT IS TIED TO THE INTERNAL OR EXTERNAL WORLD.

Refer to the skills reviewed in Chapter 13 to identify characteristics of different types of thoughts. If you're still unsure whether a thought reflects an internal or external experience, use Socratic questioning.

2.a. If the thought pertains to the external world, assess whether or not it is changeable.

STEP 3: RESPOND ACCORDINGLY.

3.a. If it is a thought reflecting the external world, and changeable, use problem-solving.

3.b. If it is a thought reflecting an internal experience, or unchangeable, engage in the alternative skills reviewed in Chapter 14 (willingness, cognitive defusion, and scheduled worry time).

3.b.1. With more distance from the thought itself, take time to reflect on the underlying needs or values reflected in that thought.

3.b.2. Consider actions that do not resolve the thought itself, but effectively help get those needs met or that move toward the highlighted value. Practice tolerating discomfort while committing to this action.

VIGNETTE

Teddy has recently been noticing the thought "What if I'm a bad friend?" This thought is upsetting, so he decides to use the Thought Decompiler to better understand it. As Teddy is unsure whether or not this thought reflects his actual quality as a friend, he refers to the Socratic questioning table. He picks five questions to aid in reflecting on the thought more deeply. To avoid getting caught in overthinking, Teddy designates 15 minutes in the evening to reflect while he is sitting outside. He sets an alarm to indicate when to switch his focus. Through this questioning process, Teddy identifies that the thought reflects his internal experience, as he does not have concrete, objective evidence that he is a "bad friend." He imagines that his friends would likely confirm that he is a good friend, and he is able to list several times that he supported his friends.

From there, Teddy moves forward with an alternative response to his thoughts, rather than problem-solving. He practices cognitive defusion when the thought arises. He reminds himself that distressing thoughts are human, and it is okay to experience this discomfort. Teddy finds that scheduled worry time before dinner works well for him; he contains the worry about whether or not he is a good friend to this scheduled time.

Now that Teddy is able to engage with the thought from a position of willingness, he is more equipped to decompile the thought to identify the underlying needs and values. He reviews the lists of values and needs in Chapter 14; he recognizes the presence of his value of loyalty. While he does not need to take actions to solve the problem of being a "bad friend," he can consider what actions he can take that are consistent with loyalty.

Teddy considers how he has been so worried about being a bad friend that he has avoided necessary conflict. One of his friends recently made a hurtful comment. Teddy has tried to ignore the comment and tell himself that it didn't bother him. Being honest with himself, he acknowledged that the comment did hurt his feelings. Considering his value of loyalty, Teddy noted that addressing the comment with his friend would actually be an act of loyalty. He is aware that trying to suppress these feelings might lead to future resentment, and ultimately hurt the relationship. Teddy then considers how to broach the concern with his friend in a way that serves the relationship, maintaining empathy and curiosity in the conversation.

By identifying whether the thought reflects the internal or external world, Teddy is able to decide whether or not to engage in problem-solving. By willingly experiencing the distressing thought with defusion, he is more equipped to understand the underlying needs and values of the thought. When he has access to this valuable data, he can make decisions and take actions that best serve him.

IDENTIFYING NEXT STEPS

The material covered in this section of the book challenges what many believe to be true about the nature of thoughts. Incorporating this new information to relate to thoughts is a gradual process. Some people become fused with their thoughts even after they have mastered the material. Instead of striving for perfection, focus on growth. The Thought Decompiler (and its elements) will likely feel challenging at first. The process of identifying and categorizing thoughts will become easier with time.

For example, if you have a tendency to experience thoughts

consistent with the cognitive distortion called mind reading, then over time, you'll be able to quickly identify these familiar thoughts as cognitive distortions instead of taking their content as true. From there, you can gain clarity on how to effectively engage with the thoughts. In the meantime, while building insight into patterns of thought and learning the inner workings of the mind, we encourage you to practice self-compassion. Thoughts are messy; it is only natural that learning how to respond to them will be messy as well.

EXERCISE: IDENTIFYING NEXT STEPS

1. Fill out the Integrating Skills Planning Activity to assess each skill.

Integrating Skills Planning Activity

Skills	Read each statement, then rate confidence level.	Confidence level rating: 1 (not confident) - 4 (very confident)	Tools and resources for skill development
Awareness of Thought Patterns	*I am aware of the thought patterns and cognitive distortions that are familiar to me (i.e., catastrophizing, all-or-nothing thinking).*		*Cognitive Behavioral Therapy (CBT); CBT reading material; mindfulness exercises*

Skills	Read each statement, then rate confidence level.	Confidence level rating: 1 (not confident) - 4 (very confident)	Tools and resources for skill development
Mindfulness	*I am able to notice my internal and external experiences on purpose, in the present moment, and non-judgmentally.*		*Apps; retreats; mindfulness-based therapy*
Socratic Question	*I am able to differentiate thoughts that are regarding internal versus external events.*		*Cognitive Behavioral Therapy (CBT) reading material; CBT therapy*
Willingness	*I am willing to experience discomfort. I believe that my distress is part of common humanity. I believe that thoughts and feelings are temporary.*		*Acceptance and Commitment (ACT) reading material; media that normalizes the internal experiences of others; friendship; therapy*
Cognitive Defusion	*I am able to observe my thoughts without taking them literally. I am able to notice the difference between myself and my thoughts.*		*Acceptance and Commitment Therapy reading material (ACT); ACT therapy; mindfulness exercises*

Skills	Read each statement, then rate confidence level.	Confidence level rating: 1 (not confident) - 4 (very confident)	Tools and resources for skill development
Scheduled Worry Time	*I am able to contain my worry to specific times and not get consumed by unhelpful worry or rumination throughout the day.*		*Cognitive Behavioral Therapy (CBT) reading material; CBT therapy; a scheduled worry time plan*
Committed Action	*I am able to identify an action that is consistent with my values or core needs and commit to the action, even when uncomfortable emotions or thoughts arise.*		*Acceptance and Commitment Therapy reading material (ACT); ACT therapy; Values List (see Decompiling Emotions Section); Personal Values Card Sort (Miller et al., 2001)*
Values Clarification	*I am able to describe my values and what is most important to me. I am willing to endure discomfort and face my fears in order to pursue these identified values.*		*Acceptance and Commitment Therapy (ACT): books and videos; Values Sort Cards*

2. Based on this review of the identified skills, list one or two skills that you are most motivated to work on.

3. Brainstorm a list of actions to take to foster that skill(s). Do not commit to any one action yet. The more ideas the better.

4. Identify one action on the list that you are most drawn to.

5. Frame the identified action to meet the characteristics of a SMART goal: Specific, Measurable, Attainable, Relevant, and Timely (Doran, 1981).

   - Specific (e.g., "use a mindfulness tool like the Headspace app" versus "learn mindfulness")

   - Measurable (e.g., "use the mindfulness tool three times a week")

   - Attainable (e.g., "use the mindfulness tool three times a week for ten minutes")

   - Relevant (e.g., "use the mindfulness tool to develop skills to better regulate my emotions")

   - Timely (e.g., "start using the mindfulness tool today at 5 p.m.")

6. Compose the identified action into a succinct SMART goal (e.g., "I will use Headspace app three times per week for ten minutes at a time to help me build skills for emotion regulation. I will start this practice today at 5 p.m.").

SUMMARY

While it is common to perceive thoughts as within one's control and reflective of oneself, it is more complicated than that. Researchers and psychologists have found ways to organize thoughts to bring a bit more clarity. We hope that these constructs serve as a baseline of knowledge to support the process of decompiling your thoughts.

The next steps of experiencing and figuring out how to effectively respond to those thoughts takes practice. Rather than sticking with old patterns of suppressing thoughts or overthinking, we have offered alternative skills. Willingness, cognitive defusion, and scheduled worry time are all effective ways to experience thoughts. By engaging with thoughts in these new ways, you can access the valuable data that underlies them. Decompiling this data permits better values-based and needs-based decisions.

The next and final section will provide an overview of themes we have observed with our engineering clients. We will demonstrate how the skills provided in both the decompiling emotions and thoughts sections can be applied to these trends.

SECTION III

APPLYING SKILLS

WE BEGAN THIS BOOK WITH THE METAPHOR OF A software decompiler, taking the "machine code" that runs our daily mental processes and expanding it to show the underlying scripts and functions in a human-readable way. In the last two sections, we applied this process to both emotions and thoughts. We hope you can now see them both more clearly, as you decompile the layers of interconnected beliefs, values, needs, and instincts that feed those emotions and thoughts.

Self-awareness is a beautiful thing. But as we have said from the beginning, there is more to this process than just achieving self-knowledge. An engineer who sets out to read the decompiled code behind a program is probably not just doing it to slake curiosity; there is probably something about the program that is causing challenges. Having read the code, they can either find a way to improve it, or else, by understanding the origins of the issue, adjust their own approach and expectations to find a way forward.

In our years of work with engineers, we have seen certain themes emerge over and over again as our clients face challenges in their lives or areas that they want to improve. These common themes are: perfectionism, need for connection, struggle with uncertainty, and the impostor phenomenon. This section will review each of these themes and offer alternative ways of responding to the challenges, pulling in lessons from the sections of this book related to decompiling emotions and thoughts, to demonstrate how those skills can be applied in these specific areas. We will highlight a few skills for each of the themes, but please note that these are not the only ways to respond more effectively; all of the skills reviewed in this book will directly or indirectly support progress in each of these areas.

In addition, each of the common themes intersects with the other themes and content in the book. For instance, perfectionism does not occur in a vacuum; it may arise as a response to uncertainty or the impostor phenomenon, and it may indirectly negatively impact relationships. Comprehending and changing behaviors as they relate to each of these topics will likely not be a linear process, in the same way that one rarely debugs code by simply reading line-by-line and correcting errors in order.

In therapy, we often encourage clients to conceptualize the growth process as a large, complicated knot of yarn. Pulling one end of the yarn and expecting the knot to be unwound is not effective. Rather, unknotting the yarn requires a slight tug on one end, a pull on a different area, and an incomplete loosening in another area. Over time using this back-and-forth process, the knot of yarn will gradually become looser and eventually, unwind. (We are told that debugging an app or hunting for the burnt-out component on a misbehaving circuit board can feel much the same.)

These themes are not completely universal; not all engineers experience these concerns, and for those who do, these concerns are often experienced in subjectively different ways. We encourage you to approach each topic with curiosity and reflection to consider if you have observed these patterns in yourself.

You might decide to direct your attention towards perfectionism, and then take action to address your interpersonal relationships. You might see that as your relationships improve, you notice an ease of the pressures to be perfect. After that, you might want to take some time to reflect on your relationship with uncertainty. As you grow more comfortable with uncertainty, you can become more able to apply those skills to your interpersonal relationships. While it might feel frustrating that each theme cannot be addressed in full before moving toward another theme, inherent in each step toward gradually shifting old patterns is the momentum toward change in other areas.

It is time to put your new self-knowledge to work!

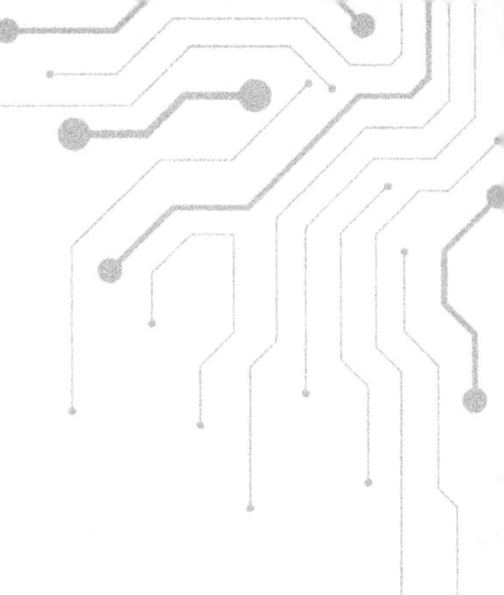

<h1 style="text-align:center">CHAPTER 16</h1>

PERFECTIONISM

WHAT DOES THE WORD "PERFECTIONISM" BRING UP? What associations does this word have? The answers to these questions are impacted by a variety of factors such as one's upbringing, interpersonal experiences, and environment. Maybe this topic even gives you pause...Take a moment to reflect: is there a part of you that feels nervous reading about this topic? And if you have a long list of ambitious goals, challenging perfectionistic tendencies might, understandably, feel threatening to success.

Perfectionism can be described as "a disposition to regard anything short of perfection as unacceptable" (Merriam-Webster, n.d.f). Our anecdotal observations of perfectionism amongst engineers clearly and consistently support that this disposition is present. A wider search of blogs and articles reveals that our observations are common. Even if you do not have a tendency for perfectionism, pressures to be perfect will likely crop up within an engineering role. It can be difficult to tease out any causal relationship; does the field attract those in pursuit of perfection, or does it shape and mold individuals into this way of being with its emphasis on eliminating errors? Perhaps it is both.

Signs of Perfectionism

- You do not view a task as finished until you deem the result perfect.

- You do not engage, or you have difficulty engaging in a task unless you are confident that you can do it perfectly (which can lead to procrastination).

- You have difficulty delegating because you cannot trust others to do a task correctly.

- It takes you significantly longer than others to complete tasks.

- You use the word "should" a lot because you follow a particular set of unspoken rules.

- You focus on the result as opposed to the process of completing a task or learning.

- You perceive your sense of worth through achievement.

- You make decisions motivated by a fear of failure.

We want to be *very* clear that the purpose of this discussion is not to pathologize high standards and achievement. In fact, our aim is quite the opposite. Studies suggest that manifestations of perfectionism are likely to prevent one from achieving higher levels of success (Dahl, 2014; Greenspon, 2014). We invite you to approach this topic with an open mind. If you feel protective of perfectionism, we encourage you to mindfully notice that experience. If you feel stuck and skeptical that anything about your relationship with perfectionism can change, observe these emotions and thoughts. And if you find yourself approaching this topic with the goal of completely and thoroughly "fixing" all of your perfectionism challenges, allow yourself to smile at the irony.

FUNCTION OF PERFECTIONISM

Instead of viewing perfectionism as "good" or "bad" (a black-or-white thinking style), let's look through the lens of function. Long-term patterns of behavior are present for a reason and often serve a purpose, regardless of whether they elicit pleasant or unpleasant emotions. In her book *Acceptance and Commitment Skills for Perfectionism and High-Achieving Behaviors,* Patricia E. Zurita Ona, PsyD (2022) explores the function of perfectionistic tendencies and humans' wiring for fear-based emotions, evasion from painful emotions, careful behaviors, and the ability to prepare for worst-case scenarios. These built-in features have one thing in common: preventing errors with the goal of survival. While all human brains are oriented to survival, different people utilize different strategies to get there. Perfectionism is one of those strategies.

In addition to nature, Zurita Ona (2022) also explores "nurture": how one's upbringing and life experiences can have a profound impact on their relationship with perfection. Humans are wired to seek attachment from a young age. When children receive messages that closeness with their caregivers can be obtained by accomplishing or achieving enough, they can perceive perfection as their ticket to life. The messaging can also be less explicit, with the caregivers displaying their own perfectionistic behaviors that they might assume go unnoticed by their children. Children are sponges, however, and merely watching a caregiver's relationship with mistakes can have a profound impact on their impressionable brains.

Perfectionistic tendencies are also rooted in human history. The human mind is primed to pay attention to what could go wrong and has been working hard to help things go right, physically, psychologically, and socially. Mistakes become a natural enemy when the mind believes that they threaten access to these needs.

Perfection is one way to attempt to meet human needs including closeness, acceptance, status, success, security, partnership, and support.

Aspects of the engineering profession can also nurture perfectionistic thinking. In our work with engineering students, we have noticed a subset of perfectionism: optimization. "Optimization" is defined by the "act, process, or methodology of making something (such as a design, system, or decision) as fully perfect, functional, or effective as possible" (Merriam-Webster, n.d.d). In other words, there is a fixation on finding the best possible solution, no matter how difficult it is or how long it takes. We have learned how important this concept is for engineers and the work they do both as a tool and as a goal in and of itself.

One of the first important applications of calculus a student learns is how to optimize a function to find its maxima and minima. Complex theoretical calculations rely on numerical methods (like gradient descent) to find optimal solutions. Algorithms are designed around decision rules like Minimax ("**min**imizing the **max**imum possible losses"). And of course, there is an entire subfield of "design optimization" that seeks to make everything from wing shapes to circuit power consumption profiles function in the absolutely best possible way.

Given the way optimization works in the engineering world, we have witnessed attempts to apply this concept to any and all decisions. For example, one of our friends, who happens to be an engineer, claims to have applied the Minimax principle to his previous romantic relationship (We don't know how that works day-to-day!) From finding a new dentist to deciding where to take a date, many of our clients spend copious amounts of time systematically searching for "perfect."

Perfectionism can also exist as a way of keeping discomfort (i.e., uncertainty, failure, judgment, shame) at bay. Perfectionistic avoidance strategies may be hidden behind labels such as "dedication" or "responsibility." For example, consider an engineer who is praised for staying on top of the latest research, frequently spendings late nights at the office completing the workload of several employees, and never turning in a report or sending an email with grammatical errors. On the surface, this employee might receive feedback that they are "going above and beyond"; they might even discover that their supervisor wants to give them a promotion.

Beneath the surface, the employee, however, could be crumbling while attempting to do everything perfectly in order to prove to others (and themselves) that they are not "stupid." They could also be trying to show others that they belong, because they cannot bear to experience the thoughts and emotions that accompany disapproval. In this example, the perfectionistic behaviors have less to do with their passion for their work and more to do with their desire to be accepted by their peers. In a results-oriented environment, it is very easy to tie outcomes to worth, perpetuating perfectionistic patterns.

DISPROPORTIONATE IMPACT

Cultural pressures related to perfectionism can also disproportionately impact underrepresented populations in engineering professions, with women engineers as one example. After all, it was not too long ago that women's employment rights were nonexistent, and unfortunately, there are stark remnants of that history embedded in the fabric of today's workplace. In her blog post titled "The Problem of Perfect: How Quality is Hurting Equality and What to Do About It," civil engineer Andi DuMont argues that "perfectionism is endemic to how girls are socialized," leading to gender gaps in confidence (DuMont, 2019). This idea is also explored by Kay and Shipman (2014), in an article in *The Atlantic,* when they comment on how women tend to feel less self-assured compared to men, despite their achievements and competence.

With a long history of exclusion and racism in STEM, Black students, too, face the demands of perfectionism far beyond their internal standards. Research shows that Black students often feel pressure to work harder than their non-Black peers in order to prove their belonging in these spaces (McGee, 2018). These external pressures are a burden and lead to "serial excelling," including a laser focus on achievement and no room for mistakes. Unfortunately, success does not guarantee that others will stop doubting their abilities.

We briefly referenced just two examples of how perfectionism can be experienced by underrepresented groups. Next, we will explore some of the ramifications of perfectionism. Keep in mind that experience of perfectionism can vary, person-to-person. We invite you to consider your own identity and life experiences and how they affect your own experience of perfectionism.

CONSEQUENCES OF PERFECTIONISM

People develop perfectionistic tendencies in an attempt to meet core human needs. And yet, the consequences of perfectionism are undeniable. To start, sometimes striving to be perfect means limiting one's goals to those which seem to guarantee success. Consequently, success can come at the cost of pursuing endeavors which are meaningful, albeit risky. The perfectionist may find themselves bored or may never discover their potential. Finding emotional safety within these limits, they could live their entire life without making significant mistakes or failing. Limiting goals in pursuit of perfection often requires the sacrifice of other values.

Sometimes perfectionists avoid tasks altogether while others wait until the last minute to complete them. In this way, the same thoughts and feelings that drive perfectionism can drive procrastination behaviors such as avoiding or delaying the work. This is often confused with laziness. However, it is not laziness or apathy that causes avoidance, but rather an attempt to cope with the stress that comes with high expectations.

Perfectionism also breaks down in assuming a "perfect" outcome. Perfection is not something that can be easily defined or measured, and outcomes that one person strives for might be completely different for another. For instance, what would a "perfect" work meeting entail? Would it mean that everyone contributes equally? Would it mean that there is time for social connection? Or perhaps, it is perfect because there is no small talk, and the focus is on the work.

To put it in the language of an engineer, a well-defined optimization problem requires an objective function to extremize. How certain are you that you can articulate a single objective function for your own personal and professional goals? And if you have more than one objective, how sure are you that these goals never conflict? The complex problems entailed by human hopes and dreams are unlikely to have Pareto-optimal solutions.

DIMINISHING RETURNS

Although living flawlessly in all areas of life is an unachievable goal, the truth is that some people seem to get pretty darn close in certain domains. Consider someone who wants to construct the "perfect email," agonizing over the greeting, tone, level of formality, periods versus exclamation points, and the perfect sign off (Does "Sincerely" sound too cliche? Is "Regards" too dry?) At the end of this process, they might look at their grammatically correct, four-sentence-long masterpiece with pride as they hit "Send." Although they did not send a final draft to *The New York Times,* did they reach their goal of crafting the perfect email? Well, sort of. There is no rubric for such an abstract opinion, and yet, they were completely satisfied with their email.

But their achievement tells only part of the story. An arguably more important question to ask in this case is, "Was it worth it?" Even if we could all agree on the anatomy of a perfect email, is perfect better than simply "good enough?" According to the law of diminishing returns, the level of additional benefits gained might not justify the amount of additional effort required.

The law of diminishing returns, traditionally used in economics, can be applied to many areas of life: an athlete's time spent training versus performance improvement, number of people working together in an escape room game versus time it takes to escape, and number of cookies consumed versus enjoyment of consuming said cookies. Over time, productivity and efficiency decrease to a point where there is less value for those efforts. At that point, more time spent is not likely to improve your email by much, if at all.

The Law of Diminishing Returns

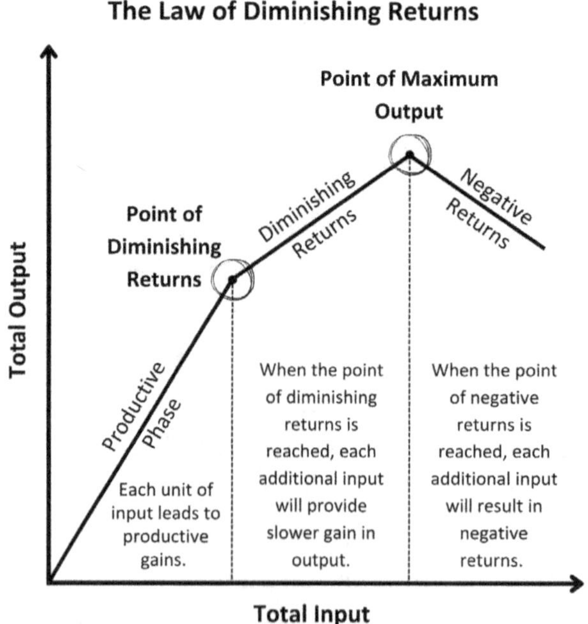

Take a moment to reflect: if you struggle with perfectionism, can you think of times your efforts reached a point where your resources were no longer efficiently utilized? Maybe it was an all-nighter to review four practice exams. You later realized you could probably have stopped studying after the second practice exam without losing much knowledge. If you could have gained the same results after practicing less than half the time, was it worth the additional effort?

The phenomenon of diminishing returns often shows up in engineering spaces given the field's emphasis on quality. The nature and pressure of the work—often involving public and environmental safety—naturally pulls engineers towards perfection. DuMont states, "To sooth our anxiety with this uncertainty, we develop an auto-pilot response to over-analyze and ruminate on the problem, a tenant of perfectionism. It's become an industry-revered analytical response to an emotional problem" (DuMont, 2019).

While approaching projects in a meticulous manner can be rewarding, even necessary, it can also be costly if the details are unimportant. Not only can this drive for quality and perfectionism sacrifice productivity and result in diminishing returns, but it is also possible to creep closer to reaching a point of *negative* returns on resources. When this happens, additional increase in input leads to a decrease in output. In this case, spending all night attempting to memorize terms could backfire when, the next day, your sleep-deprived brain has difficulty accessing all of the information you attempted to cram into it.

Another consequence of perfection is that it requires sacrificing the time that could be devoted to other important things. As we've mentioned previously, an employee who is considered to be going "above and beyond," consistently keeping up with research, frequently spending late nights at the office, and always sending perfect emails, is making a huge investment of time. Everyone has the same number of hours in a day; the only difference is how they choose to spend them. So, let's take a moment to consider what this employee is not doing when they are maintaining this rigorous routine. The consistent effort toward perfection likely requires sacrificing some of their time for hobbies, self-reflection, and connection.

Alison writing here: let's talk about how connection can sometimes be at odds with perfectionism. When I had been fighting a cold, I was also meeting a client for the first time, and they were expressing to me that they were feeling self-conscious and embarrassed about the challenges they were going through (Of course, I cannot and will not provide any details about this client or their challenges. These details are not relevant anyway; what is relevant here is my own experience during our first session.) In this session, I found myself speaking ... a lot. Attempting to be the perfect therapist, I tried to put them at ease and communicate that my office is a safe, judgment-free zone. When I perceived that my approach was not helping, I spoke more. I searched and searched for the perfect words to say, hoping that I could help them feel more comfortable.

About halfway through the session, all of this talking caught up with me. My throat started feeling scratchy, which caused me to cough. I reached for my water and gulped it down. Somehow this only made things worse. Soon, I was in a full-on coughing fit. And then...silence. I lost my voice completely. But that didn't keep me from trying to speak! With each attempt, nothing came out except for what can only be described as croaks interspersed with a high-pitched squeaking sound.

As my client and I locked eyes, I shrugged my shoulders and conceded my defeat. With a pen and piece of paper, I scribbled, "Now I'm the one who's feeling embarrassed." At that moment, we both burst out in laughter and arranged a different time to meet. My client, now looking relaxed, thanked me and left my office. As I sat there, I was stunned by the irony of trying to connect with my client by saying and doing all of the "right" things as a mental health professional, only to find that real, genuine connection occurred when we shared a moment of imperfection.

AN ALTERNATIVE APPROACH

Before we dive into alternatives to perfectionistic behaviors, we want to highlight the importance of context. There are forces—interpersonally, societally, and globally—out of our control when it comes to professional expectations. Perfectionism can be a pragmatic response to the work environment. Supervisors, advisors, or colleagues can demand flawless work, complicated by the presence of challenging power dynamics. For some engineers, the stakes are as high as they can get, perhaps even with human lives relying on the quality of their work. In such cases, we are not suggesting that you do anything to jeopardize safety or success. You know your situation best, and we encourage you to use your own judgment as you apply your new skills. Context is important, and approaching every situation in the same way is like using the same formula for different problems.

Perfectionism inherently requires drive, dedication, and resilience, all qualities that generate excellence. So, what exactly is the goal? To live a life without these qualities? Changing your relationship with perfection does not mean giving up on the qualities that have led to success. In fact, the goal is to honor those qualities even more by being mindful of your time and energy. Focusing effort on what *truly* matters conserves the resources to live a life aligned with personal values.

EXERCISE: PERFECTIONISM REFLECTION

Take some time to reflect on how changing your relationship with perfectionism might serve you. If you were to loosen your grip on perfection, what might you have more time and energy for? How might your life look different?

Considering Your Values

Examining values is an important starting place in reassessing a relationship with perfectionism. We can be pulled in all kinds of directions if unclear about what we care about. Chasing perfectionism by running from failure could mean ending up in an unintended, random place. We might even reach an impressive destination, but if that destination is not based on our own values, we can end up prioritizing some else's values over our own. Sorting out values can help bring clarity surrounding decisions and behaviors, whether they are driven by perfectionism or personally meaningful principles.

Further, values *can* inform our priorities and time management; but because there is only so much time and energy available in a day, treating every task as equal (extending the same amount of effort regardless of importance or urgency) will only lead to frustration and defeat. For example, attempting to achieve complete perfection in a slide deck might leave less time for drafting a grant proposal, a grant that might allow research aligned with the value of sustainability.

How can you determine when to trade perfection for excellence? If you are working on a high-priority project, based on your values, you might hold off on other projects (if possible) until it is completed. You might need to communicate your needs to a supervisor. Or you might make a change outside of work or school, such as saving time and energy by eating takeout. Small changes can add up quickly!

Keep in mind that priorities need not be stagnant. As circumstances change, priorities can shift from month to month, week to week, and day to day. For instance, priorities might be centered on an urgent safety task, and the next week, work pressures lift to allow refocusing on family and friends. Connection and safety are both values. These priorities, informed by those values, are flexible within a changing context. Clarity and flexibility within changing contexts can help to set priorities and to practice intentional imperfection.

Exchanging Perfectionism for Productivity

Both productivity and quality are important in engineering, yet these factors can be at odds with one another. According to the phenomenon of diminishing returns, you then might ask, "What actions can I take to have the greatest impact?" Often "good enough" is better than perfect. Unfortunately, it is not always clear when good enough is acceptable. When unsure about external expectations, we suggest speaking to a supervisor or colleague about discerning which tasks require perfection versus a "good enough" effort.

This discernment is only the beginning. The shift to doing what is good enough requires willingness to experience the uncomfortable emotions that arise while loosening the grip on perfection. These emotions are not a sign that something is wrong. Instead, they are a sign of doing something different. In order to understand and respond effectively to these emotions, refer to the Emotion Decompiler:

The Emotion Decompiler

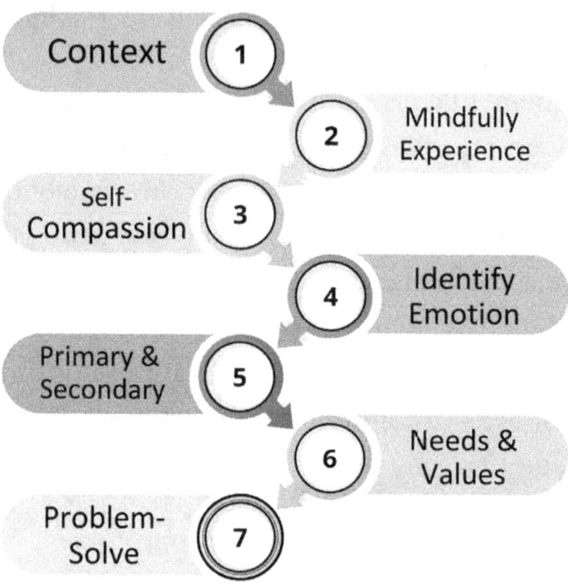

Considering the Impact of Cognitive Distortions

We all experience thoughts that can impact how we view the world. As you may recall from the Decompiling Thoughts section, the thoughts themselves are neither good nor bad. They are just thoughts. When unchecked, however, we can interpret thoughts as ultimate truths and make decisions based on them. "Should statements," a type of cognitive distortion, are common for those with perfectionistic tendencies. Should statements involve thoughts, beliefs or ideas which include words like "should" and "need to" to indicate some type of personal rule to follow. Rules for yourself might also include extremes such as "always" or "never" (black-or-white thinking).

Imagine writing a paper and having the familiar thought "I should finish this section before I stop writing." Let's say that this is how you have always approached your writing. But maybe this rule does not make sense that day. Imagine already being late to dinner with friends, having run out of mental and creative energy and being so hungry that your mind continues to wander thinking about food. Taking this "should" thought literally could leave you feeling frustrated as you push yourself to write under impossible conditions. The quality of the writing will likely suffer. You might even end up missing dinner!

Stepping back and noticing the thought "I should finish this section before I stop" through a lens of cognitive defusion gives you an opportunity to pause before you decide how to move forward. In fact, you probably do not need to finish a whole section every time, and taking a break might generate more momentum later, allowing you to approach it with a renewed sense of energy.

Noticing thoughts with cognitive defusion can help you recognize when cognitive distortions are arising. From there, continuing the decompilation of thoughts can allow you to make decisions based on your underlying needs and values. This process can help you decide what challenge to take on. Sometimes the more disciplined behavior (such as deviating from an ingrained habit or pattern of behavior) looks like a less disciplined one (such as taking a break).

EXERCISE: DECOMPILING PERFECTIONISM

Try the following steps to decompile perfectionism.

1. Consider thoughts and rules related to perfectionism (e.g., I should always be on time; If I don't overdeliver, I'm underdelivering; I can never make mistakes; I need

to always have the answer; I can't start a task unless I know exactly what I'm doing). Identify any cognitive distortions among them.

2. Take a few minutes to practice mindfully noticing these thoughts using the skill of cognitive defusion, observing thoughts without taking them literally, as if they were characters on a movie screen. Set a timer for between two and ten minutes to engage in this mindfulness activity.

3. After mindfully noticing these thoughts, reflect on their function(s) and what they say about underlying needs. For instance, what need might the brain be trying to meet (perhaps connection, belonging, being seen), or what might the brain be trying to protect against (maybe shame or embarrassment)?

4. Reflect on other, more effective ways to get this need met. If the mind is trying to protect against challenging emotions, consider the underlying values and what it might look like to willingly experience thoughts and emotions while moving toward what matters.

VIGNETTE

DeAndre, an industrial engineer, recently graduated and started a new job at a well-known company. As a graduate of a prestigious university with several awards and research publications behind him, DeAndre is eager to show his team and supervisor his capabilities. But after just three months, DeAndre finds himself extremely stressed, exhausted, and anxious. He looks around at others with amazement, wondering how some of his colleagues can appear to be so calm. While unsure of what exactly is going on, he knows that he needs some type of support, or he will not be able to stay at this job much longer.

DeAndre meets with his friend Ramona, who has been in the industry for a long time and once had a similar role. As DeAndre describes his daily workload, feelings of overwhelm, and anxiety surrounding the tasks he needs to complete, Ramona immediately recognizes DeAndre's perfectionistic tendencies. In particular, Ramona notices DeAndre's "should statements" and the rigid sets of rules he has established for himself. According to DeAndre, he "should always" answer emails within two hours as he wants to be a dependable colleague, even though the expectation from the company is 24 hours. He "needs" to be the last one to leave the office each day to show his supervisor that he cares about his job. DeAndre also "should" eat his lunch at his desk to maximize productivity.

Ramona provides DeAndre with feedback that it seems he's following the rule "Not over-delivering is underdelivering." At first DeAndre is taken aback as he believes he has simply been trying to do good work and make a good impression. The more he thinks about it, though, the more he recognizes additional, personally held rules he has for himself. When Ramona and DeAndre discuss ways his perfectionistic rules have impacted him, DeAndre confesses that he has recently been considering quitting his job. Given his stress and mental exhaustion, DeAndre worries he is going to drop the ball soon and does not want others to see him fail. He does not want to see himself fail.

DeAndre is not familiar with cognitive defusion. Ramona

explains how the self is separate from thoughts, and how noticing this separation can create room to make decisions. DeAndre takes a moment to imagine his should statements typed out on a movie screen, a screen to which he can give his attention and from which he can turn away. The two engineers discuss the function of DeAndre's thoughts and rules. DeAndre discovers that behind his perfectionism lies a desire to be seen. Having grown up with six siblings, throughout his childhood he constantly had to fight for moments of one-on-one connection with his parents. When he was in middle school, his parents took notice of his impeccable grades and praise from teachers. DeAndre was labeled "gifted." He quickly discovered that the more he achieved, the more praise and time he received from his parents. DeAndre realizes that at this new job, he has been hoping to receive similar praise and time with leadership of this company.

Ramona suggested that DeAndre take some time to think about how he can be more flexible with his rules. For starters, DeAndre reflects on how he can practice cognitive defusion throughout his workday during times of stress. Now that he recognizes his cognitive distortions, he can pause before making reactive decisions based on those distortions. DeAndre considers that his need underlying these perfectionistic beliefs is connection. Based on the recognition of this need, DeAndre considers more effective ways to meet this need, pledging to slow down just a bit and try to get to know his colleagues. He plans to start by inviting his officemate to lunch instead of eating at his desk.

SUMMARY

Engineers are some of the most determined, hard working people we know. Throughout this chapter, we hope to have conveyed our desire to support excellence and the pursuit of your passions. Attempting to cope with uncomfortable thoughts and emotions with perfectionistic behaviors likely takes you further away from what matters. Decompiling thoughts and emotions, to better understand what is most important, promotes decision-making consistent with your personal needs and values.

CHAPTER 17

CONNECTION

ALL HUMANS NEED CONNECTION AND, UNFORTUNATE-
ly, all humans experience barriers to this need from time to time.
Connection and related interpersonal skills include so many
subtopics, including conflict management, intercultural communication, self-advocacy, intimate relationships, and supervisory
skills. Given this, we acknowledge that interpersonal connection
is a vast topic that cannot be fully addressed within the context
of this book. Here, we will offer a bird's-eye perspective on what
we have observed.

Joanna Burchfield, PhD and April Kedrowicz, PhD (2023)
argue that instilling skills which support connection is an important part of preparing engineers for the workforce, as well as
a means of enabling them to meet the growing demand for civic
engagement. Despite the significance of these skills, engineering
curriculums in higher education tend to neglect the development
of interpersonal skills (Willmot & Colman, 2016).

Often the concerns that clients share at the start of therapy are
different from the concerns that emerge over time. For instance,
an engineering student may seek support for procrastination
and low motivation. Through unpacking those concerns, the
deeper, more impactful concern might be revealed as a lack of

self-confidence. While their self-doubt presents as procrastination and avoidance of the work, the emphasis in therapy becomes addressing low self-confidence in addition to finding strategies to get the work done.

Loneliness and a lack of connection are exceedingly common underlying concerns that arise through the therapeutic process. Even if our clients are not initially aware of how their symptoms relate to a lack of connection, deepening relationships often becomes foundational to the clinical goals. To be clear, these are not engineering-specific concerns. Loneliness is a concern confronted by all disciplines and was determined by US Surgeon General Vivek Murthy, MD (2023) to be an epidemic. In this chapter, we will review the importance of connection, what it can look like when it is lacking, and how the skills of this book can be applied to developing more effective connection.

FUNCTION OF CONNECTION

It makes sense that the need for connection often shows up in therapeutic space, because from an evolutionary perspective, connection is vitally important. Humans, like many other mammals, evolved to need social connection and community as a basis for survival. Living in community with others increased early humans' ability to get their basic needs met. When working together, hunters were able to go after larger animals and could more effectively fend off predators. In fact, predators were less likely to attack large groups of people in the first place. Ultimately, there was—and continues to be—strength and safety in numbers. Due to the necessity of connection, many emotions are relationally-based, including embarrassment, shame, and guilt. The function of these emotions is to motivate humans to build and maintain community.

In the modern world, most humans no longer rely on hunter-gatherer communities of one hundred or so people to get by. Assuming that they can access them, technology and delivery services exist that can fulfill many survival needs that were formally met by the tribe. This modern infrastructure leads people to believe (erroneously) that they do not need others, or at least that they do not need others in the way that was necessary for most of human existence.

While humans technically might not need community to meet *immediate* practical needs such as food and shelter, human psychology continues to be oriented around relationships with others. In fact, Harlow (1958) demonstrated the importance of physical connection relative to the basic need of food, with an experiment that, though it would not pass muster with today's ethical review boards, was striking in its findings. In his study, monkeys were socially isolated. Two surrogate mothers were manufactured—one with soft sponge rubber and terry cloth, and another made of wire which offered milk. When the monkeys were allowed to choose which surrogate to spend their time with, the soft surrogate was preferred. The manufactured mother with milk was visited briefly, but the monkeys spent most of their time with the soft surrogate. While the milk is a biological need for these monkeys, their preference for the soft mother illuminated the crucial nature of physical bonding.

Because interpersonal connection is no longer necessary to immediately meet daily needs (e.g., food, warmth, or water), for many, it is not always obvious when a lack of connection becomes a problem. A client might describe feeling depressed or anxious early in the therapeutic work. Identifying the feeling of loneliness often takes longer to recognize. A vague sense of malaise might take over, but, because their immediate physical needs are met, it is often not clear that the malaise is related to their lack of connection.

Despite the lack of conscious awareness regarding the impact of disconnection, research shows how a lack of connection continues to be a significant detriment to long-term human survival (lack of saber-tooth tigers notwithstanding). In 2010, a team of scientists performed a meta-analysis by carefully parsing the statistics on social isolation in 148 different studies, comprising data from over 300,000 studied individuals (Holt-Lunstad, 2010). The combined power of the analysis allowed them to carefully control for things like age, sex, geography, prior health conditions, and more. What the researchers found was unmistakable: not only was social isolation strongly associated with early mortality, but it was also actually more significant in predicting an early demise than factors like obesity and physical inactivity. On the whole, they found that having adequate social connections improved one's odds of survival from year to year by about the same amount as quitting a smoking habit.

Subsequent research continues to bolster the assertion of human connection as a vital part of human health. A more recent study in 2015 found a potential association between social isolation and a lowered immune system which creates vulnerability to disease and viruses (Hawkley & Capitania, 2015). Researchers have also discovered a link between isolation and up to a 30% increased chance of heart disease and stroke (Valtorta et al., 2016). While connection is not always necessary to meet practical daily demands, it is a key biological need.

COPING WITH A LACK OF CONNECTION

Human brains creatively work hard to try to protect us from pain and to meet needs. This is especially true when experiencing loneliness, an emotion that, as we've shared, is often not consciously recognized. Rather than recognizing the signs of loneliness and responding with behaviors that go straight to the source and directly address the needs for connection and community, many find indirect methods of coping. In code repositories, for example, sometimes dozens of programmers have, over the years, piled more and more creative patches onto a buggy substructure, because no one has had the time to sit down and address the real underlying weaknesses in the code. Unfortunately, in life as in software, these indirect methods of coping often just end up making things more unstable and unmanageable and may ultimately exacerbate the issue.

Of course, methods vary based on personalities, context, upbringing, and beliefs that have been adopted regarding what fosters connection. Consider some examples of strategies we have observed while working with engineers. If you do not relate to the examples listed, that does not mean that the brain is not pursuing indirect methods for connection. It might instead mean that the brain is quite creative, and you might be engaging in completely different methods!

Examples of indirect methods to connection include:

- **"If I am perfect, I'll be accepted."** Some clients we work with express exceedingly high expectations of themselves. They exhibit a lot of self-criticism and do not allot room for mistakes. On the surface, these clients often come to therapy because they want to do "better" and are frustrated by their perceived personal limitations. These clients hold the (typically unconscious) belief that avoiding mistakes will lead to acceptance (connection) and making mistakes will lead to rejection (separation). They hold themselves to a high standard in order to evade both self-criticism and criticism from others. For these clients, efforts toward perfectionism are indirect attempts to receive and maintain connection. After seeking solutions to

improve their performance, their deeply rooted need
for belonging and acceptance is later recognized.

- **"If I achieve, I will be liked."** These clients describe
  high ambitions. They might not expect perfection, but
  they have career and personal ambitions that are at the
  core of their identity. Often, their presenting concerns
  might be stress, anxiety, and burnout. They might also
  express despair that a certain goal was not met. In
  working with clients to understand what is feeding this
  ambition, the belief that achievement earns connection
  is unveiled. Perhaps, as children, they gained
  acceptance from others for performing well on an exam
  or in a soccer game. On the surface, their ambition is
  attributed to their passion for the field or their value
  of hard work. While their hard work and passion are
  authentic, it is also true that their need for connection
  is attached to their predilection for achievement.

- **"If I suppress my needs, I won't be a burden to
  others."** Many of our clients have a difficult time
  accessing emotion and possibly pride themselves on
  their logical disposition. They might voice a concern
  that expressing emotion is a burden to others, and
  therefore, maintain a stoic presentation that conveys
  self-reliance. They often describe having a difficult time
  asking for help or expressing vulnerability, as they fear
  that they will be perceived as weak or needy. Over time,
  their loneliness becomes clearer, and they realize that
  they have been trying to maintain connection through
  logic and emotional independence.

Embedded in each of these examples are amazing traits and
authentic values, such as challenging oneself, attention to detail,
ambition, hard work, stoicism or stability, and self-responsi-
bility. In recognizing the importance of each of these traits, it
is also beneficial to understand how these traits might be used

as indirect attempts at connection. Whatever one's profession, doubling down on certain aspects of one's personality to try to foster connection can be ineffective. While these strategies are likely helpful to some degree in fostering belonging, they quickly become convoluted and miss the mark on connection that is deeply meaningful and authentic.

Although it can be surprising to realize that identity is often related to the need for connection, connection is a core source of human motivation. Referring back to the evolutionary function of connection, it makes sense that this need for support and belonging is central to much of what people do. That said, we encourage you to use self-compassion skills if any self-criticism or painful emotions arise as you consider ways you have indirectly pursued connection.

EXERCISE: CONNECTION

Consider the following prompts about ways that you might be indirectly seeking connection. Please keep in mind that these questions might be overwhelming to reflect on all at once. When reviewing the question, if you are outside of the Window of Tolerance and feeling overwhelmed, or if you experience any sense of dysregulation (i.e., panic, numbness, despair, and so on), we encourage you to revisit the prompts when you are within your window. This will help to regulate the emotions that arise (i.e., noticing the sensations, taking deep breaths, naming the emotions, exhibiting self-compassion). It might also be useful to review the questions with a trusted therapist, close friend, or loved one who can provide support and emotional regulation.

1. What parts of my personality do I like?

2. What parts of my personality do I try to hide from others?

3. What traits do I strive for in myself?

4. What messages did I receive in childhood about what fosters belonging and acceptance?

5. Based on your responses to the first four questions, what are some ways you might be trying to indirectly foster connection? This insight often takes time to unpack, so it's okay if you do not have clear answers right away.

6. In what ways are these attempts effective in fostering connection? In what ways are these attempts ineffective?

ALTERNATIVE WAYS TO FIND CONNECTION

When considering how to move forward in a way that fosters connection and more meaningful interpersonal relationships, the skills in the first two sections of this book are building blocks to relate better to others. The more knowledge you have about your internal experience and how to effectively respond, the more you can incorporate these skills into your relationships. In the following segments, we will elaborate on how some of the skills covered in the first two sections can be applied to building connections with others.

Decompile Emotions

Building and maintaining relationships can be challenging. Whether it is a relationship with a coworker, a friend, or a spouse, navigating communication and differences will inevitably bring up a range of emotions. As emotions are a source of data about one's needs, processing and identifying the function of emotion can help get those needs met. Responding to an emotion using the Emotion Decompiler can help with regulation. After mindfully experiencing the sensations tied to the emotion, responding with self-compassion, identifying the emotion, and considering whether it is a primary or secondary emotion, you can become curious about the function of the emotion(s).

The Emotion Decompiler

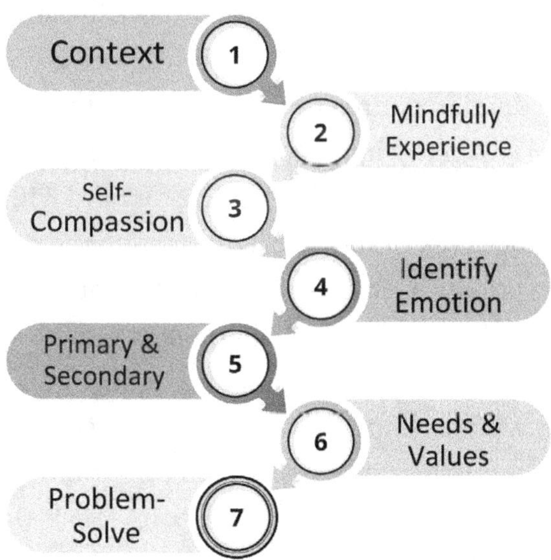

The Functions of Emotions table and the Identifying Needs table in Chapter 3 can help you deepen your understanding of your emotional experience. Next is problem-solving. For instance, the emotion of guilt (as a primary emotion) might signal a need to repair the relationship. If so, you can problem-solve ways to mend the relationship and possibly apologize.

While the emotion of guilt feels unpleasant, feeling it and being curious supports approaching the relationship in a way that can serve the emotional needs and the relationship itself. In another case, anger might be a primary emotion. In this case, the Emotion Decompiler can point to ways to meet the needs reflected in anger. Often, anger is a body cue that a boundary needs to be set. After riding the wave of emotion, problem-solving can then be used to create effective methods for boundary setting.

Consider the Context

Consider the context before completing the Emotion Decompiler. Just as processing and expressing emotions is not effective in all contexts, context also matters when considering when and how to deepen relationships. Considering the level of trust is important to deepen connection while protecting both parties. For instance, *gradually* increasing vulnerability is a necessary skill for meaningful connection; moving forward with caution is wise. Vulnerability that is not met with compassion and respect can be quite harmful, so it is important to be mindful when self-disclosing. Consider both the audience and the appropriate level of vulnerability. Vulnerability always includes risk, as we cannot know with certainty how the other person will respond. Self-protection involves disclosing with intentionality.

Considering the person(s) and their previously demonstrated compassion and understanding can also help increase the chances that your vulnerability will be received with kindness. For instance, consider if they have shown openness and kindness to others. Alternatively, perhaps they gossip about and judge their peers. Also, consider the vulnerability level of the content. On a scale from one to ten, how sensitive does the content feel? Perhaps a "10" is your deepest secret, and it would feel extremely painful if others did not respond well. A "2" might be nerve-wracking, but you could recover if the other person did not respond well. The first attempts of vulnerability with a new person may begin with a "2" on the vulnerability scale. Over time, as trust builds, meaningful connection can be established by gradually raising the vulnerability level. Again, if the person responds with judgment, disrespect, or nonacceptance, pausing the practice of vulnerability is wise.

Cognitive Distortions that Affect Connection

Cognitive distortions automatically arise as a means of efficiency and safety. Given that connection is a core human need, these thought patterns often revolve around understanding others. When cognitive distortions impact your perceptions of others, there is a risk of making decisions in relationships based on those distortions. The distortion of "mind reading," for instance, might convince you that you know a person's intention, when in reality, there are likely several possible explanations for an action. Jumping to the conclusion that a person's action derives from hurtful intent will harm the connection. While it is sensible to approach deepening vulnerability and connection with caution, it is also important to consider your own "lens" and the beliefs that might get in the way.

Black-or-white thinking is another cognitive distortion that often arises when learning about others. For example, categorizing someone as a "good" or "bad" person can bring relief, as the mind no longer needs to sort through the complexity of human nature. However, categorizing others in these boxes limits curiosity about the other and blocks openness to the possibility that the relationship could change or deepen.

We want to emphasize that these cognitive distortions are normal. It is possible to both experience cognitive distortions *and* to make decisions in relationships that challenge these filters of thinking. Decompiling your thoughts and building awareness of cognitive distortions can allow you to notice them when they arise. We encourage you to consider how these distortions have shown up for you previously. Noticing these thoughts with cognitive defusion can allow you to experience them without being controlled by them.

EXERCISE: COGNITIVE DISTORTIONS AND CONNECTION

Try the following steps and observe the benefits.

1. Identify a recent social interaction in which you experienced discomfort.

2. Thinking about that experience, complete Steps One through Five of the Emotion Decompiler to unpack the feelings and identify a primary emotion. If the initial emotion is a secondary emotion, repeat Steps One through Five to identify and/or focus on the primary emotion beneath the secondary emotion.

The Emotion Decompiler

Context — 1

2 — Mindfully Experience

Self-Compassion — 3

4 — Identify Emotion

Primary & Secondary — 5

6 — Needs & Values

Problem-Solve — 7

3. Reflect on what cognitive distortions might arise while making sense of the situation.

4. Return to the Emotion Decompiler to complete Steps Six and Seven.

VIGNETTE

Leilani considers a recent interaction with her coworker, Miranda, who offered her advice on a work problem. While Leilani is not sure what emotions were present at the time, she recognizes that she felt "weird." Leilani takes time to complete Steps One through Five of the Emotion Decompiler. Leilani decides to wait until after work in order to give herself space to effectively process her emotions. She mindfully experiences the sensations arising in her body. She notices thoughts and redirects her attention toward the sensations in her body. While Leilani has a tendency to be self-critical, she practices self-compassion by reminding herself that experiencing uncomfortable emotions in relationships is human.

Using the Emotion Decompiler, Leilani identifies the emotion of anger. She feels angry that Miranda offered unsolicited advice. When exploring whether this anger is a primary or secondary emotion, Leilani reviews the Feeling Wheel to see if any other emotions resonate for her. In this process, Leilani recognizes that the emotion "envy" stands out to her and realizes that she feels envy toward Miranda, who is a talented engineer and never seems to struggle. Leilani repeats Steps One through Five, focusing on envy.

Leilani then considers which cognitive distortions might be arising. Leilani notices the thought "Miranda thinks I am stupid." Reviewing the list of cognitive distortions, Leilani considers that this thought is likely an example of mindreading, assuming she knows what Miranda is thinking.

Leilani returns to the Emotion Decompiler to complete Steps Six and Seven. While considering the function of envy, she is initially stumped. How can this feeling be helpful? She decides to speak to a trusted friend to help her unpack what envy might be trying to do for her. In that conversation, she realizes that her envy helps her understand what she wants; Leilani admires Miranda's talent and wants to develop that competency. Given this, Leilani identifies that she needs support and resources to help her build her competence.

After giving it some thought, Leilani recognizes that asking Miranda for support could actually be a solution. Considering the context of the existing relationship with Miranda, Leilani determines that it is appropriate to invite her to coffee in order to ask her follow-up questions about the advice. In addition to building her engineering skills by working with Miranda, she can also enhance her connection with her coworker. While the initial "weird" feeling Leilani experienced might have led her to avoid connection with Miranda, processing it in this way allows her to feel more connected at work and increase her competency.

SUMMARY

Given the importance that connection had in the survival of early humans, it makes sense that the need for interpersonal support persists today. While the environment in which humans access community looks different in modern times, it is nonetheless necessary to meet this human need for psychological well-being. Using the emotion and thought skills in this book serves as a foundation for building, maintaining, and deepening your connection with others.

Considering the function of emotions to better meet your needs, considering the context of the relationship, and building insight into cognitive distortions are all skills that can contribute to the quality of relationships. Just as developing skills to recognize and respond to emotional and cognitive distress occurs on a learning curve, the same is true for the development of interpersonal skills.

We encourage self-compassion and patience while building these skills and deepening connections with others. Changing neurological patterns related to interpersonal relationships is not easy; however, each additional pathway creates access to new, future ways of relating.

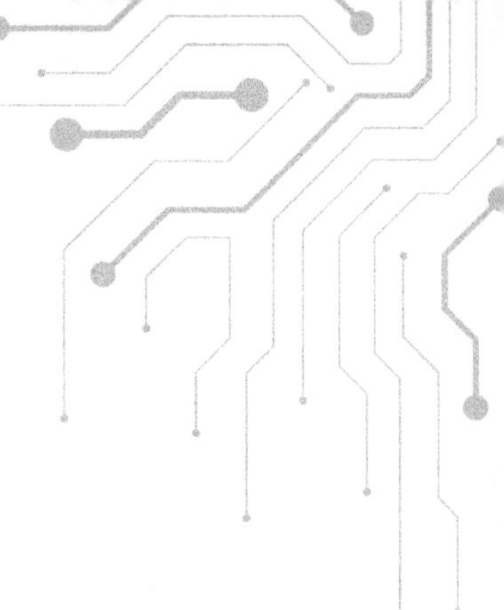

CHAPTER 18

UNCERTAINTY

OUR CLIENTS BRING CONCERNS TO THERAPY SUCH AS procrastination, romantic relationship struggles, and persistent ruminations. We work hard to support clients and address whatever concerns are most impactful. Part of our support includes considering ways that they can improve their immediate circumstances. Another part of this process is to build insight into deeper, underlying concerns.

In the previous chapter, we discussed how the need for connection is one of these common underlying concerns. Another underlying concern that often arises is difficulty tolerating and navigating uncertainty. Uncertainty is embedded in a range of areas, including career, academics, health, family, financial well-being, and relationships. Naturally, the discomfort of uncertainty tends to arise around the things of most importance.

While the discomfort of uncertainty is a human experience and not unique to engineers, we have noticed that engineers have a unique perspective. Many are tasked with decreasing uncertainty in their day-to-day work. For example, they are responsible for increasing the certainty that a device or code will work as intended and reduce the chance of undesired outcomes. Accepting uncertainty in these roles can be dangerous and can

283

even result in safety and liability issues, so it is imperative that they work to minimize uncertainty as much as possible. In other words, fighting uncertainty is both productive and rewarded.

While engineers must remain vigilant at work, carefully detecting uncertainty in order to increase consistent outcomes, applying this same vigilance to uncertainty in other areas of life is often associated with increased distress and mental health symptoms. According to Boswell et al. (2013), there is a positive correlation between the intolerance of uncertainty and depressive symptoms, worry, panic disorder, and Generalized Anxiety Disorder (GAD). Just as the avoidance of painful experiences is associated with an increase in distress, the same is true of the unwillingness to experience uncertainty. Engineers' capacity to solve and prevent uncertainty serves them extremely well in their work, but this same skill, when applied to their wellness and personal lives, can have the opposite effect.

Added to the mixed messages about the usefulness of "fixing" uncertainty are the beliefs that surround it. For some, uncertainty can be interpreted as a sign of insufficiency. Others might view it as a personal failure. Interpreting uncertainty as failing can add layers of self-blame and self-doubt. In that case, not only is the person experiencing fear of the unknown, but also layers of shame, guilt, or anxiety. If they perceive the uncertainty as their fault, rather than perceiving it as an inevitable experience of being human, uncertainty becomes an especially painful experience.

FUNCTIONS AND THE IMPACTS OF THE MODERN WORLD

Like the need for connection, physical safety is a core human need. Emotions such as guilt, shame, and love are oriented to motivate the creation and maintenance of connection, whereas emotions including fear, anxiety, and anger function to create physical safety. Fear drives us to react and protect ourselves in times of imminent threat, anxiety pushes us to prepare and prevent potential future dangers, and anger allows us to guard against someone threatening either ourselves or our resources.

When it comes to safety, uncertainty is a liability. Uncertainty about our next meal or where we will sleep signals that our safety needs are at risk. Human emotions that arise in response to this risk are necessary to motivate action that helps achieve safety. When safety is on the line, feeling comfortable or content is not the body's priority; emotions that arise in response to safety risks typically do not feel "good." Human brains, then, are wired to underestimate their capacity to handle uncertainty and to overestimate the level of threat that is associated with the uncertainty, as a function of survival.

One research study demonstrates this very phenomenon. The experiment involved 45 volunteers participating in a computer game which evoked varying levels of uncertainty. In the game, participants were tasked with guessing whether or not there were snakes under rocks before turning them over (de Berker et al., 2016). When snakes were present, they received an electric shock. As time went on, participants learned which rocks were more likely to have snakes under them. However, these odds changed throughout the game, causing the degree of uncertainty to fluctuate throughout the study.

As they played, researchers measured the participants' level of stress by tracking their perspiration and pupil dilation (de Berker et al., 2016). Their observations allowed them to predict the participants' stress response to both the shocks and the uncertainty the participants experienced when they were not sure if they would receive a shock. The study revealed that people had a greater stress response when they felt *uncertain* about whether or not they would receive a shock versus knowing a shock was coming.

In the modern, complex world, uncertainty isn't just tied to our immediate surroundings; the global view expands the awareness and impact of uncertainty. In addition to exposure to world news—which often highlights uncertainties such as elections, international war, climate change, and supply chain struggles—we've seen how the world has become increasingly interdependent. This increased interdependence means it is not only local officials, family members, and neighbors that impact safety; people on the other side of the world can have an effect. An election abroad, the manufacturing process for an imported food product, or international policies around sustainable energy are all examples of how global interdependence can impact us and our safety.

The modern unknowns and reliance on global systems for safety and resources mean that more aspects of safety and uncertainty are outside of the individual's control, at least compared to an early human ancestor. Of course, early humans also experienced factors outside their control, such as finding prey or receiving rainfall. However, these factors occurred in their immediate environments and were typically temporary. (Eventually it would rain, and eventually they would catch prey.) On this smaller scale, acting on the instincts that accompanied their anxiety was reasonably effective. Anxiety would drive them to take action on what they could control: preparing, planning, and conserving resources. These actions were useful for temporary periods of time, until the transient uncertainty passed, and the emotion of relief washed the anxiety away.

COPING WITH UNCERTAINTY

In the modern world, where many uncertainties are chronic and evolving, relying on instinctual urges which accompany anger, fear, and anxiety is not sufficient. The anxiety that comes with dangerous international conflicts or a political battle tells the body to act, yet actions taken at an individual level will rarely resolve the uncertainty at the global level. Emotions such as anger, anxiety, and fear might motivate individual actions such as voting, donating, and advocating for a cause. These individual actions are often consistent with one's values, but they will not end the uncertainty that is so pervasive in the global world. The resulting stress of persistent uncertainty can be exhausting and unsustainable. While the human mind is wired to handle this stress for short periods, the mind is less equipped to effectively cope when uncertainty is everlasting. When uncertainty is chronic, the mind needs to find alternative ways to cope.

One way the mind copes with prolonged uncertainty is by redirecting the anxiety and fear to helplessness and apathy. This response is natural and logical; if anxiety is not working, try something else! In part, helplessness and apathy are productive as they help preserve one's energy when the energy of anxiety is not leading to relief. While these emotions can help the mind achieve a reprieve from prolonged anxiety and stress, they can also remove the motivation to take values-based action.

Sometimes, the mind copes by attempting to achieve certainty indirectly. As people often subconsciously attempt to meet their need for connection through indirect actions (such as pursuing perfection, accomplishments, and emotional independence), the same is true for safety and certainty. For instance, someone might attempt to reach an anxiety-free future by focusing on achievement. There is sometimes a subconscious belief that meeting a particular level of accomplishment will remove all psychological pain. Focusing on building wealth or extensively preparing or researching can actually be attempts to avoid uncertainty. While these indirect methods help one to remain motivated and to avoid feelings of helplessness and apathy, they are based on illusions. Being successful, knowledgeable, exceedingly prepared, or wealthy, does not mean that you can avoid the uncomfortable emotions tied to uncertainty.

Another illusion that can arise is the denial of uncertainty or possible future danger. Have you ever met a young, healthy person who believed they were indestructible? Perhaps you, yourself, are that person! If you have never experienced significant health concerns, it makes sense that you might struggle to imagine that your youth and health are not guaranteed. While it is likely not helpful to obsess about every possible illness, a lack of awareness of mortality does not make one immortal.

An especially risky coping method is the reliance on extremist groups. Hogg et al. (2013) discuss the relationship between the presence of uncertainty and motivation to identify with extremist groups. When uncertainty is overwhelming, deferring to groups that promise to provide concrete, uncomplicated answers to the world's problems is tempting. A sense of belonging and clarity can come from these groups, even if their outlook is based in illusion. Confirmation bias can strengthen individuals' beliefs and adherence to these groups. Of course, like many coping methods, this approach is a subconscious process.

EXERCISE: UNCERTAINTY

Consider how you handle uncertainty using the following steps.

1. Identify a few areas that bring up uncertainty (e.g., family, academics, work, health).

2. What emotions do you tend to feel when you are experiencing uncertainty (such as anxiety, nervousness, shame, guilt, etc.)?

3. What thoughts do you tend to experience in response to the uncertainty (for instance: "I should have done better," "I am not smart enough," or "Uncertainty is normal in this situation")?

4. How do you tend to cope with the uncertainty (by planning, asking for help, distracting yourself with other tasks or activities, ruminating, achievement, trying to convince yourself that things are certain)?

AN ALTERNATIVE RESPONSE

Tolerating uncertainty is necessary in today's world, but what does that look like? How might we respond to uncertainty in a way that does not feed into illusions, lead to feeling helpless and apathetic, or generate chronic unmanageable anxiety?

Willingly Experiencing Uncertainty

As I (Audrey) am writing, I am experiencing a moment of uncertainty. This is a vast topic, and I feel the pressure to offer solutions to make the experience of uncertainty feel more palatable. I am feeling overwhelmed and unsure how to approach writing this in a way that achieves the optimal benefit to the reader. I, too, dislike the feelings that come with uncertainty, and I would love to be able to wave a magic wand to rid myself (and you, the reader) of it. I am noticing an urge to walk away from the computer and avoid this sensation. I feel a pit in my stomach as I face the fact that I am not sure how this content will be perceived by others.

I am noticing that thoughts of self-doubt arise in response to this uncertainty.

While part of me wants to avoid this discomfort by telling my co-author Alison that we should delete this topic, I also know that a value of mine is mental health. Shedding light onto the experience of uncertainty is an important way to help people cope effectively and to support their mental health; it is a way that I can act in line with this value. I am now faced with the decision to either move away from my pain by deleting this topic or to move toward my value of mental health. Moving away from my pain would require me to bypass this opportunity. Moving toward this value would require me to experience anxiety and thoughts of self-doubt while acknowledging the uncertainty that I cannot know how others will receive this section. It would require me to tolerate the uncertainty while I continue to put words to the page.

Given that you are reading this section, it is clear that I decided to move toward my value and to tolerate the discomfort. While the pit in my stomach persists, I am anchored in my value of mental health to remind myself why I am willing to experience these sensations and thoughts of self-doubt. I am tapping into my skills of cognitive defusion to notice the thoughts of self-doubt that arise, without interpreting them as necessarily reflective of reality. I am holding a both/and attitude, recognizing that it is possible for me to *both* experience thoughts of self-doubt *and* to communicate my knowledge and skill.

I am offering compassion to myself, as it is painful to feel these sensations and thoughts that arise with this uncertainty. I am also reminding myself that the experience of uncertainty is human and inevitable and is not a reflection of my personal failure. I will act according to my value of mental health by self-disclosing my own experience of uncertainty and modeling a way to tolerate that discomfort. While I will likely take a break at some point in the process of writing, I will do so in a way that allows me to recover from the cognitive effort this task requires and to revisit this topic with a fresh perspective, rather than with the aim to avoid the discomfort.

This is what it can look like to experience uncertainty without pushing it away. Uncertainty is not going anywhere, and it is human-nature to feel overwhelmed by it from time to time. As previously discussed, this discomfort serves a purpose: motivating actions to maintain safety. Sometimes, however, there is no additional action to take, as the uncertainty is chronic and largely outside of our control. Instead, anchoring by clarifying values can allow persistence with purpose. The ability to accept and willingly experience uncertainty can be the difference between living a fearful, limited life and one which is full and meaningful.

Mindfulness

Uncertainty can sometimes feel like an overstimulating arcade, with hundreds of lights and sounds happening at the same time. Trying to anticipate every possible outcome is like trying to register all of the sensory inputs at once to find clarity in the chaos. Mindfulness can provide grounding by noticing the "what" and slow the "why" and "how" questioning and rumination. From a position of mindfulness, it is not your responsibility to identify why you are having a certain reaction. For instance, you do not need to question "why" you are experiencing self-doubt; rather you can notice that you are experiencing the specific thought "What if I can't handle this?" You do not need to consider "how" to stop feeling anxious, but rather notice the anxiety as it comes and goes. Mindfulness allows detachment in the present moment, rather than getting swept away in all of the future "what if" questions.

Self-Compassion

With clients, we find that emphasizing self-compassion in response to uncertainty is essential. We often hear engineers blaming themselves for not being able to find the answers they are looking for. They believe that if they were to plan better, try harder, or be more knowledgeable, they wouldn't have to endure uncertainty. Of course, planning and effort can create more certainty. But even with all the planning in the world, some uncertainty is inevitable. Remembering and reflecting on our common humanity (one of the three components of self-compassion) can be validating. The experience of uncertainty is evidence of that humanity; no one is alone in that discomfort. Offering self-kindness, rather than self-criticism, in response to uncertainty can lessen the burden. While uncertainty is inherently uncomfortable, compounding uncertainty with self-criticism is not helpful.

Assess the Changeability of the Problem

In the Decompiling Thoughts section, we responded to stress by considering the changeability of the problem. For problems that can be fully or partially addressed, tapping into engineering skills like problem-solving is effective. For problems outside of your control, though, focusing on acceptance and willingness is more useful. The same can be applied to distress tied to uncertainty.

For instance, when working on an engineering design, some aspects are changeable: more research, implement quality assurance testing, and getting feedback from colleagues. These tasks decrease the odds that negative outcomes will occur. While focusing on the aspects of the work that are changeable, there are still possible negative outcomes that are not changeable: how the users will like the product, whether or not they follow the directions accurately, and so on. Discerning what aspects of uncertainty are and are not within your control is essential to decide how to respond effectively.

EXERCISE: COMMITTED ACTION AMIDST UNCERTAINTY

Let's build a plan to practice tolerating uncertainty.

1. Identify one value (e.g., kindness, family, generosity, competence).

2. Identify one possible action that would be consistent with that value. Pick an action that is specific and takes between five minutes and two hours (e.g., volunteering, visiting a family member, practicing a new skill).

3. What uncertainty might be experienced to pursue that action? What aspects of the uncertainty are changeable and what aspects are not (e.g., not knowing what others will think, deciding how much time is spent preparing, etc.)?

4. Mindfully notice the feelings and thoughts while completing the action. Respond to arising discomfort with self-compassion. With willingness, continue to complete the task.

VIGNETTE

Shane builds a plan to practice tolerating uncertainty. They pick their value of "learning" for this exercise. Shane has been feeling bored in their job recently and reflects on how applying for a management role within their company could be a good opportunity to move toward their value. The role includes responsibilities that Shane has not previously performed, so there would be a steep learning curve. When applying for the job, Shane would need to experience the uncertainty of how the hiring committee perceives their application. They would be uncertain about whether or not they would be invited for an interview and how it would feel if they were not selected.

Aspects of this uncertainty could be alleviated by closely reading the job description, requesting to have an informational interview with Sylvia (the person who formerly held the position), and updating their resume. Shane is not able to control what the hiring committee thinks of their application, the quality and actions of the other applicants, and what emotions will arise if they are not hired.

In preparation for submitting an application, Shane decides to reach out to Sylvia. While sending the email, Shane notes feeling nervous and notices the thought "She will think I am not ready for the job." While updating their resume, Shane also notices that the nerves come and go. They notice self-critical thoughts about their experience, including "My lack of experience is embarrassing."

After hitting "Send" on the application, Shane notices the emotion of excitement. Shane is excited about the possibility to try a new role and learn something new. Shane also notices waves of anxiety. Shane remembers that the anxiety and excitement reflect that this action is consistent with their value of learning. While Shane waits for a response, they feel proud of themself for willingly experiencing discomfort as they pursue their value.

SUMMARY

Being human means experiencing uncertainty. While engineers are uniquely qualified to minimize uncertainty, this skill is not fully effective in all contexts. Discerning when to focus on reducing uncertainty and when to accept and tolerate it is a key skill for wellness. Tolerating uncertainty encompasses several of the skills discussed previously: recognition of values, mindful awareness of emotions and thoughts, willingness, cognitive defusion, and self-compassion. Embracing a both/and perspective can foster the ability to tolerate uncertainty. Developing these skills is a gradual process and applying them will be challenging at first. Progress in building tolerance of uncertainty is not a straight, upward-facing 45-degree line (that is, a monotonically increasing function). Rather, progress will be a series of ups, downs, and plateaus, at times deferring to old patterns such as denial, helplessness, or illusions of control. However, each moment of practice gradually deepens the neural pathways that will contribute to the capacity to tolerate uncertainty.

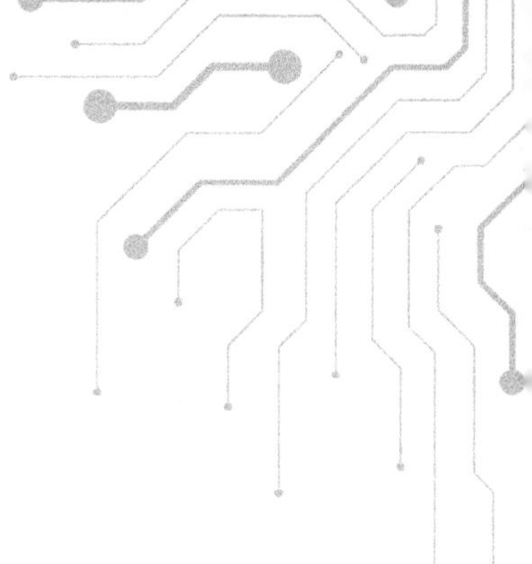

CHAPTER 19

THE IMPOSTOR PHENOMENON

DO YOU EVER FEEL LIKE YOU ARE THE ONLY PERSON in the group who does not know what they are doing, the only person who struggles to keep up with the workload, or who actually needs to work hard for their success while everyone else is naturally intelligent? And yet, despite this perceived imbalance in competence, you have somehow managed to succeed. You have fooled everyone, you believe, and they think you have it all together while you are still figuring it all out. If only they knew!

The impostor phenomenon is "characterized by persistent doubt concerning one's abilities or accomplishments accompanied by the fear of being exposed as a fraud despite evidence of one's ongoing success" (Merriam-Webster, n.d.a). This phenomenon, first documented by Pauline Clance, PhD and Suzanne Imes, PhD (1978), is certainly not unique to engineers. We have chosen to use their terminology "impostor phenomenon" as opposed to the impostor "syndrome" term used in pop psychology. The impostor phenomenon is not pathological. While the impostor phenomenon can accompany clinical anxiety and depression (Huecker et al., 2024), it is not a mental disorder. There is no diagnosis for the impostor phenomenon in the *Diagnostic and Statistical Manual* (DSM) or *International Classification of Diseases, Tenth Revision* (ICD-10).

Diagnosis or not, the impostor phenomenon is a common experience among engineers. Some common signs include:

- Dismissing and distrusting of positive feedback
- Over-reliance on constant external validation
- Feeling unworthy of success
- Attributing success to luck or over-preparation
- Constantly striving for perfection
- Having goals that are unrealistic
- Self-sabotaging (i.e., avoiding promotions, not challenging oneself)
- Being unable to internalize accomplishments
- Experiencing persistent fear of being "found out" as an impostor

Those who experience the impostor phenomenon can become very skilled at hiding their self-doubt. While they may be able to identify their own internal experiences and perception of themselves as an impostor, the external clues—what everyone around them can see and notice—are often minimal. We encourage you to keep this in mind when your peers appear confident. Comparing your internal experience to their external presentation might lead to faulty conclusions about how they actually feel *and* how they perceive you.

Because the impostor phenomenon coexists with high achievement and success, it can be experienced by amateurs and professionals alike, impacting anyone from a first year student in college to a veteran in the field. Anecdotally, we have spoken to many engineers who believed obtaining a PhD would miraculously erase all traces of so-called "impostordom," only to find that they felt no different with the additional degree. In fact, the impostor phenomenon often appears during times of growth—when one enters uncharted territory and accepts new challenges. For example, someone who is generally confident in their abilities might find that they perceive themselves as an impostor when awarded a promotion.

While initially believed to be unique to professional women (Clance & Imes, 1978), subsequent research has indicated that the experience is quite universal. Not only are there numerous research studies showing that the phenomenon has an equal impact across genders (Bravata et al., 2019), but according to the *International Journal of Behavior Science,* the impostor phenomenon is estimated to impact 70% of all people at some point in their careers (Sakulku & Alexander, 2011). It is more difficult to meet someone who hasn't experienced the phenomenon at some point in their life.

Statistics regarding the impostor phenomenon are only as good as the validity of the research and assessments, which, unsurprisingly, often included only a small number of individuals belonging to minoritized ethnic groups (Bravata et al., 2019). So, while various studies and reports note that the phenomenon is also common in these groups (Huecker, 2024), historical and cultural context is often left out (Tulshyan & Burey, 2011). For many marginalized groups, feeling like an outsider goes far beyond a *feeling.* Instead, questioning one's belonging is a reasonable response to actual (past or present) discrimination on an individual, social, or systemic level. Which begs the question: is it the imposter phenomenon, or is it racism?

In the article "Racism Camouflaged as Impost[e]rism and the Impact on Black STEM Doctoral Students," McGee et al. (2022) examined ways in which 54 Black engineering and computing students experienced self-doubt regarding their intellect. This qualitative study found that 94.4% of the students "attributed their feelings of exclusion to how race and racism positioned them as impost[e]rs" (McGee et al., 2022, p. 494). With a long history of racial bias and perceived intellectual inferiority, it is clear that the experiences of the majority of these Black doctoral students were shaped by interactions with others, policies, practices, and institutional factors. There is a distinction between this experience and that of the impostor phenomenon: the former involves working hard so that others will recognize one's true self (i.e., one's intellect and contributions), while the latter involves working hard so that others do **not** discover one's true self (i.e., one's perceived fraudulence). For these doctoral students, then, the battle is to gain the respect of others rather than to maintain it.

The authors ultimately came to the conclusion that the impostor phenomenon is a "myth" and a "cover to mask relations of power and privilege in STEM fields" (McGee et al., 2022, p. 499). We agree that not all feelings of fraudulence are best described by the impostor phenomenon and encourage readers who experience self-doubt to pause and reflect on how their identities and environments play a role. Later in this chapter we will provide tools to examine and address behavioral patterns stemming from beliefs of impostordom. Please keep in mind that this chapter focuses on navigating internal experiences rather than the role of institutions.

If you believe your feelings of fraudulence have more to do with your external environment as it relates to your held identities, this topic may not be as relevant to you. If so, we invite you to skip ahead to the "Engineering Culture" portion or to skip this entire topic, as needed. If unsure whether your experience is the result of the impostor phenomenon in addition to the impact of institutional and structural racism or discrimination, consider:

- Am I worried that people would discover who I truly am, a "fraud," despite my achievements? If the answer is "yes," you might be experiencing the impostor phenomenon.

- Am I worried that people will not recognize my talents and contributions? Are my abilities being unjustly questioned? If the answer is "yes," this experience is more in line with the impact of an unsupportive, inequitable, and discriminatory environment. Consider opportunities to expand or deepen communities that can offer support.

BELIEFS ABOUT COMPETENCE

Those who fear that they are impostors are skilled at coming up with reasons why they are undeserving of what they have accomplished, or ways they have tricked everyone into thinking that they are professionals. Therefore, achieving more and more is not a solution. In fact, continuing to achieve without addressing the underlying belief system might even exacerbate fears of being discovered as a fraud (i.e., "I've achieved so much for so long, my luck will soon run out!" or "I'm fooling everyone").

According to Valerie Young, EdD, author of *The Secret Thoughts of Women: Why Capable People Suffer From Impostor Syndrome,* people who worry they are impostors have a distorted view of what it means to be "competent," which plays a large role in perpetuating self-doubt (Young, 2011). This distorted perception, along with the "rules" behind it, has a profound impact on one's ability to *feel* competent. If the standard of competence is idealistic or unrealistic, professionals will likely have difficulty feeling satisfied with their work and with internalizing their achievements. Young suggests that bringing awareness to one's "competence type" is an important step towards changing self-perception. She outlines five different competence types, which highlight the rules that people often unknowingly abide by. These rules include words which live in the extremes, such as "should," "don't," "always," and "never."

Check-in with yourself: what type(s) resonates? Can you relate to any experiences in the following list?

1. The Perfectionist: "Everything should be perfect." There is little, if any, room for error. Competence is based on *how* work is completed as well as its final result. Even minor mistakes are signs of failure. This rule can result in inaction.

2. The Expert: "I should know everything." Competence is measured by *what* and *how much* they know or accomplish. While briefly finding comfort in knowledge, they ultimately learn that what they have learned is never "enough" as the knowledge base and issues evolve. Often, this rule delays action and can even be used as a means of procrastination.

3. The Soloist: "I should do it alone." Soloists take self-reliance to an extreme. Competence is measured by *who* completes the task; asking others for help can open them up to being discovered as incapable. This rule can limit the benefits gained from collaboration and lead to isolation.

4. The Natural Genius: "Success should come easy to me." They are likely to have grown up as star students who received a lot of positive feedback for their achievements. Competence is measured by *how* and *when* one achieves; they focus on ease and speed. Effort is a sign of incompetence. If they are not naturally skilled at something, they feel bad about themselves. They tend to limit themselves to things they are good at, as they constantly worry that they will be found out.

5. The Superhuman: "I always have to go above and beyond in everything I do." Competence is measured by *how many* roles in which they can manage and excel. They are often referred to as a workaholic, giving all they have got to prove themselves to others. Their focus is on the *process* of working instead of the work itself, a stance which can lead to overwhelm and burnout.

If you are interested in reading more about the types, Dr. Young's book is a valuable resource, containing strategies to work through each type and rewrite the related "inner rules." Importantly, Dr. Young notes that despite the title *The Secret Thoughts of Successful Women,* male-identified individuals can also find the book relevant and useful.

EXERCISE: COMPETENCE TYPES

Consider your struggle with the impostor phenomenon. For each type you relate to ask the following questions:

1. How long have I held these beliefs about competence?

2. Where did I receive this message?

3. What function does this expectation or rule serve in my life?

4. Are these beliefs and expectations protecting me from any uncomfortable experiences, emotions, or thoughts?

THE FUNCTION OF THE IMPOSTOR PHENOMENON

Our brains want us to stick to what we know. The more we stick to the known, the less brain power we use. When met with a task that requires moving from automatic thinking to one which requires more effort, the brain might give some pushback. The impostor phenomenon is an example of automatic processing taking the lead and relying on assumptions that do not require analysis. All of those doubts and fears serve a purpose: to keep the status quo, keep things stable, and to stick to what takes less effort (For those who have never felt like impostors in one way or another, their brains have likely found other effective shortcuts.)

Let's explore the role that the impostor phenomenon might have played for early humans, including potential survival and reproductive advantages. Researchers suggest that the impostor phenomenon is a manifestation of "anticipatory anxiety" (Chrousos et al., 2020). Anticipatory anxiety activates a physiological response in humans to prepare for fight, flight, or freezing in place. In this modern day, anticipatory anxiety might look like putting forth a significant amount of energy to avoid exposure as a "fraud" or disengaging from perceived threatening situations altogether.

Additionally, avoidance of anxiety-producing tasks related to the impostor phenomenon might be driven by a fear of success. In this context, success can feel threatening as it draws extra attention and has the potential to create more future expectations from others (Cavenar & Werman, 1981). From an evolutionary perspective, success can threaten one's social status or acceptance. Consequently, such fear can lead to difficulty internalizing achievements as proof of competency; if one is competent, then their future selves may be at risk. People might instead view their personal accomplishments as flukes and not representative of their abilities, thereby allowing them to remain in a safety net of predictable expectations and outcomes.

ATTEMPTS TO COPE WITH THE IMPOSTOR PHENOMENON

Clance's conception of the impostor phenomenon cannot be fully understood without also understanding her Impostor Cycle (Clance, 1985; Sakulku, 2011). This cycle begins when a task is assigned in a setting which includes evaluation and opportunity for achievement. Someone who experiences the impostor phenomenon then becomes activated by the upcoming evaluation, experiencing physiological changes related to the fight, flight, or freeze response, often accompanied by emotions such as anxiety and self-doubt. This response then elicits some type of action or inaction designed to manage the discomfort, typically in the form of either over-preparation or procrastination (then followed by frantic preparation). Once the task is completed, one might feel relaxed and even accomplished. Unfortunately, this part of the cycle is often short-lived.

The "impostor" rejects any positive feedback or messages they receive from others as incongruent with their view of themselves. Notions of success become skewed as the journey to the destination does not match what it "should have" looked like. For example, someone who over-prepared might believe they were only successful because they worked really hard—which, according to people who think they are impostors, is not indicative of their ability (Clance, 1985). Someone who procrastinates, and then rushes to finish their work just in time, might chalk their success up to luck. In either case, the individual is unable to internalize their achievements, and instead, they compare their experiences to a romanticized idea of what "true" success looks and feels like.

Often anxiety, self-doubt, and other uncomfortable emotions are absent from this fantasy, as they hold the belief that one cannot experience these feelings and succeed at the same time.

The Impostor Cycle

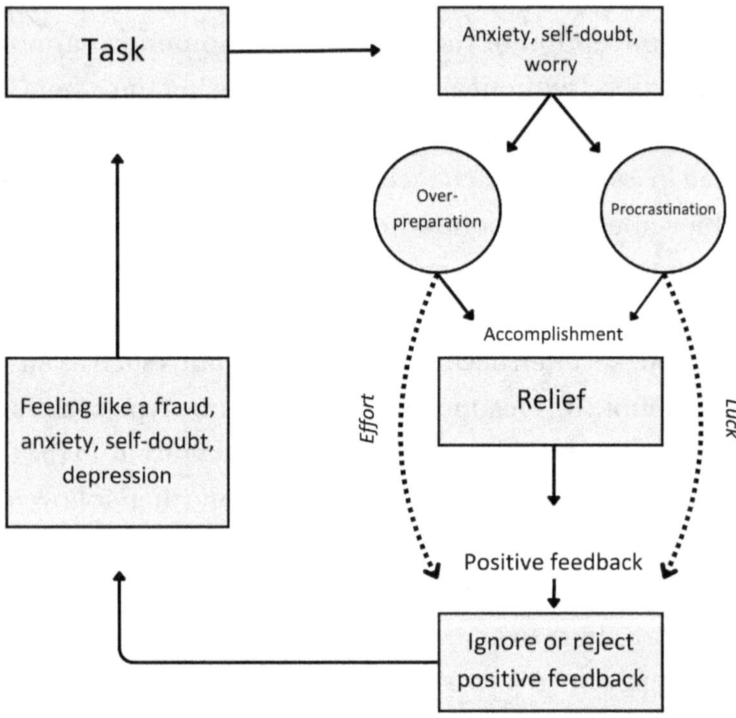

For access to enlarged, color images, go to appliedwellnessinitiatives.com.

An individual's perception that they somehow scraped by and did well enough to fool others into thinking they belong can feel unbearable. Because they over-prepared or procrastinated, not only do they perceive their success as invalid, but they now have an additional concern: others might expect them to reproduce the same (or better) results. How long, they wonder, can they keep up this charade? The space between one's expectations of success and the reality of success fuels the fire of self-doubt. When a new task or opportunity comes along, the perceived impostor enters a lose-lose situation in which success is explained away by external factors, and the failure narrative is reinforced because their process does not meet idealized expectations.

EXERCISE: THE IMPOSTOR PHENOMENON

Take a moment to reflect on your experience, if any, with the impostor phenomenon and cycle. When does it usually appear? Is it when you are challenging yourself or beginning a new job or role? What is your typical way of coping?

THE ENGINEERING CULTURE

Changes in individual mindset, while valuable, are not enough to combat the impostor phenomenon. Many factors beyond the individual can result in the experience of feeling like an impostor. Culture, defined as "the values, beliefs, language, rituals, traditions, and other behaviors that are passed from one generation to another within any social group" (American Psychological Association, n.d.a) can influence one's feeling of competence and belonging. As we take a look at pressures that engineers face that contribute to the impostor phenomenon, we encourage you to reflect on the subtle (and not-so-subtle) messages you have received.

Intelligence

The emphasis on individual intelligence is abundant in the field. This emphasis has extended to a larger societal narrative about engineering and its mental rigors. Researchers and authors of *Smartness in Engineering Culture: An Interdisciplinary Dialogue,* explore the interactions between the psychological perception of so-called "smartness" (which highlights individuals' beliefs about intelligence) and the anthropological perception (which views intelligence and ability as culturally constructed) (Dringenberg et al., 2019). Perhaps unsurprisingly, the authors found that the two lenses are intertwined. Ideas of smartness in engineering and academia draw from personal experiences as well as cultural norms and criteria.

The engineering culture's narrative around smartness fuels beliefs about belonging (Dringenberg et al., 2019). Often, science and math skills are valued over "soft" skills, such as creativity, communication, and art. This leads to a limited picture of what it looks like to be an engineer. According to researchers, the message that engineering is "not for everyone" has had detrimental consequences for underrepresented populations. For example, there is a large overlap in traits revered in academia and traits which are traditionally linked to masculinity (e.g., rationality, objectivity, seriousness) (Dringenberg et al., 2019; Gutierrez y Muhs et al., 2012). Unfortunately, women and underrepresented racial minorities are less likely to participate in a field which is perceived to require innate intelligence (Leslie et al., 2015). While intelligence is indeed necessary for engineering work, rigid beliefs about what constitutes intelligence and assumptions about who fits the engineering mold can be harmful to individuals and the profession more broadly. As we peel back the layers of how intelligence came to be defined in a cultural context, it is easy to see how narrow the definition truly is, leaving room for all kinds of "impostors" who do not fit the biased and stereotypical mold.

Displays of intelligence and confidence—authentic or not— are valued in engineering environments. In many ways, these displays are used as a means of social survival. From our observations, when engineering students choose to project smartness over seeking opportunities to learn (either by speaking up as a means of displaying their intelligence or by staying silent when they feel confused or unsure), two things can happen. First, the student misses out on actual learning and is instead focused on how others might perceive them. Second, they create an external version of themselves which is incongruent with their internal experience, perpetuating the personal and cultural story of their identity as an impostor. Outwardly projecting intelligence to others then backfires, as the individual inevitably encounters situations in which they do not have the answers. Instead of using these moments as opportunities to learn and grow, those who feel unsafe expressing their lack of knowledge view them as further evidence that they do not belong.

The Measure of Merit

It is useful to have a system which rewards accomplishments and draws in talent and potential. Exam scores, GPAs, research grants, publications, and project assignments can be helpful measures of ability, providing institutions and employers with useful information about the people on their projects and teams. On a personal level, success in these areas can lead to individuals feeling accomplished, recognized, and motivated. In its purest form, such a system provides opportunities for anyone to be rewarded for their achievements.

The principle of meritocracy arose in the United States as an offering of equality. At least, it was intended that way. Meritocracy is "a system, organization, or society in which people are chosen and moved into positions of success, power, and influence on the basis of their demonstrated abilities and merit" (Merriam-Webster, n.d.b). The idea that opportunities are presented as long as natural ability and effort exist became the bedrock of US culture. The belief that effort and smarts will always be awarded proportionally is enticing. But in fact, meritocracy does not exist in a vacuum and, in practice, is more complex.

By ignoring the history of systemic inequity among people of different political, economic, racial, religious, ethnic, and gendered groups, meritocracy empowers the privileged to believe that everyone starts on equal ground. This belief further perpetuates another belief of meritocracy, namely that "If some people are not succeeding, they should just work harder." In his article "Challenging the Meritocratic Ideology in Engineering Education," Professor Robert P. Loweth (2023) of Purdue University posits that meritocratic systems require equitable and fair access to opportunities through fair competition. He then argues that the academic system fails at this requirement. As it turns out, it is impossible to understand a person's strengths when the measurement tools do not account for all they have to offer.

Loweth (2023) uses the example of the Grade Point Average (GPA), a number that is constantly conflated with merit. Systemic advantages (which often go unrecognized in measurements of GPA) play a huge part in helping this number climb. Advanced Placement courses, for example, which are not distributed evenly amongst high schools, allow some students to earn a GPA above 4.0. For these students, their schools weigh the AP courses on a scale of 5.0 rather than the traditional 4.0. In well-funded and prestigious high schools, it is not uncommon for several students to have GPA's well over 4.0 due to access to these courses. The students who attend such schools are typically financially secure and can devote themselves to their studies, or they have access to private tutoring. While hard work is definitely involved in the process, there is no denying that the playing field for college admission is not level.

For students who do not have access to these resources, advancement relies heavily on their institutions' sensitivity to equity in order to counteract the unjust system. Because systems of meritocracy often overlook inequitable practices, students can be shamed, silenced, and tricked into ignoring how inequitable contexts shape their experience. The system thereby explicitly and implicitly encourages students to place blame on themselves and internalize its flaws. As a result, students might come to doubt their intellect, their capacity for hard work, and, ultimately, to feel that they are impostors. While people rising to their potential and being credited for their abilities is not bad or unwarranted, the rigid and erroneous measures of merit are taken out of context.

A CASE AGAINST CONFIDENCE

As Albert Einstein famously said, "The more I learn, the more I realize how much I don't know." Diving deep into a subject we are familiar with can help uncover layers about the subject that we didn't even know existed. While our confidence is likely to take a hit, a lack of complete confidence is not so bad. What do we mean by this?

The Dunning-Kruger effect is a type of cognitive bias in which people overestimate their abilities, often due to a deficit in self-awareness and failure to recognize the level of others' expertise. In 1999, David Dunning and Justin Kruger of Cornell University provided random subjects with tests on humor, grammar, and logical reasoning. As it turned out, those who ranked in the bottom 25% believed that they were at the top of the pack, while those in the top 25% believed their scores to be lower than they were (Kruger & Dunning, 1999). The researchers used the term "dual burden" to describe the experience of ignorance and of their ignorance of that ignorance.

As in the following graph, when experiencing this cognitive bias, the competence journey starts with a steady build toward confidence. A student or employee in this situation might not only feel really confident, but they are also likely to exude it. If you were to observe someone experiencing the Dunning-Kruger effect, you might notice this self-assurance. And if you are deep in the throes of the impostor phenomenon, you might even envy them, perhaps wondering "What must it be like to experience confidence, knowing that you are capable?"

The Dunning-Kruger Effect

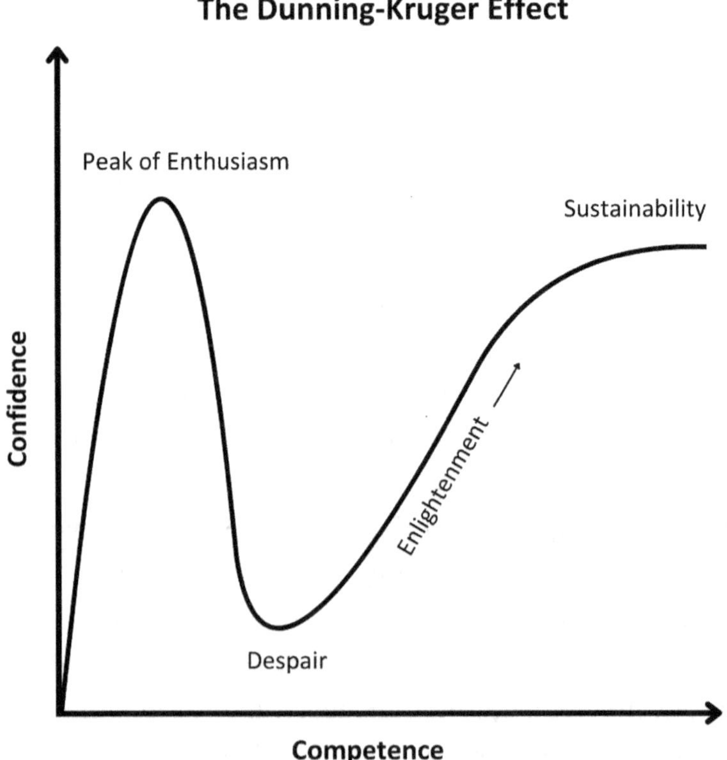

While engineers located at the "Peak of Enthusiasm" have grasped knowledge vital to building a foundation for deeper learning, the knowledge itself is incomplete. But these confident, biased engineers don't know what they don't know, so they move forward, satisfied with their rudimentary understanding of concepts. They continue unperturbed while the "impostors" fixate on and stress over the details—details that the confident, biased engineer is unaware of. They might even push back when others try to correct them or present novel ideas. From the impostor's perspective, seeing the confidence they desire in another person while feeling unsure themselves deepens their fraudulent narrative.

Eventually, the confident, biased engineer will hit a wall as they begin to realize that their grasp of various concepts only scratches the surface. Following this realization is a steep descent into "Despair." Here, it is crystal clear that there is more to master. Interestingly, amidst the anguish, they hold significantly more wisdom than they did when their confidence was at its peak. But because they previously conflated their high confidence with wisdom, they are at risk of confusing low confidence with incompetency. If they can allow themselves to learn, to tolerate the discomfort, they are able to see their confidence climb back up. And this time, confidence is joined by knowledge.

AN ALTERNATIVE RESPONSE

The impostor phenomenon is much larger than the individual, and not everyone reading this book is in a position of power. But for those who are, we invite you to consider how the system measures and facilitates success and ways to contribute to cultural changes that promote growth while facilitating an accurate perception of confidence. Here are just a few ideas:

- Celebrating the development of skills along the way rather than waiting until evaluations or grades are submitted

- Normalizing mistakes by discussing personal experience

- Responding compassionately and with curiosity when others disclose their own struggles

- Taking time to consider who might not be seen, heard, or recognized in your organization and consider ways to elevate those voices (elevation does not mean speaking on behalf of others, but rather giving them a platform to speak to their experiences)

For those who experience the impostor phenomenon on a personal level (whether or not in a position of great power), we invite you to recognize the extent to which systems can have a major influence on feelings of fraudulence. There are factors outside of your control, but certain skills help to combat the Impostor Cycle.

When considering alternative responses to the impostor phenomenon, keep in mind that the goal is not and cannot be to get rid of the impostor phenomenon altogether. This impostor phenomenon is made up of thoughts and emotions which, as we have established, cannot be controlled. Instead, we hope to help you relate with the phenomenon more effectively and to take control of your behavior and response to this internal experience.

Use Socratic Questioning

In the midst of the impostor phenomenon, it can be difficult to determine the validity of the anxiety and self-doubt. Sometimes, anxiety can indicate that one is underprepared. For instance, students may find relief from their test anxiety after learning and implementing more effective study practices. On the other hand, many engineering clients are consumed with self-doubt and anxiety even when they continue to demonstrate competency across the board. At times, this anxiety can reflect a need for more preparation, and at other times, the anxiety can be indicative of the impostor phenomenon. Given this, how can the individual determine the trustworthiness of this anxiety and self-doubt?

Using the skill of Socratic questioning can help assess the trustworthiness of such thoughts. For instance, consider the thought "Everyone here knows what they are doing, and I don't." Some Socratic questions to unpack this thought include:

- "Is my concern fear-based?"
- "Is there evidence for this concern?"
- "Is it possible I'm misinterpreting the evidence?"
- "Could my thought be an exaggeration of what's true?"
- "How likely is this thought to be true?"
- "Is my brain coming up with the worst-case scenario?"

Through this questioning process, you might realize that the thought reflects the cognitive distortion of mind reading (believing that we know what others think). This insight helps reframe the thought as reflecting an internal experience rather than being objectively accurate.

And although exaggerated, there might be a hint of truth embedded within the thought. Perhaps you *are* underprepared for one aspect of the work. In this case, you might respond with problem-solving in order to meet your employer's standards. Outside of the hint of truth, remember that the impostor phenomenon is at work.

As the famous physicist is also reported to have said, "The exaggerated esteem in which my lifework is held makes me very ill at ease. I feel compelled to think of myself as an involuntary swindler." Einstein, a swindler? Of course, no one besides Einstein would ever think so! The impostor phenomenon is not indicative of low intelligence or ability. Instead, it more likely indicates that you are challenging yourself, growing, or trying something new. When the discomfort arises in the process, know that you are in good company.

Avoid Emotional Avoidance

In the first section of this book, we reviewed two strategies people use to avoid emotions: suppression and intellectualization. How are the responses to uncomfortable emotions in the Impostor Cycle forms of avoidance? Procrastination is a way to suppress emotion for as long as possible, and overpreparation is a strategy to distract the self from uncomfortable feelings by engaging the intellect. One thing we know about emotional avoidance is that it does not free us from the impact of the emotion forever. The body and mind hold on to the emotions as they build and intensify.

Despite the individual's best efforts, procrastination and over-preparation do not "get rid" of the uncomfortable emotions, and instead intensify feelings of impostordom when the success can be discounted and explained away. Anxiety, worry, and feelings of self-doubt themselves are not the issue. Although uncomfortable, all are normal emotional responses to challenging situations. In the Impostor Cycle, the real issue is the *response* to the uncomfortable emotions.

An alternative approach to coping with the impostor phenomenon is to decompile the thoughts and feelings in order to understand the underlying needs and values. Allow the uncomfortable emotions to come and go. Create room between the emotions and any resulting behavior. Rather than reactively acting on the emotions, know that you are destined to have feelings. Rather than relying on automatic responses to these thoughts and feelings, consider what actions might serve the underlying needs and values.

Maybe they are attempting to point to values, to motivate you to do a satisfactory job, or to help you avoid mistakes. Thank your brain for the assistance, take what is helpful, and leave the rest.

Access Self-Compassion

If you experience the impostor phenomenon, even listing achievements on a resume or curriculum vita (CV) can be distressing. Anxiety and self-doubt might arise while reflecting on what you have "technically" accomplished, feeling as though the words on the page are an exaggerated reflection of your competence. What if employers get the wrong idea and obtain an inflated notion of your capabilities? The impostor phenomenon makes it difficult to own and internalize those abilities as items listed on a piece of paper.

An alternative, self-compassionate approach to internalizing your abilities is to reflect on invisible personal triumphs. These can be big or small, perhaps related to school or work, or to life outside the two. Maybe you demonstrated resilience in the face of a long, difficult challenge. Or perhaps you did something you never thought you could. Maybe you completed a project which ended up being mediocre, but the experience and the process gives you strength still today. Maybe you feel proud of a failure because you grew as a person in a profound way. This different kind of resume or CV will reflect the personal strengths developed throughout life instead of a checklist of external accomplishments. Examples of strengths include creativity, open-mindedness, accountability, leadership, kindness, humility, persistence, authenticity, discipline, preparedness, bravery, resilience, and justice. Notice any overlap between these strengths and your own values.

As you may recall from the Decompiling Emotions section, common humanity is one of the tenets of self-compassion. Common humanity encompasses pain as part of the human process.

As such, there will be times when you fall short of your goals, correct course, fail, disappoint others, and disappoint yourself. While vital to your professional life, a traditional resume or CV does not capture this common humanity. But your humanity makes you who you are. There is so much more to your story than achievement. Connecting with the parts of yourself that others cannot see—strengths, growth, and wisdom—will help connect to the *person* capable of all those achievements.

The Impostor Cycle

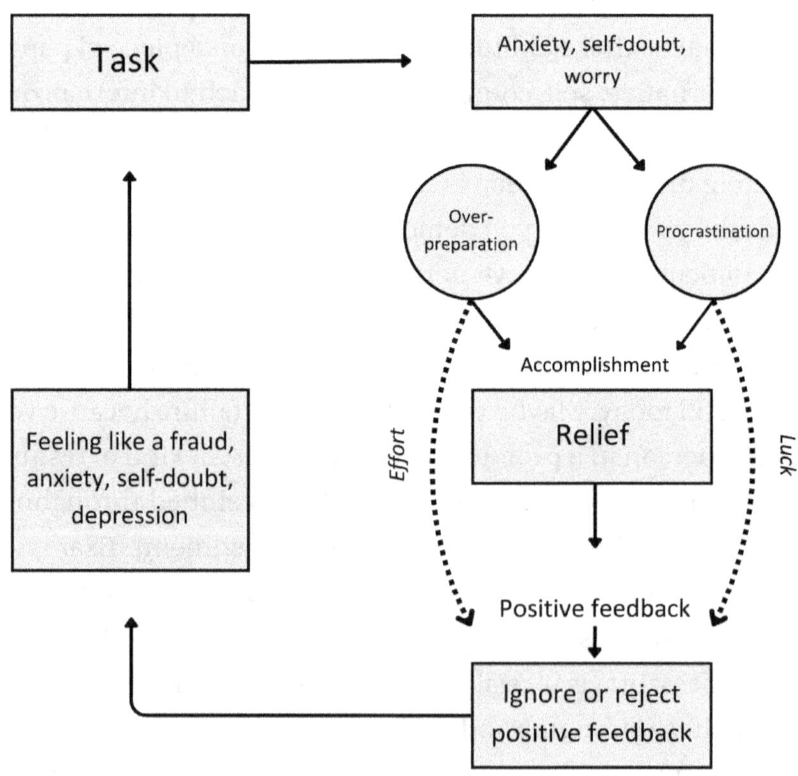

EXERCISE: ALTERNATIVE RESPONSE

These steps can help generate alternative responses to the experience of the impostor phenomenon.

1. Identify a situation in which you are experiencing the impostor phenomenon. If you cannot think of a current situation, use a past experience.

2. Which emotions accompany that experience?

3. What urges arise in response to these emotions? Do you feel compelled to over-prepare? Do you experience an urge to procrastinate?

4. Engage in the Emotion Decompiler to identify relevant needs or values. When doing problem-solving in Step Seven of the Decompiler, consider ways to gradually challenge any procrastination or overpreparation tendencies.

VIGNETTE

Zoe has been developing electronics for various projects during her first year with the company. The work has gone well and reminds her of college projects; she feels competent and well-prepared. However, at the start of her second year, a project manager who was impressed with her work suggests that she be transferred to the company's autonomous vehicle division. The autonomous vehicle projects are considered a more prestigious assignment and attract more public attention. Zoe is flattered and excited by the offer, but also worried. Her role would be to develop electronics packages for new experimental sensors, work which is outside her comfort zone.

The project manager says she is sure Zoe can handle it, but Zoe is very aware that the project will involve equipment and techniques that she has no experience with. She is worried that she should have learned them by now. The thought that haunts her the most is "A 'real' engineer would have no trouble quickly learning these skills." Zoe already feels like a failure even though this is an old story she has held about herself, and there is no evidence to support this idea. At this moment, she recognizes her internal experience as the impostor phenomenon.

Zoe checks in with herself and notices that she is feeling anxious. Zoe observes the urge to retreat, avoid, and procrastinate. She receives an email from her project manager, which includes accolades and details about the new role. She gets halfway through the email before having the thought "I can't do this" and abruptly closing her laptop.

Zoe directs her attention back to her emotions and asks herself what they are trying to do for her. She thinks about how much the new role would help her career, that it would come with a promotion and challenge her in ways she has been missing in her current position. Zoe thinks about her anxiety's attempt to prepare her for every possible barrier standing between her and all of the positive things this new role can offer. She notices that in addition to her anxiety, she is also experiencing excitement. She recognizes how this emotion points to her values of growth, financial security, and learning.

Zoe opens her laptop to read the rest of the email, allowing uncomfortable thoughts and emotions to come and go. Wanting to make a decision informed by her needs and values instead of by reactively acting on her impulses, she sets up a meeting with her supervisor to get her questions answered and to learn as much as she can about this job prospect. Setting up this meeting is a concrete way that Zoe is challenging her tendency toward procrastination. She continues to breathe, reminding herself that she can choose whether or not to act on that urge.

SUMMARY

Life is full of changes and change is often a significant elicitor of the impostor phenomenon. A new job, a new relationship, or a move across the country can feel destabilizing, leaving you questioning your competence all over again. If this concept resonates with you, consider the strategies in this book and think about how you might allow yourself to feel the uncomfortable thoughts and feelings as you continue to move towards your values.

CONCLUSION

THE WORLD IS CHANGING EVERY DAY, GROWING IN-creasingly sophisticated and developing technology about which early humans could never have dreamt. And yet, the mind has been slow to update its programming. Although useful and efficient in many ways, the brain contains its original operating system, making it difficult to make sense of the thoughts and emotions in this modern context.

If you are an engineer, you are likely skillful in problem-solving and systematic reasoning. Alongside this logical perspective, you hold automatic and deeply ingrained human instincts and systems that sometimes contradict this rational demeanor. While you cannot change the neurological systems inherent to the brain, increasing your understanding of these systems can inform decisions and actions that will better serve you.

The most effective approach is both contextual and flexible. And discerning when to implement typical engineering skills and when to take an alternative approach can be a challenging task. With this understanding, the Emotion and Thought Decompilers are designed to approach these decisions with intentionality and effectiveness. By decompiling these psychological processes, you can respond to those experiences in a way that does not exacerbate the distress and moves you closer to your needs and values. Given the inner workings of the human mind, building these skills is a gradual process.

Practice, repetition, and incorporating the skills within different contexts will be necessary in order to create habitual patterns. We encourage you to use the Integrating Skills Planning Activities, provided at the end of the Decompiling Emotions and Decompiling Thoughts sections, to identify manageable next steps for practicing these skills. We also encourage you to explore these skills with those you trust, as learning deepens within relationships.

Over time, this new self-knowledge and these alternative responses will become more automatic. Each time you implement the Decompilers or use a skill within these processes, you lay the groundwork for a new neural pathway. And each time these new neural pathways are used, they will be easier to access, not requiring as much intentional, controlled thinking (which uses a lot of mental energy) as when first implementing these approaches.

Additionally, developing these skills is an expansive process; one skill will set you up to learn another. Practicing mindfulness will lay a foundation for practicing self-compassion more fluidly. Developing self-compassion leads to curiosity about underlying needs and values. Curiosity about needs and values, in turn, supports the skill of mindfulness. All of these skills will bolster efforts to move toward a more fulfilling life. This learning process can gradually update one's mental code.

We recognize that the effort and time required to engage in this work can feel difficult alongside other responsibilities. In today's world, engineers are often looked up to and relied upon to navigate the changing world and fast-evolving technologies. These technologies can bring hope in the realms of healthcare, renewable energy, climate change, and space travel, to name only a few! Along with hope, these changes bring uncertainty, pressure, and stress. How effective will the solutions be? What are the potential side-effects of those technologies? What harms could be unintentionally created?

Engineers are uniquely equipped to navigate these technological changes and challenges. Society needs people who can anticipate and solve problems in order to improve the lives of humans today and humans to come. While that might feel like a lot of pressure, we wrote this book to support you and your human mind to face such expectations. True to a both/and perspective, we honor and support your ability to engineer solutions for the modern world **and** acknowledge the needs of your non-modern human mind. We hope this book continues to point toward a perspective that is both adaptive to the changing world and accepting of how the human mind functions.

Picture a scenario in which you can sustain motivation while also moving toward the things you care most about, toward your values. Consider how this new relationship with your thoughts and emotions could highlight opportunities to feel more connected, engaged, and fulfilled. Decompiling your mind to better understand your needs and values can foster effective engineering by supporting your ability to identify and meet your needs, in order to become resourced and energized for that work. While solving crucial problems, you can also be positioned to handle this stress in a way that protects your wellbeing and sustains your passion.

While the goal of this book is to present useful information in an effective way, humans are extraordinarily unique. Not every methodology will resonate with every reader. Not all engineers (or humans, for that matter) possess the same resources, desires, motivations, fears, difficulties, support, barriers, beliefs, or goals. As therapists, we are typically granted the chance to discover individual differences in the therapy room and to tailor our approaches to each client. Therapy is a collaborative process, and writing requires us to fill in the gaps by imagining what your personal experience might be. We hope to have struck a balance between a concrete, digestible approach and one which leaves room for individual differences and nuance.

We invite you to bring your own knowledge and insight to this process of decompiling your mind. Honoring that inner knowledge, we encourage you to reflect on next steps. Perhaps you will want to deepen this exploration with a therapist. Maybe you will talk to friends or fellow-engineers about what you learned. You know yourself best, so consult with yourself (and your values!) as you consider where to go from here.

ACKNOWLEDGEMENTS

WE WOULD LIKE TO EXPRESS OUR DEEP APPRECIATION to all of the people who provided support throughout the writing process. To start, we offer our gratitude to our engineering clients, who provided the inspiration for this book. Your insights, questions, and openness to the therapeutic process energizes the work we do.

To our friends and colleagues, thank you for your encouragement over the last two years. While we cannot recognize everyone by name, your presence has not gone unnoticed. Instead, it has allowed us to persist through the highs and lows of the writing process. We are so grateful to have so many amazing humans in our corner.

Colleen Ehrnstrom, thank you for believing in this project from the very beginning. It's hard to quantify how much we learned from you in this process. From your ACT expertise, to your guidance in the book-writing process, to embodying what it truly means to live out your values, it's clear that we couldn't have done this without you. Your voice (and wisdom) echoed in our heads many times over the years–propelling us forward when things felt uncertain.

And Stacy Gerberich, we are so fortunate to share a professional space with someone who possesses so much knowledge and passion for this work. Your invaluable feedback helped shape a (very) rough draft into a final product we're proud of. Your investment in this project–all of that time and energy–will never be taken for granted.

Lisa West, thank you for your generosity with your time as the final reviewer of this book. It was a huge relief to know that we could rely on your attention to detail and editing expertise to catch errors before releasing the book out into the world. Your grammar skills and knowledge are unmatched.

Thank you to Alicia Sepulveda and Beatriz Salazar for your exuberant support and consultation regarding the marketing of this book. You both have so much wisdom, of which we are honored to be the beneficiaries.

We are also extremely grateful to Kathy and Mike McCoy. Thank you for your belief in this project, alongside your financial investment. Your support ensured that, from the beginning, we had access to the very best editors and formatters and could produce a book that lived up to our lofty goals.

To Laura Pasquale and Taryn Nergaard, a big thank you for editing and formatting this book. You both went above and beyond in helping us navigate the self-publishing process. We'll be in touch for book number two!

We will try our best to capture our appreciation for Colin West. As our engineering liaison, your input helped us bridge the gap between the psychological and STEM perspectives. But of course, this was just a drop in a very large bucket of contributions. Your countless hours of editing, consulting, brainstorming, proofreading, and childcare were all a driving force to make this book happen. Not only did you wear multiple hats in this process, but you did so with conviction and enthusiasm. As this book transforms into its final, tactile version of itself, we know that you will join us in a collective, deep exhale. We did it!

AUDREY WOULD ALSO LIKE TO EXPRESS APPRECIATION to her family. To Joel, thank you for your genuine enthusiasm for this project and for cheering me on along the way. In my moments of self-doubt, your support helped me stay motivated. I loved our weekend cafe dates, working side-by-side on our separate projects. Your company (along with the excessive amount of caffeine) made the time spent writing fly by. Thanks for generously sharing our weekends with my writing time, even today, on your birthday!

To my parents, Eric and Dawn, my siblings, Quinn and Sophie, and my sister-in-law, Sarah - thank you for always listening to my latest updates and sharing in my excitement for the book. Some of the best ideas came from our conversations during our yearly family trips. Particular thanks go to my dad, Quinn, and Sarah for sharing your engineering perspectives. Your logical, strategic advice was essential in the writing process. Thanks for always being receptive to my calls and texts asking for your feedback (I promise, this will be the last book cover I ask you to review!) I also want to express appreciation to my in-laws, Jodi, Brett, Ashlynn, and Julia, who I am lucky to have. Thank you for being so understanding when I had to sneak away to write during our visits.

And to my friends who have offered direct and in-direct support to me during the writing process, I am so grateful for you. I do not take for granted how lucky I am to have a community of people who are so kind, intelligent, and genuine.

And finally, thank you so much to Alison - my colleague, friend, and co-author. These last few years have been a wild ride, and it is hard to fully wrap my mind around the fact that we wrote a WHOLE BOOK together. In this time, not only have you become a co-author to me, but you have become a close friend. I am thankful for your attention to detail, your artistic creativity (shout out to all of our images!), and your ability to understand my jumbled words before I have had the chance to organize my thoughts. Your authenticity and calm nature along with your sense of humor contributed to my confidence that we would find our way through the moments of uncertainty. As hard as writing this book has been, it has been easy to work with you.

LIKEWISE, ALISON WOULD LIKE TO EXPRESS THE DEEP-est gratitude to those who share her home and were constantly on the receiving end of the phrase, "Hold on a minute, I'm writing!" Colin, it is not hyperbole to say that this book only exists because of the kind of life-partner you are. You provided more than was ever fair for me to ask for–keeping our house afloat while I scrambled to meet deadlines (all while wearing the multiple aforementioned hats). I'm not sure how I got so lucky to marry such a caring and talented person, and at this point I'm too afraid to ask.

And to my boys: I'm incredibly proud to be your mom. Calvin, even though you have "written" several books in the time that it took me to write one, you have shown me so much patience and grace throughout this process. Russell, thank you for laying on my keyboard when I clearly needed to take breaks. Although you're a toddler of few words (because you're one), you know just how to get a point across. I hope both of you boys know that you'll always be my "why."

To my parents, Kathy and Mike, my brother Chris, sister-in-law Brianne, and parents-in-law Lisa and Paul, thank you for your un-wavering support, enthusiasm, and genuine interest in this book. I cherish the conversations the book has sparked at our family dinners over the years. And thank you to Evan and Sam, whose love and support I've felt all the way from Oregon!

And thank you, Rosalyn. You've been an amazing resource; thank you so much for answering all of my questions about the publishing process (and swapping pumpkin beer recommendations).

Thank you to all of my friends, near and far, who have cheered me on. I can't possibly name everyone who has supported me over the years–shaping the person who wrote this book. One of my biggest sources of pride comes from with whom I've chosen to surround myself, in both professional and personal contexts.

And finally, a huge thank you to my co-author, colleague, and dear friend Audrey. In the early days, when the book was just an idea we were dreaming up, I found myself wondering if it was all too good to be true. Did we really share the same vision? I later came to realize that the answer was no, we didn't. The truth was that I hadn't been dreaming big enough. Your tenacity, ability to think a step ahead, and courage to take risks is taking this book further than I ever thought possible. I'm thankful for your big-picture perspective, and your ability to mercilessly "kill (my) darlings." While we're joined by others in celebrating the highest of highs with this book's release, only you and I will know and understand the lows and what it really took to get here. Thank you for being such a solid confidant through it all.

REFERENCES

Al-Atabi, M. (2014). *Think like an engineer: Use systematic thinking to solve everyday challenges & unlock the inherent values in them: Dream big, be different, have fun.* Createspace Independent Publishing Platform.

American Psychological Association. (n.d.a). *Culture.* APA Dictionary of Psychology. American Psychological Association. https://dictionary.apa.org/culture

American Psychological Association. (n.d.b). *Dissociation.* APA Dictionary of Psychology. American Psychological Association. https://dictionary.apa.org/dissociation

American Psychological Association. (n.d.c). *Emotion.* APA Dictionary of Psychology. American Psychological Association. https://dictionary.apa.org/emotion

American Psychological Association. (n.d.d). *Intrusive thoughts.* APA Dictionary of Psychology. American Psychological Association. https://dictionary.apa.org/intrusive-thoughts

American Psychological Association. (n.d.e). *Mood.* APA Dictionary of Psychology. American Psychological Association. https://dictionary.apa.org/mood

American Psychological Association. (n.d.f). *Rumination.* APA

Dictionary of Psychology. American Psychological Association. https://dictionary.apa.org/rumination

American Psychological Association. (n.d.g). *Thought.* APA Dictionary of Psychology. American Psychological Association. https://dictionary.apa.org/thought

American Psychological Association. (n.d.h). *Trauma.* APA Dictionary of Psychology. American Psychological Association. https://dictionary.apa.org/trauma

American Psychological Association. (n.d.i). *Worry.* APA Dictionary of Psychology. American Psychological Association. https://dictionary.apa.org/worry

American Psychological Association. (n.d.j). *Mindfulness.* American Psychological Association. https://www.apa.org/topics/mindfulness#:~:text=Mindfulness%20is%20awaeness%20of%20one's,judging%20or%20reacting%20to%20them

Andrews, P. W., & Thomson, J. A. (2009). The bright side of being blue: Depression as an adaptation for analyzing complex problems. *Psychological Review, 116*(3), 620–654. https://doi.org/10.1037/a0016242

Arnold, A. C., Wilkins-Yel, K. G., Bekki, J. M., Bernstein, B. L., Natarajan, M., Randall, A. K., & Owku, E. C. (2020, January). Examining the effects of STEM climate on the mental health of graduate women from diverse racial/ethnic backgrounds. *Proceedings of the 2020 American Society for Engineering Education Conference.*

Barrett, L. F. (2006). Are emotions natural kinds? *Perspectives on Psychological Science, 1*(1), 28-58. https://doi.org/10.1111/j.1745-6916.2006.00003.x

Beck, J. (2015, February 24). *Hard feelings: Science's struggle to define emotions.* The Atlantic. https://www.theatlantic.com/health/archive/2015/02/hard-feelings-sciences-struggle-t-define-emotions/385711/

Bench, S., & Lench, H. (2013). On the function of boredom. *Behavioral Sciences, 3*(3), 459–472. https://doi.org/10.3390/bs3030459

Boswell, J. F., Thompson-Hollands, J., Farchione, T. J., & Barlow, D. H. (2013). Intolerance of uncertainty: A common factor in the treatment of emotional disorders. *Journal of Clinical Psychology, 69*(6), 630–645. https://doi.org/10.1002/jclp.21965

Brandrick, C., Hooper, N., Roche, B., Kanter, J., & Tyndall, I. (2020). A comparison of ultra-brief cognitive defusion and positive affirmation interventions on the reduction of public speaking anxiety. *The Psychological Record, 71*(1), 109–117. https://doi.org/10.1007/s40732-020-00432-z

Bravata, D. M., Watts, S. A., Keefer, A. L., Madhusudhan, D. K., Taylor, K. T., Clark, D. M., Nelson, R. S., Cokley, K. O., & Hagg, H. K. (2019). Prevalence, predictors, and treatment of Impostor Syndrome: A systematic review. *Journal of General Internal Medicine, 35*(4), 1252–1275. https://doi.org/10.1007/s11606-019-05364-1

Breines, J. G., & Chen, S. (2012). Self-compassion increases self-improvement motivation. *Personality and Social Psychology Bulletin, 38*(9), 1133–1143. https://doi.org/10.1177/0146167212445599

Burchfield, J. G., & Kedrowicz, A. A. (2023, June 25-28). *Engineering is personal: Interpersonal communication for the 21st-century engineer* [Conference paper]. American Society for Engineering Education (ASEE). Baltimore, MD. https://nemo.asee.org/public/conferences/327/papers/38205/view

Burgo, J. (2012). *Why do I do that? Psychological defense mechanisms and the hidden ways they shape our lives.* New Rise Press.

Cash, E., Salmon, P., Weissbecker, I., Rebholz, W. N., Bayley-Veloso, R., Zimmaro, L. A., Floyd, A., Dedert, E., & Sephton, S. E. (2015). Mindfulness meditation alleviates fibromyalgia symptoms in women: Results of a randomized clinical trial. *Annals of Behavioral Medicine, 49*(3), 319–330. https://doi.org/10.1007/s12160-014-9665-0

Cachia, R. L., Anderson, A., & Moore, D. W. (2016). Mindfulness in Individuals with Autism Spectrum Disorder: a Systematic Review and Narrative Analysis. *Review Journal of Autism and Developmental Disorders, 3*(2), 165–178. https://doi.org/10.1007/s40489-016-0074-0

Cavenar, J. O. & Werman, D. S. (1981). Origins of the fear of success. *American Journal of Psychiatry, 138*(1), 95–98. https://doi.org/10.1176/ajp.138.1.95

Choi, E., Farb, N., Pogrebtsova, E., Gruman, J., & Grossmann, I. (2021). What do people mean when they talk about mindfulness? *Clinical Psychology Review, 89,* 102085. https://doi.org/10.1016/j.cpr.2021.102085

Chrousos, G. P., Mentis, A.-F. A., & Dardiotis, E. (2020). Focusing on the neuro-psycho-biological and evolutionary underpinnings of the imposter syndrome. *Frontiers in Psychology, 11.* https://doi.org/10.3389/fpsyg.2020.01553

Clance, P. R. (1985). *The impostor phenomenon: Overcoming the fear that haunts your success.* Peachtree Publishers.

Clance, P. R., & Imes, S. A. (1978). The imposter phenomenon in high achieving women: Dynamics and therapeutic intervention. *Psychotherapy: Theory, Research & Practice, 15*(3), 241–247. https://doi.org/10.1037/h0086006

Cribb, G., Moulds, M. L., & Carter, S. (2006). Rumination and experiential avoidance in depression. *Behaviour Change, 23*(3), 165–176. doi:10.1375/bech.23.3.165

Dahl, M. (2014, September 30). *The alarming new research on perfectionism.* The Cut. https://www.thecut.com/2014/09/alarming-new-research-on-perfectionism.html

Danckert, J., Mugon, J., Struk, A., & Eastwood, J. (2018). Boredom:

What is it good for? In *The Function of Emotions* (pp. 93–119). Springer International Publishing.

de Berker, A. O., Rutledge, R. B., Mathys, C., Marshall, L., Cross, G. F., Dolan, R. J., & Bestmann, S. (2016). Computations of uncertainty mediate acute stress responses in humans. *Nature Communications, 7*(1). https://doi.org/10.1038/ncomms10996

Dippel, A., Brosschot, J. F., & Verkuil, B. (2023). Effects of worry postponement on daily worry: A meta-analysis. *International Journal of Cognitive Therapy, 17*(1), 160–178. https://doi.org/10.1007/s41811-023-00193-x

Doran, G. T. (1981). There's a S.M.A.R.T. way to write management's goals and objectives. *Management Review, 70,* 35–36.

Dringenberg, E., Secules, S., & Kramer, A. (2019). *Smartness in engineering culture: An interdisciplinary dialogue.* 2019 ASEE Annual Conference & Exposition Proceedings. https://doi.org/10.18260/1-2--33272

Driscoll, R. (1989). Self-condemnation: A comprehensive framework for assessment and treatment. *Psychotherapy: Theory, Research, Practice, Training, 26*(1), 104.

DuMont, A. (2019, August 6). *The problem of perfect: How quality is hurting equality and what to do about it.* https://www.andromedadumont.com/p/the-problem-of-perfect

Dryman, M. T., & Heimberg, R. G. (2018). Emotion regulation in social anxiety and depression: A systematic review of expressive suppression and cognitive reappraisal. *Clinical Psychology Review, 65,* 17–42. https://doi.org/10.1016/j.cpr.2018.07.004

Eagleman, D. (2017). *The brain: The story of you.* Vintage Books.

Eifert, G. H., & Forsyth, J. P. (2005). *Acceptance & commitment therapy for anxiety disorders: A practitioner's treatment guide to using mindfulness, acceptance, and values-based behavior change strategies.* New Harbinger Publications.

Ekman, P. (1971). Universals and cultural differences in facial expressions of emotion. *Nebraska Symposium on Motivation, 19,* 207-283.

Ekman, P., & Friesen, W. V. (1971). Constants across cultures in the face and emotion. *Journal of Personality and Social Psychology, 17*(2), 124–129. https://doi.org/10.1037/h0030377

Faustino, B., Vasco, A. B., Farinha-Fernandes, A., & Delgado, J. (2021). Psychological inflexibility as a transdiagnostic construct: Relationships between cognitive fusion, psychological well-being and symptomatology. *Current Psychology, 42*(8), 6056–6061. https://doi.org/10.1007/s12144-021-01943-w

Frank, D. W., Dewitt, M., Hudgens-Haney, M., Schaeffer, D. J., Ball, B. H., Schwarz, N. F., Hussein, A. A., Smart, L. M., & Sabatinelli, D. (2014). Emotion regulation: Quantitative meta-analysis of functional activation and deactivation. *Neuroscience & Biobehavioral Reviews, 45,* 202–211. https://doi.org/10.1016/j.neubiorev.2014.06.010

Freeston, M. H., Rhéaume, J., Letarte, H., Dugas, M. J., & Ladouceur, R. (1994). Why do people worry? *Personality and Individual Differences, 17*(6), 791-802.

Gilbert, P. (1998). The evolved basis and adaptive functions of cognitive distortions. *British Journal of Medical Psychology, 71*(4), 447–463. https://doi.org/10.1111/j.2044-8341.1998.tb01002.x

Godfrey, E., & Parker, L. (2010). Mapping the cultural landscape in engineering education. *Journal of Engineering education, 99*(1), 5-22.

Greenberg J., Romero, V.L., Elkin-Frankston, S., Bezdek, M.A., Schumacher, E.H., & Lazar, S.W. Reduced interference in working memory following mindfulness training is associated with increases in hippocampal volume. *Brain Imaging Behavior.* 2019 April, *13*(2):366-376. Doi: 10.1007/s11682-018-9858-4. Erratum in *Brain Imaging Behavior,* 2019 June,

13(3):878. Doi: 10.1007/s11682-018-9890-4. PMID: 29549665; PMCID: PMC6141345.

Greenspon, T. S. (2014). Is there an antidote to perfectionism? *Psychology in the Schools, 51*(9), 986–998. https://doi.org/10.1002/pits.21797

Gross, J. J. (2002). Emotion regulation: Affective, cognitive, and social consequences. *Psychophysiology, 39*(3), 281–291. doi:10.1017/S0048577201393198

Gross, J. J., & John, O. P. (2003). Individual differences in two emotion regulation processes: Implications for affect, relationships, and well-being. *Journal of Personality and Social Psychology, 85*(2), 348–362. https://doi.org/10.1037/0022-3514.85.2.348

Gutierrez y Muhs, G., Niemann, Y. F., Gonzalez, C. G., & Harris, A. P. (Eds.), (2012). *Presumed incompetent: The intersections of race and class for women in academia.* Utah State University Press.

Hallis, L., Dionne, F., Knäuper, B., & Cameli, L. (2012, July 22-25). *Integrating Acceptance and Commitment Therapy (ACT) into traditional Cognitive Behaviour Therapy (CBT)* [Poster presentation]. Association for Contextual Behavioral Science (ACBS) Annual World Conference 10, Washington, D.C.

Harlow, H. F. (1958). The nature of love. *American Psychologist, 13*(12), 673–685. https://doi.org/10.1037/h0047884

Hawkley, L. C., & Capitanio, J. P. (2015). Perceived social isolation, evolutionary fitness and health outcomes: A lifespan approach. *Philosophical Transactions of the Royal Society B: Biological Sciences, 370*(1669), 20140114. https://doi.org/10.1098/rstb.2014.0114

Hayes, S. C. (2004). Acceptance and commitment therapy, relational frame theory, and the third wave of behavioral and

Cognitive Therapies. *Behavior Therapy, 35*(4), 639–665. https://doi.org/10.1016/s0005-7894(04)80013-3

Hayes, S. (2022). *Get out of your mind and into your life: The new acceptance and commitment therapy.* New Harbinger Publications Inc.

Heidel, J. A. (2020, November 12). *Why the Practice of Mindfulness Might Backfire on Autistic People.* Jaime a. Heidel - the Articulate Autistic. https://www.thearticulateautistic.com/why-the-practice-of-mindfulness-might-backfire-on-autistic-people/

Hogg, M. A., Kruglanski, A., & van den Bos, K. (2013). Uncertainty and the roots of extremism. *Journal of Social Issues, 69*(3), 407–418. https://doi.org/10.1111/josi.12021

Holt-Lunstad, J., Smith, T. B., & Layton, J. B. (2010). Social relationships and mortality risk: A meta-analytic review. *PLoS Medicine, 7*(7). https://doi.org/10.1371/journal.pmed.1000316

Huecker, M. R., Shreffler, J., McKeny, P. T., & Davis, D. (2024). *Imposter phenomenon.* StatPearls Publishing. https://www.ncbi.nlm.nih.gov/books/NBK585058/

Huron, D. (2018). On the functions of sadness and grief. In Heather C. Lench (Ed.), *The function of emotions* (pp. 59–91), Springer International Publishing A.G.

Hutton, S. (2020, October 8). *Learning to celebrate neurodiversity in mindfulness.* Mindful. https://www.mindful.org/learning-to-celebrate-neurodiversity-in-mindfulness/

James, W. (1890). *The Principles of Psychology, Vol I.* https://doi.org/10.1037/10538-000

Jensen, K. J., Mirabelli, J. F., Kunze, A. J., Romanchek, T. E., & Cross, K. J. (2023). Undergraduate student perceptions of stress and mental health in engineering culture. *International Journal of STEM Education, 10*(1). https://doi.org/10.1186/s40594-023-00419-6

Jepsen, M. (2012, January 2). *Thought/emotional avoidance and acceptance: Ball in a pool.* Association for Contextual Behavioral Science. https://contextualscience.org/thoughtemotional_avoidance_and_acceptance_ball_in

Kabat-Zinn, J. (2016). *Mindfulness for beginners: Reclaiming the present moment and your life.* Sounds True.

Kabat-Zinn, J. (1994). *Wherever you go there you are: Mindfulness meditation in everyday life.* Hyperion.

Kahneman, D. (2011). *Thinking, fast and slow.* Farrar, Straus, and Giroux.

Kapp, S. K., Steward, R., Crane, L., Elliott, D., Elphick, C., Pellicano, E., & Russell, G. (2019). 'People should be allowed to do what they like': Autistic adults' views and experiences of stimming. *Autism, 23*(7), 1782–1792. https://doi.org/10.1177/1362361319829628

Karnaze, M. M., & Levine, L. J. (2018). Sadness, the architect of cognitive change. In Heather C. Lench (Ed.), *The function of emotions* (pp. 45–58). Springer International Publishing A.G.

Kay, K., & Shipman, C. (2014, May). The confidence gap. *The Atlantic.* https://www.theatlantic.com/magazine/archive/2014/05/the-confidence-gap/359815/

Klinger, E. (1975). Consequences of commitment to and disengagement from incentives. *Psychological Review, 82*(1), 1–25. https://doi.org/10.1037/h0076171

Kross, E., Berman, M. G., Mischel, W., Smith, E. E., & Wager, T. D. (2011). Social rejection shares somatosensory representations with physical pain. *Proceedings of the National Academy of Sciences, 108*(15), 6270–6275. https://doi.org/10.1073/pnas.1102693108

Kruger, J., & Dunning, D. (1999). Unskilled and unaware of it: How difficulties in recognizing one's own incompetence lead to inflated self-assessments. *Journal of Personality and Social*

Psychology, 77(6), 1121–1134. https://doi.org/10.1037/0022-3514.77.6.1121

Kuyken, W., Hayes, R., Barrett, B., Byng, R., Dalgleish, T., Kessler, D., Lewis, G., Watkins, E., Brejcha, C., Cardy, J., Causley, A., Cowderoy, S., Evans, A., Gradinger, F., Kaur, S., Lanham, P., Morant, N., Richards, J., Shah, P., ... Byford, S. (2015). Effectiveness and cost-effectiveness of mindfulness-based cognitive therapy compared with maintenance antidepressant treatment in the prevention of depressive relapse or recurrence (prevent): A randomised controlled trial. *The Lancet, 386*(9988), 63–73. https://doi.org/10.1016/s0140-6736(14)62222-4

Lally, P., van Jaarsveld, C. H., Potts, H. W., & Wardle, J. (2009). How are habits formed: Modelling habit formation in the real world. *European Journal of Social Psychology, 40*(6), 998–1009. https://doi.org/10.1002/ejsp.674

Lench, H., & Carpenter, Z. K. (2018). What do emotions do for us? In Heather C. Lench (Ed.), *The function of emotions* (pp. 1-7). Springer International Publishing A.G.

Leslie, S. J., Cimpian, A., Meyer, M., & Freeland, E. (2015). Expectations of brilliance underlie gender distributions across academic disciplines. *Science, 347*(6219), 262-265.

Levenson, R. W. (2003). Blood, sweat, and fears. *Annals of the New York Academy of Sciences, 1000*(1), 348–366. https://doi.org/10.1196/annals.1280.016

Lieberman, M. D., Eisenberger, N. I., Crockett, M. J., Tom, S. M., Pfeifer, J. H., & Way, B. M. (2007). Putting feelings into words. *Psychological Science, 18*(5), 421-428. https://doi.org/10.1111/j.1467-9280.2007.01916.x

Loweth, R. (2023, July 17). *Challenging the meritocratic ideology in engineering education.* ASEE Commission on Diversity, Equity, and Inclusion. August 26, 2024, https://diversity.asee.org/deicommittee/2023/07/17/

challenging-the-meritocratic-ideolog-in-engineer-ing-education/

MacCormack, J. K., & Lindquist, K. A. (2019). Feeling hangry? When hunger is conceptualized as emotion. *Emotion, 19*(2), 301–319. https://doi.org/10.1037/emo0000422

Marcks, B. A., & Woods, D. W. (2005). A comparison of thought suppression to an acceptance-based technique in the management of personal intrusive thoughts: A controlled evaluation. Behaviour Research and Therapy, 43(4), 433-445.

Masuda, A., Twohig, M. P., Stormo, A. R., Feinstein, A. B., Chou, Y.-Y., & Wendell, J. W. (2010). The effects of cognitive defusion and thought distraction on emotional discomfort and believability of negative self-referential thoughts. *Journal of Behavior Therapy and Experimental Psychiatry, 41*(1), 11–17. https://doi.org/10.1016/j.jbtep.2009.08.006

McGee, E. (2018). "Black genius, Asian fail": The detriment of stereotype lift and stereotype threat in high-achieving Asian and black stem students. *AERA Open, 4*(4), 233285841881665. https://doi.org/10.1177/2332858418816658

McGee, E. O., Botchway, P. K., Naphan-Kingery, D. E., Brockman, A. J., Houston, S., & White, D. T. (2022). Racism camouflaged as impostorism and the impact on black stem doctoral students. *Race Ethnicity and Education, 25*(4), 487–507. https://doi.or g/10.1080/13613324.2021.1924137

Merriam-Webster (n.d.a). *Impostor syndrome definition & meaning.* Merriam-Webster. https://www.merriam-webster.com/ dictionary/impostor%20syndrome#:~:text=noun,evidence%20 of%20one's%20ongoing%20success

Merriam-Webster (n.d.b). *Meritocracy definition & meaning.* Merriam-Webster. https://www.merriam-webster.com/dic-tionary/meritocracy

Merriam-Webster (n.d.c). *Neurodivergent definition & meaning.*

Merriam-Webster. https://www.merriam-webster.com/dictionary/neurodivergent

Merriam-Webster (n.d.d). *Optimization definition & meaning.* Merriam-Webster. https://www.merriam-webster.com/dictionary/optimization

Merriam-Webster (n.d.e). *Overthink definition & meaning.* Merriam-Webster. https://www.merriam-webster.com/dictionary/overthink#:~:text=%3A%20to%20think%0too%20much%20about,overthink%20a%20situation%2Fproblem

Merriam-Webster (n.d.f). *Perfectionism definition & meaning.* Merriam-Webster. https://www.merriam-webster.com/dictionary/perfectionism

Merriam-Webster (n.d.g). *Stimming definition & meaning.* Merriam-Webster. https://www.merriam-webster.com/dictionary/stimming

Miller, W. R., Miller, C'de Baca, J., Matthews, D. B. & Wilbourne, P. L. (2001). *University of New Mexico Department of Psychology.*

Murthy, V. (2023). *Our epidemic of loneliness and isolation.* US Public Health Service.

Neff, K. D. (2003). The development and validation of a scale to measure self-compassion. *Self and Identity, 2*(3), 223–250. https://doi.org/10.1080/15298860309027

Neff, K. (2011). *Self-compassion: The proven power of being kind to yourself.* HarperCollins Publishers.

Neff, K. D., & Rude, S. S., & Kirkpatrick, K. (2007). An examination of self-compassion in relation to positive psychological functioning and personality traits. *Journal of Research in Personality, 41,* 908-916.

Parsafar, P., & Davis, E. L. (2018). Fear and anxiety. In Heather C. Lench (Ed.), *The function of emotions* (pp. 9–23). Springer International Publishing A.G.

Pinto-Gouveia, J., Dinis, A., Gregório, S., & Pinto, A. M. (2018).

Concurrent effects of different psychological processes in the prediction of depressive symptoms: The role of cognitive fusion. *Current Psychology, 39*(2), 528–539. https://doi.org/10.1007/s12144-017-9767-5

Powers, T. A., Koestner, R., & Zuroff, D. C. (2007). Self–criticism, goal motivation, and goal progress. *Journal of Social and Clinical Psychology, 26*(7), 826–840. https://doi.org/10.1521/jscp.2007.26.7.826

Quartana, P. J., & Burns, J. W. (2010). Emotion suppression affects cardiovascular responses to initial and subsequent laboratory stressors. *British Journal of Health Psychology, 15*(3), 511–528. https://doi.org/10.1348/135910709x474613

Rachman, S. (1998). *Anxiety.* Psychology Press.

Radomsky, A. S., Alcolado, G. M., Abramowitz, J. S., Alonso, P., Belloch, A., Bouvard, M., Clark, D. A., Coles, M. E., Doron, G., Fernández-Álvarez, H., Garcia-Soriano, G., Ghisi, M., Gomez, B., Inozu, M., Moulding, R., Shams, G., Sica, C., Simos, G., & Wong, W. (2014). Part 1: You can run but you can't hide: Intrusive thoughts on six continents. *Journal of Obsessive-Compulsive and Related Disorders, 3*(3), 269–279. https://doi.org/10.1016/j.jocrd.2013.09.002

Rakshit, D. (2023, May 4). *Why meditation works for some people, but not others.* The Swaddle. https://www.theswaddle.com/why-meditation-works-for-some-people-but-not-others

Reed, L. I., & DeScioli, P. (2017). The communicative function of sad facial expressions. *Evolutionary Psychology, 15*(1), 147470491770041. https://doi.org/10.1177/1474704917700418

Roseman, I. J. (2018). Functions of anger in the emotion system. In Heather C. Lench (Ed.), *The Function of Emotions* (pp. 141–173). Springer International Publishing A.G.

Santanello, A. W., & Gardner, F. L. (2006). The role of experiential avoidance in the relationship between maladaptive perfectionism and worry. *Cognitive Therapy and Research,* *31*(3), 319–332. https://doi.org/10.1007/s10608-006-9000-6

Sakulku, J. (2011). The impostor phenomenon. *The Journal of Behavioral Science, 6*(1), 75–97. https://doi.org/10.14456/ijbs.2011.6

Sakulku, J., & Alexander, J. (2011). The imposter phenomenon. *International Journal of Behavioral Science, 6*(1), 75–97.

Schneider, W., & Shiffrin, R. M. (1977). Controlled and automatic human information processing: I. Detection, search, and attention. *Psychological Review, 84*(1), 1–66. https://doi.org/10.1037/0033-295x.84.1.1

Schneider, W., & Shiffrin, R. M. (1977a). Controlled and automatic human information processing: I. Detection, search, and attention. *Psychological Review, 84*(1), 1–66. https://doi.org/10.1037/0033-295x.84.1.1

Self (2024, July 25). Compassion: Dr. Kristin Neff. https://self-compassion.org/

Siegel, D. J. (1999). *The developing mind: How relationships and the brain interact to shape who we are.* The Guilford Press.

Siegel, E. H., Sands, M. K., Van den Noortgate, W., Condon, P., Chang, Y., Dy, J., Quigley, K. S., & Barrett, L. F. (2018). Emotion fingerprints or emotion populations? A meta-analytic investigation of autonomic features of emotion categories. *Psychological Bulletin, 144*(4), 343–393. https://doi.org/10.1037/bul0000128

Steffen, P. R., Austin, T., & DeBarros, A. (2017). Treating chronic stress to address the growing problem of depression and anxiety: Biofeedback and mindfulness as simple, effective preventive measures. *Policy Insights from the Behavioral and Brain Sciences, 4*(1), 64–70. https://doi.org/10.1177/2372732216685333

Storbeck, J., & Wylie, J. (2018). The functional and dysfunctional aspects of happiness: Cognitive, physiological, behavioral, and health considerations. In Heather C. Lench (Ed.), *The Function of Emotions* (pp. 195–220). Springer International Publishing A.G.

Strack, F., & Deutsch, R. (2004). Reflective and impulsive determinants of social behavior. *Personality and Social Psychology Review, 8*(3), 220–247. https://doi.org/10.1207/s15327957pspr0803_1

Substance Abuse and Mental Health Services Administration (n.d.). *What is mental health?* https://www.samhsa.gov/mental-health

Sutton, J. (2020, June 19). *Socratic questioning in psychology: Examples and techniques.* PositivePsychology.com. https://positivepsychology.com/socratic-questioning/

Taylor, J. B. (2006). *My stroke of insight: A brain scientist's personal journey.* Penguin Random House LLC.

Thomas, E., Moss-Morris, R., & Faquhar, C. (2006). Coping with emotions and abuse history in women with chronic pelvic pain. *Journal of Psychosomatic Research, 60*(1), 109–112. https://doi.org/10.1016/j.jpsychores.2005.04.011

Treleaven, D. A., & Britton, W. (2018). *Trauma-sensitive mindfulness: Practices for safe and transformative healing.* W.W Norton & Company.

Tseng, J., & Poppenk, J. (2020). Brain meta-state transitions demarcate thoughts across task contexts exposing the mental noise of trait neuroticism. *Nature Communications, 11*(1). https://doi.org/10.1038/s41467-020-17255-9

Tulshyan, R., & Burey, A. (2021, February 11). *Stop telling women they have imposter syndrome.* Harvard Business Review. https://hbr.org/2021/02/stop-telling-women-they-have-imposter-syndrome

Valtorta, N. K., Kanaan, M., Gilbody, S., Ronzi, S., & Hanratty, B. (2016). Loneliness and social isolation as risk factors for coronary heart disease and stroke: Systematic review and meta-analysis of longitudinal observational studies. *Heart, 102*(13), 1009–1016. https://doi.org/10.1136/heartjnl-2015-308790

van Middendorp, H., Lumley, M. A., Jacobs, J. W. G., van Doornen, L. J. P., Bijlsma, J. W. J., & Geenen, R. (2008). Emotions and emotional approach and avoidance strategies in fibromyalgia. *Journal of Psychosomatic Research, 64*(2), 159–167. https://doi.org/10.1016/j.jpsychores.2007.08.009

Watkins, E. (2023). Rumination. In D. J. A. Dozois & K. S. Dobson (Eds.), *Treatment of psychosocial risk factors in depression (pp. 305–331)*. American Psychological Association. https://doi.org/10.1037/0000332-014

Wegner, D. M., Erber, R., & Zanakos, S. (1993). Ironic processes in the mental control of mood and mood-related thought. *Journal of Personality and Social Psychology, 65*(6), 1093–1104. https://doi.org/10.1037/0022-3514.65.6.1093

Wegwarth, O., Gaissmaier, W., & Gigerenzer, G. (2009). Smart strategies for doctors and doctors-in-training: Heuristics in medicine. *Medical Education, 43*(8), 721–728. https://doi.org/10.1111/j.1365-2923.2009.03359.x

Werner, A. M., Tibubos, A. N., Rohrmann, S., & Reiss, N. (2019). The clinical trait self-criticism and its relation to psychopathology: A systematic review—update. *Journal of Affective Disorders, 246*, 530–547. https://doi.org/10.1016/j.jad.2018.12.069

Wilke, A. & Mata, R. (2017). *Cognitive bias.* Reference Module in Neuroscience and Biobehavioral Psychology. https://www.sciencedirect.com/topics/psychology/cognitive-bias

Willcox, G. (1982). The feeling wheel. *Transactional Analysis Journal, 12*(4), 274–276. https://doi.org/10.1177/036215378201200411

Williams, L. A. (2018). Emotions of excellence: Communal and agentic functions of pride, moral elevation, and admiration.

In Heather C. Lench (Ed.), *The Function of Emotions* (pp. 235–252). Springer International Publishing A.G.

Willmot, P., & Colman, B. (2016, December 4-7). *Interpersonal skills in engineering education* [Conference paper]. Australasian Association for Engineering Education (AAEE) 2016 Conference, Coffs Harbour, Australia. https://core.ac.uk/download/pdf/288370315.pdf

Wrosch, C., Scheier, M. F.; Carver, C. S., & Schulz, R. (2003). The importance of goal disengagement in adaptive self-regulation: When giving up is beneficial. *Self and Identity, 2*(1), 1–20. https://doi.org/10.1080/15298860309021

Young, V. (2011). *The secret thoughts of successful women and men: Why capable people suffer from impostor syndrome.* Penguin Random House LLC.

Zou, Y., Li, P., Hofmann, S. G., & Liu, X. (2020). The mediating role of non-reactivity to mindfulness training and cognitive flexibility: A randomized controlled trial. *Frontiers in Psychology, 11.* https://doi.org/10.3389/fpsyg.2020.01053

Zurita Ona, P. (2022). *Acceptance and commitment skills for perfectionism and high-achieving behaviors: Do things your way, be yourself, and live a purposeful life.* Routledge.

ABOUT THE AUTHORS

**Alison West, MA, Licensed Professional Counselor (LPC),
Licensed Addiction Counselor (LAC)
Co-Founder of Applied Wellness Initiatives**

ALISON EARNED HER MASTER'S IN COUNSELING AND human services at the University of Colorado at Colorado Springs (UCCS). Alison's clinical training and background reach far and wide across the mental health care system. From working with individuals in crisis, to providing ongoing therapeutic care, and helping vulnerable populations navigate convoluted systems, Alison has seen up close the variability of needs within the mental health continuum. One of Alison's greatest passions is providing mental health support for engineering students, who in her opinion, are some of the most driven, resilient, and delightful people she has ever met. In addition to providing individual therapy, Alison works closely with faculty, staff, and student leaders to respond to the unique challenges of engineers–developing personalized programming and resources. Her passion for tailored approaches to mental wellness is what led Alison to co-found Applied Wellness Initiatives. Her special interests include mindfulness, emotion regulation, addiction, and collective efforts to support and destigmatize mental health. Alison spends most of her spare time chasing around her two rambunctious sons, pretending to be a dinosaur; she also enjoys drawing, listening to podcasts, and playing her drumset.

Audrey Gilfillan, MA, Licensed Professional Counselor (LPC)
Co-Founder of Applied Wellness Initiatives

AUDREY EARNED HER MASTER'S IN EDUCATIONAL PSYchology from the University of Minnesota-Twin Cities. Audrey has experience in a broad range of professional disciplines including psychotherapy, career counseling, academic coaching, consulting, training, and supervision. In this work, she has developed a speciality in supporting engineers and their mental health while they continue to pursue their professional goals. As a co-creator of the Scaffolded Mental Health Support Model, Audrey also specializes in helping non-clinical professionals support the mental health of their students and employees within occupational settings. Building on her therapeutic skills for engineers and her systems approach to psychological wellness in work spaces, Audrey co-founded Applied Wellness Initiatives to consult with and support engineering groups around emotional wellness. Her special interests include emotional regulation, supporting leaders as they support the mental health of their teams, neurodiversity, values-based decision making, executive functioning skills, and effective communication. In her free time, Audrey enjoys hiking, reading, and spending time with friends and family (and pets!).